Other publications from Crowbar Press

Inside Out | Ole Anderson, with Scott Teal

Wrestlers Are Like Seagulls
James J. Dillon, with Scott Teal

Assassin: The Man Behind the Mask
Joe Hamilton, with Scott Teal

"Is That Wrestling Fake?"
Ivan Koloff, with Scott Teal

Bruiser Brody |
Emerson Murray, edited by Scott Teal

Wrestling with the Truth
Bruno Lauer, edited by Scott Teal

The Solie Chronicles
Bob Allyn, with Pamela S Allyn & Scott Teal

Wrestling in the Canadian West | Vance evada

Long Days and Short Pays
Hal West, edited by Scott Teal

Drawing Heat | Jim Freedman

ATLAS: Too Much, Too Soon
Tony Atlas, with Scott Teal

The Last Laugh | Bill De Mott, with Scott Teal

HOOKER | Lou Thesz, with Kit Bauman

The Last Outlaw | Stan Hansen, with Scott Teal

NIKITA | Nikita Koloff, as told to Bill Murdock

The Strap | Roger Deem

BRISCO | Jack Brisco, as told to Bill Murdock

The Mighty Milo | Phillips Rogers

"I Ain't No Pig Farmer!"
Dean Silverstone, with Scott Teal

The Hard Way | Don Fargo, with Scott Teal

Whatever Happened to Gorgeous George?
Joe Jares

"It's Wrestling, Not Rasslin'!"
Mark Fleming, edited by Scott Teal

BRUISER:
   The World's Most Dangerous Wrestler
Richard Vicek, edited by Scott Teal

The Mat, the Mob & Music
Tom Hankins, edited by Scott Teal

BREAKING KAYFABE
THEY CALL ME BOOKER
Jeff Bowdren, edited by Scott Teal

BATTLEGROUND VALHALA
Michael Majalahti, edited by Scott Teal

Florida Mat Wars: 1977
Robert D. VanKavelaar, with Scott Teal

When It Was Real
Nikita Breznikov, with Scott Teal

The Annotated Fall Guys
Marcus Griffin, annotated by Steve Yohe & Scott Teal

Pain Torture Agony
Ron Hutchison, with Scott Teal

Raising Cain: From Jimmy Ault to Kid McCoy
Raising Cain:
   From The Inferno to The Great Mephisto
Frankie Cain & Scott Teal

Master of the Ring | Tim Hornbaker

Tonight! Tonight! Tonight!
Bert Prentice & Scott Teal

Wilbur Snyder:
   The World's Most Scientific Wrestler
Richard Vicek & Steven Verrier

Ed Don George: From Farm to Fame
Dan Murphy

We Wrestled, We Brawled, We Started It All
Joel Goodhart & Scott Teal

Wrestling Archive Project — Scott Teal
Vol. #1 • Vol. #2 • Vol. #3

Through the Lens ... Through the Ropes
Compiled by Scott Teal
Vol. 1 — Southeastern Championship Wrestling
Vol. 2 — Championship Wrestling from Florida
Vol. 3 — All South Wrestling Alliance

— **The Great Pro Wrestling Venues** —
Vol. 1 — **Madison Square Garden**
   Scott Teal & J Michael Kenyon
Vol. 2 — **Nashville, Tennessee, vol. 1**
   Scott Teal & Don Luce
Vol. 3 — **Alabama: 1931-1935**
   Jason Presley
Vol. 4 — **Japan: The Rikidozan Years**
   Haruo Yamaguchi,
   with Koji Miyamoto & Scott Teal
Vol. 5 — **Knoxville: 1905-1960**
   Tim Dills & Scott Teal
Vol. 6 — **Amarillo: 1911-1958**
   Kriss Knights & Scott Teal
Vol. 7 — **St. Louis: 1873-1927**
Vol. 8 — **St. Louis: 1928-1936**
   Scott Teal

— **Classic Arena Programs** —
Vol. 1 — SLAM-O-GRAM, Volume 1
Vol. 2 — SLAM-O-GRAM, Volume 2
Vol. 3 — Florida, 1970
Vol. 4 — Florida, 1971
Vol. 5 — Knoxville, Southeastern
Vol. 6 — St. Louis, 1943-1945
Vol. 7 — St. Louis, 1946-1948
Vol. 8 — St. Louis, 1949-1951
Vol. 9 — St. Louis, 1945-1949 (Sam Muchnick)
Vol. 22 — Jacksonville: July 1976-July 1977
Vol. 23 — Jacksonville: July 1977-May 1978
Vol. 24 — Jacksonville: May 1978-July 1980

Pro Wrestling and the
Tennessee Athletic Commission
Tim Dills, with Scott Teal

MOVIES & ENTERTAINMENT
Herschel (Chuck) Thornton

DURANGO • Charles Starrett

Joel A. Goodhart & Scott Teal

Gallatin, Tennessee

Copyright © 2025 by Joel Goodhart & Scott Teal

All rights reserved. No part of this book may be reproduced or transmitted in any form or by any means, electronic or mechanical, including photocopying, recording, or by any information storage and retrieval system, without permission in writing from the publisher.

Published by Crowbar Press
106 Tattnal Court
Gallatin, Tennessee 37066.

http://www.crowbarpress.com

Book layout and cover design by Scott Teal

Library of Congress Cataloging-in-Publication Data

Goodhart, Joel / Teal, Scott
    We Wrestled, We Brawled, We Started It All | by Joel Goodhart & Scott Teal

1. Sports—United States—Biography. 2. Wrestling—United States—History.
  I. Goodhart, Joel II. Teal, Scott III. Title

Printed in the United States of America
ISBN 978-1-940391-49-6

First Edition / May 2025

TABLE of CONTENTS

Acknowledgments	6
Foreword by Tod Gordon	7
1. Out of the Wrestling Closet	10
2. The Squared Circle	16
3. Watching a Radio Broadcast	25
4. Jim Cornette and the King of Prussia	33
5. Autographed Underwear	49
6. The Long-Haired, Snakeskin-Booted, Seriously Sunglassed, 36-year-old Insurance Salesman	64
7. Tri-State Wrestling Alliance	77
8. Mr. Sandman Sleep Center	91
9. "For twenty-five dollars, she'll do anything!"	101
10. Phone Call from the Sheik	117
11. The Biggest Payday! | The Smallest Gate!	131
12. Five-Foot-Seven ... in Both Directions!	146
13. The City of Brotherly Hate	150
14. The Bones That Talked	161
15. Hot Oil Wrestling	165
16. The Dream Match	171
17. Taking a Financial Bath	179
18. Sleeping Well at Night	190
19. Goodhart, Blackhart and Friendlyhart	198
20. The Legacy	202
21. Go-Go Professional Wrestling	204
22. It's Chubby Dudley's Fault	210

Acknowledgments
by Joel Goodhart

There are so many people that I just have to acknowledge, but I won't go into detail because I mention most of them in the book.

First of all, my announcers ... Tod Gordon, Michael Tearson and Chris Cruise.

Larry Winters & Ron Shaw, my two full-time instructors and partners in the Ringmasters wrestling school.

Elliott Murnick & Jim Ross, the two people who helped me get a foothold in the NWA, which gave me the contacts and knowledge necessary to promote wrestling.

My dear friend and co-host of "Rasslin' Radio," Carmella Fedrico Panfil Foss, and my radio producer, Ike Richman.

My first employee at the Square Circle store, Jeannie Peletsky Siciliano.

Roger Krone, who gave me my first big break in radio.

Dominic DeNucci, my first booker, and Larry Winters, who booked the TWA shows to perfection.

My "men in the middle," my referees, John Finegan (my lead referee), Joe Zanolle, Rich Ingling, Jim Molineaux, and Sal Corrente.

Steve Truitt & Ron Daignault, who handled the sound for my shows and events.

Four photographers who were at most of my shows and put TWA on the map nationally through the wrestling magazines were Bill Apter, George Napolitano, Mike Lano, and Craig Prendergast.

The memories and knowledge of TWA wrestling by Craig Prendergast, Jimmy Jannetty and Bay Ragni were invaluable as they helped my co-author, Scott Teal, identify wrestlers in photos and determine on what date those photos were taken.

Larry Gallone, who created the arena programs and flyers that helped promote TWA.

My three children, Ross, Marc and Danielle. Ross and Marc sold the programs at my shows and loved being there with their dad. Danielle was born two weeks after I got out of the wrestling business, so she never experienced what I did. Years later, when she looked at the videos of my shows, she wanted to know what I had been smoking. ?!?!?!

Larry Winters, D.C. Drake, Tony Stetson and Johnny Hotbody, the four guys who really put TWA on the map.

The three feuds that people still talk about to this day ...
  Cactus Jack vs. Eddie Gilbert
    The Sheik (the original) vs. Abdullah the Butcher
      Jerry Lawler vs. Terry Funk

Then there's Bay Ragni and Ryan Kavanaugh, who have done so much to help bring our upcoming show, "One and Done," to fruition.

Finally, thanks to Dan Murphy for his friendship and for introducing me to Scott Teal, the guy who helped me put this all together. Scott doesn't leave a stone unturned and held my feet to the fire when it came to remembering things that happened.

Foreword
by Tod Gordon

I grew up watching WWWF pro wrestling with my grandfather, but I never dreamed I would ever be involved in the business. It wasn't until 1989 that I stumbled across a wrestling program on radio station WIP-AM 610. I was stunned that a wrestling show would be on a major radio station in a city like Philadelphia. Up to that time, wrestling was almost an underground kind of thing. That was a time when almost nobody admitted to being a wrestling fan, so when I heard the show hosts talking about pro wrestling, it stopped me dead in my tracks. I became addicted to the show and, after a number of weeks, I just knew that I had to get involved in some fashion.

At the time, I was just a guy who owned Carver Reed, a downtown Philly jewelry store. I had never been to a live show and I had never met a wrestler or anyone connected to the wrestling business. One day, I heard Joel Goodhart mention that they were looking for advertisers to help support the show, so I gave him a call. Advertising was cheap. It was $75 dollars for each radio spot. I could hear the excitement in Joel's voice when I offered to sponsor Rasslin' Radio. He didn't have much advertising at the time.

We struck up a friendship and he kept telling me that if I ever wanted a wrestler to appear at my business, he could arrange it. He knew everybody! The names he threw out included former WCW wrestlers, but the names that really caught my attention were those who had wrestled for the WWWF! To be honest, I wasn't thinking about what a personal appearance could do for my business. I was excited with the idea of just meeting a WWWF wrestler. Yeah, I was a fan.

Joel and I went down the list of guys who might be available ... Bruno Sammartino, Dominic Denucci, Captain Lou Albano, David Shults, Bam Bam Bigelow. Then we looked at the WCW guys ... the Midnight Express, Tully Blanchard, Manny Fernandez. Joel had access to everybody! So, as a wrestling fan, I chose the person I thought represented pro wrestling at its finest ... Missy Hyatt! There again, that was the fan in me. I probably would have drawn a bigger crowd to the store with someone like Bruno, but Missy was drop-dead gorgeous and I wanted to meet her.

Over time, Joel and I became very good friends. I did the ring announcing for him and he even walked me through the promotion of a wrestling show that would benefit a charity I was a board member of, the Variety Club. Joel eventually brought me in as a minor partner in TWA. I wanted to support his cause because I loved his product. He presented a mix of local guys with nationally known talent. That was something that nobody else had ever done on such a grand scale.

Joel showed a strong desire to get involved with the Variety Club, so I got him a spot on the Board of Directors. Everybody on the board came to our meetings wearing suits and ties ... but not Joel! He'd show up wearing cowboy boots and dark glasses. Joel really won over the other members, though. He was funny, very glib, and gave us a lot of good ideas. He's such a bright guy.

The Variety Club benefit took place at Temple University, and that was the genesis of the TWA promotion. Joel later moved to Penn Hall at the Civic Center. But I never would have dreamed that, two years and one month after that benefit show, I would be running my own wrestling promotion in Philly. Bless his heart, Joel gave the fans much, much more than the ticket prices warranted ... and that was his undoing. Three months after he closed up shop, I was promoting my own shows at his venue, the Original Sports Bar at 8th and Market.

All that is to say that I owe everything, including the formation of Extreme Championship Wrestling, to Joel Goodhart. He inspired me and gave me the knowledge to do something I never would have dreamed of doing, and I had a heck of a lot of fun (alternating with headaches) in the process.

I was very disappointed when Joel went out of business. His demise was in the fact that he never produced a TV show, which he could have used to promote his product. If he had, he would have done really well because it would have given him the exposure he needed. In fact, I truly believe he would have been in business for many more years and ECW may never have come into existence.

When Larry Winters, Steve Truitt, and Bob Artese, Joel's booker, sound man, and ring announcer, respectively, came into my office and pitched the idea of me taking up where Joel left off, I was hesitant because Joel was a close friend. Our friendship was more important to me than a monthly bar show. I don't remember much about our conversation, but I spoke with Joel about it and he encouraged me to go ahead with it.

Joel cut all ties with the wrestling world and we didn't talk for a long time after that. When we did, he said, "*You know, it's crazy, but everybody think we hate each other.*"

I asked, "*Why do they think that?*"

He said, "*Because we haven't talked to each other in a long time.*"

I said, "*We don't have any heat at all. If it weren't for you, I never would have gotten into the business.*" Of course, I had to add, "*Then again, maybe I should hold* that *against you.*"

We both laughed.

The truth is, Joel didn't talk to *anybody* in wrestling until a few years ago. He moved on to a new chapter in his life and never looked back, so it wasn't anything personal. At least, he didn't look back until he called me about the possibility of him promoting his upcoming "One and Done" show. When we did talk, it was like no time had gone by. He was the Joel that I had always known ... upbeat and excited about future events.

For the most part, Joel and I had the same likes and dislikes. Fans in Philly getting nothing more than cartoons from the WWF, so when he offered them an alternative, I was thrilled to work with him. Joel used a lot of local talent, but he also brought in wrestlers the fans had never seen in local rings ... Cactus Jack, Eddie Gilbert, Jerry Lawler, Terry Funk. I did the same thing, although I did it a little more responsibly, and I know Joel agrees with me on that. But Joel was never concerned about making money. What drove him was to give the fans something special, something new, something exciting. In doing so, he lost a lot of money, but he was happy knowing that he had made a difference.

No, if it hadn't been for Joel, there never would have been an ECW. He's been a big part of my life and I hold him in the highest esteem. Not only for what he did for wrestling, but for his attitude. Joel has such a love for his family, and he has been through some unbelievable physical challenges during the past few years. Despite that, he's the most positive, upbeat guy I know. I don't know how he does it. It's astounding. I'm like, "*Joel, doesn't that get you down? How can you be so upbeat?*"

He just says, "*What am I gonna do? These are the cards I've been dealt. I can either go through life depressed and angry, or I can enjoy the time I have left to the fullest.*" And that's what he chooses to do. He lives every moment to the fullest. I really admire that.

Joel is truly a great guy, and if this book is even half as entertaining as he is in person, it's sure to be a great read.

From the desk of
JOEL. A. GOODHART

CAN YOU BELIEVE IT!!! The Tri-State Wrestling Alliance is now the largest independent wrestling organization in the country, when you take attendance and gate in to consideration. And you are the ones that have made it happen. As we get larger, please know that the fans are our #1 concern and that will NEVER change. This past week, the TWA had its first TV taping and I am sure that you will be pleased when you see the final product. Many of the local cable systems will be carrying this show and once contracts are signed, we will announce the stations and times on Rasslin' Radio on 610 WIP.

We have several confirmed cards in the near future.
  *June 1 - Trenton CYO, Trenton NJ
  *June 2 - Bar Wars V, Philadelphia Original Sports Bar, Philadelphia, PA
  *June 22 - Wild By Wildwood, Middle Township Memorial Field, Wildwood, NJ
  *June 23 - Bar Wars, the Premier, Baltimore Original Sports Bar, Baltimore, MD
  *July 12 Asbury Park Convention Center, Asbury Park, NJ
  *August 3 - Summer Sizzler II, Philadelphia Civic Center, Philadelphia, PA
  *August 11 - Wrestling Woodstock, Hellertown, PA

We will be announcing the lineups for these cards as soon as they are completed but I think that you will definitely want to be at Wrestling Woodstock which will run from 12 noon to 8 PM on a 25 acre tract of land with a lake, picnic grounds, live music, activities for the whole family and a lot more. We are calling this card.......PEOPLE, PICNIC, AND PUNISHMENT!!!!

Needless to say, the offices of Tri-State Wrestling Alliance are busy attempting to give you the very best professional wrestling and I want to take this opportunity to thank you for your support and I want to reaffirm our motto ... "WE WRESTLE, WE BRAWL, WE DO IT ALL!!"

JOEL GOODHART

Letter released in June 1991

1 Out of the Wrestling Closet

I can't think of any better place to start than the beginning. Where and when were you born, Joel?

Born in Philadelphia ... Aug. 28, 1953, at Jefferson Hospital. Not that it matters, but I was home grown and raised in Philadelphia. There was only one year — my freshman college year, in Hawaii, of all places — that I've lived outside the Philadelphia area.

You moved there to go to school?

Yes, at a place called Chaminade College. I don't know if it's still out, but there was a book called *Barron's Guide to Colleges*. B-A-R-R-O-N-S. Anyway, I was in high school and one day my mother asked me, "*When are you going to get serious about picking a college?*" Well, I wasn't that Ivy League student. I knew I wasn't going to go to a major university, so I got a copy of the book and looked through it.

This was back ... obviously, I was born in '53, so this was in the late '60s, early '70s. It was ten dollars to apply to a college. My father gave me a budget of $100 to pick colleges and apply. So, I always figured, "*Okay, I'm in Philadelphia, so I'll probably go to Temple or LaSalle.*" But, the first college I applied to was a college called Woodstock College.

What led you to Woodstock College?

(laughs) I thought the name was pretty cool. I had a great, logical reason for picking the colleges I did. I applied to the University of Miami because ... what the hell? Why not go to Florida where it's warm? I applied to the University of Montana because I always wanted to be a cowboy. I sent ten dollars to the University of Nevada, Las Vegas, because ... well, I loved to gamble! Why not? So I had really good reasons for picking the schools I did. Then I thought, "*Why not go to Hawaii?*" I looked up University of Hawaii and I found this college called Chaminade. I mean, it's literally across the street from the University of Hawaii, and it was a smaller school, so I applied there. Well, I sent out all those applications and the first one that came back was a letter from Woodstock College. In so many words, it said, "*Thank you for your application. However, we're a seminary and we don't think that's what you wanted to apply to.*" (laughs) Here I thought I was going to go to Woodstock College and I ended up applying to a seminary. I wouldn't have been accepted, anyway, because the second letter I got was from Chaminade. I opened up the envelope and it was the first college that accepted me. Well, I don't know about you, but if you get accepted to Hawaii, no other college is gonna cut it. So, I wrote back and accepted Chaminade.

I flew out to Hawaii on my 18th birthday. It was the first time I had ever been on an airplane. It was a direct flight from Philly to Honolulu. And so, the first time I was on a plane was for like ten hours, and I started my college career. I had so many people ask me, "*Why did you choose Hawaii?*"

My answer? "*Why not?*" I mean, look ... I knew I was going to be a B-student. That's what I was. I remember sitting at the dinner table. Our family ate dinner together every night, and on that night, my father and mother were arguing because

Chaminade was ten dollars a semester more than Temple. My father always told me, "*My job is to educate you. If you're going to be away from home, that's on you. If you choose to go to Hawaii, you better start saving up some money.*" So I worked three jobs. I was a bus boy at a restaurant here in Philly. I also worked at one of the local family supermarkets, carrying bags for ladies — you know, to their car. — and I drove a Jack & Jill Ice Cream truck. During those two summers, I saved up a couple thousand dollars, which back then was real, real money.

When I got to Hawaii, my father opened up an account at a bank called Palisades Bank and my parents put me on an allowance of $15 a week. Back then, obviously, there were no cell phones, no computers, no text, so when I landed, I had to call home collect.

The younger people reading this book won't have any idea what "call collect" means.

(laughs) You are so right. Back then, if you wanted to call outside your local area, you called long distance, or what they called "collect." When you call someone collect, the person you were calling paid for the phone call, which I believe was something like 25¢ a minute. That really added up fast and 25¢ was a lot of money back then.

Yes, it was, and I can remember when it was 75¢ a minute.

It wasn't cheap, so you didn't talk long. When I called home, my mother, my father and my sister all answered the phone because, again, that was the first time I had flown and the first time I had ever really been away from home.

Just another explanation for the younger generation, most homes back then had multiple phones in the house, all tied into the same line, so everybody could talk at the same time.

That's right. It's amazing how technology has changed since then. Anyway, I called and told them I was in Honolulu. At the time, the way they had it set up, they actually had somebody from the student body pick me up at the airport. And again, we're back to the old days when there was no Uber. The only thing close to that was taxis. Well, the person who picked me up took me on a tour of the island. You can do a round-trip in a car in about four-and-a-half hours, so for the first three, four or five hours of my days in Honolulu, I was given a road tour, which was absolutely phenomenal. Here I was coming from Philadelphia and all I'm seeing is water, beaches and hotels. It was really cool, but that's how I got started. And get this ... while I was in Honolulu, I went to watch professional wrestling — they had wrestling matches on a somewhat regular basis at the local arena [Honolulu International Center]. Sweet Daddy Siki, Johnny Barend, Moondog Mayne, and all those guys. They were big draws there.

What year was that?

That was 1971. That's when I first saw Jimmy Snuka.

Okay, let's back up a little. Did you play any sports in high school?

I played soccer, but I got hurt. I injured my leg at the beginning of the season, so I never even played in a game. So, no play, no sports. I didn't play football, I didn't play baseball. I went to high school for classes and all I wanted to do was get home when they were over.

Did your school have an amateur wrestling team? Or did that just not cross your radar at the time?

It didn't cross my radar at all. I wasn't a physical guy. That was not for me. The guys that did the wrestling were always cut [in shape]. I was never cut. I never spent time in the gym. The only thing I did in high school that was extracurricular was the acting club.

Did you not have any other hobbies as a teenager? What did you like to do?
Uh, teenager (pause) ... at that point in my life, I didn't really have any ... I was a political science freak, so I was part of the Poli Sci club. But no, I didn't have hobbies. I got into collecting coins for a little bit, but there was no serious hobby.

When was it you first realized — now this would probably have been before Hawaii, but maybe not — when was the first time you realized there was such a thing as professional wrestling. You know, your "Ah-ha!" moment?
Well, my dad took me to the matches at the Philadelphia Arena ... and that's weird because I don't remember specific matches. I just remember going ... and it was just phenomenal. I saw a match with Bruno Sammartino and ... I believe his opponent was George Steele. They wrestled inside the ring, got out of the ring, fought down the aisle, and went outside. Of course, half the crowd followed them out. Bruno slammed George down onto the hood of a car ... and it looked pretty cool. "*Oh, wow! That was really cool.*" Now, in hindsight, the car obviously was planted there, but I remember that.

Of course, they came back in. I don't remember the result. I don't remember the finish, but I remember that. I got to know Bruno really well later on and I kidded him about that. He confirmed that he did it, so I know it wasn't a faulty memory in my head. I guess everybody has somebody that they have a liking for, and for some reason, when I was growing up, Spiros Arion was my guy. Back then ... I mean, people today don't realize it, but back then it was just so different to what's being presented today. It was phenomenal. So my father was the catalyst for my love of professional wrestling.

Do you have an idea of the year you first went to a house show?
Well, it was definitely in the '60s. I'm going to say it was the late '60s. I was born in '53. I was 14 or 15 years old, so it had to be '67, '68.

Did you and your dad go to the matches regularly?
We didn't go that much. My father was always ... it was always about the dollars. But I remember going to Phillies [baseball] games with my father. We went to 76ers [basketball] games — they were the Warriors then — but we didn't have hockey until a few years later. So we went to basketball, went to baseball, went to wrestling. I'm not going to say we went every month ... maybe once every six months or so.

Before you went to Hawaii, did you ever get to talk to a wrestler, or have any interaction with anybody in the business?
Anyone? Absolutely not. I remember those days. It was just pure sport. It was cool. It was fun. We never got the good seats, because again, I think tickets back then were $3, $4 and $5. It's like, my parents argued about college admissions being $10, so we always sat in the $3 seats. We were never close enough to get near the wrestlers, so I never got to interact with them at all.

Did any of your friends at school watch wrestling?
No. It's funny. I don't know if you know this, but when I was into wrestling big-time, we had t-shirts made and we came up with the saying, "*I'm out of the closet, no longer meek, I'm finally admitting I'm a wrestling freak.*" And we sold tons of those shirts. Anyway, back then, you never communicated that you were a wrestling fan. It was something you watched on TV. It was not mainstream in any sense of the word. I remember going to Roller Derby. Roller Derby was the same way. Philadelphia Roller Derby was crazier than wrestling. Roller Derby fans were nuts. But you never admitted to people that you were a wrestling fan or anything like that, so I don't remember having conversations about wrestling. I certainly didn't go to the matches with friends. Someday, I'm going to see someone wearing

that shirt. *"I'm out of the closet, no longer meek, I'm finally admitting I'm a wrestling freak."*

I need to get a picture of that shirt for the book.

Yes! We had the TWA logo on the back of those shirts when we later promoted the Tri-State Wrestling Alliance. And when I opened up my wrestling store, which is another story that we'll get to, we sold those shirts. That was the hottest-selling shirt. People ask me if I still have any. The answer's no, but I'm sure somebody has.

Let's move forward to Honolulu. How often did you go to wrestling there?

It was just a couple of times. I got there in September and went back home at the end of the first school year, so I was there for what ... nine months? I probably went three times.

Honolulu was a hot promotion at that time. Johnny Barend was the man.

Oh, my god. He was! Sweet Daddy Siki is the one guy I truly remember. He was a black guy with white hair, you know. At the time, there were no black guys with white hair. It was just ... you know, back then, you didn't appreciate what you saw. You just didn't! I wish I had gone to every match. I wish I had gotten involved earlier. But yeah, those matches were wild.

Carmela Panfil shows off one of the t-shirts.

When you look back on the talent in the ring at the time, we loved it, but we really took it for granted. We didn't realize it at the time, but we were pretty spoiled by the talent that came in and out of the various territories.

Oh, we really were. Back then, the opening match was just two guys in wrestling trunks. I mean, it was just ... the ring didn't have TNA or WWE on it. It was just a plain ring. The ropes weren't red, white and blue. The ropes and turnbuckles were plain black. It was what was happening in the ring that made that whole thing work.

Absolutely. So you were there for just one year before you went back to Philly?

Exactly. I did my first year and then I came back to Philly for my sophomore year.

Did you continue your college education somewhere else?

Yeah. I went to Temple University for my sophomore year and did three years. I got my Bachelor of Arts degree in Political Science.

What did you do after you graduated, and did you go to the wrestling matches during those three years?

No. Again, it was weird. I don't recall going to the matches on any kind of a regular basis at all. I mean, I completely lost touch with wrestling. I watched it on TV, but it wasn't something that I would go down to the Spectrum — or wherever it was at the time — to go to the matches. They used to do TV shoots in Philadelphia, but I didn't go to any of them. I was one of those typical wrestling fans from afar who watched it on TV. I remember watching TV and seeing [Larry] Zbyszko slam Bruno with a chair. I never had a desire to go to the matches. But, yeah. That was really weird ... to have no interest in going and then wind up doing what I did. I was a regular watcher of the television program, though.

Did you work a job when you were in college?

Yeah, I worked a couple of jobs while I was in college, but think about this. I graduated in 1975, and in the '70s, political activism was on the rise. The Vietnam

War was coming to an end. I grew a 13-inch ponytail and morphed into a hippy — which I guess was the term everybody used back then. My mother used to argue about me all the time. To my father, I could never do anything wrong. My mother, I could never do anything right. My mother would say, "*He can't get a job with a ponytail!*" My father would say, "*It's what's in the head that counts!*"

Anyway, this leads up to the time when I was politically active. There was a guy by the name of Herb Denenberg, which wouldn't mean anything to you, but Herb was very popular in Pennsylvania and he decided to run for the U.S. Senate. When he did, I got involved with his campaign. At the time, he was the commissioner of the Pennsylvania Department of Insurance, but he was also an attorney by trade. In fact, he taught law at Temple University. I got to know Herb fairly well and I would sit in on the planning meetings. At the time, he had meetings at the Victory Building at 10th and Chestnut.

One day, I pulled Herb aside and told him I was a college graduate, but I wasn't sure exactly what I wanted to do. He said, "*Why don't you try the insurance industry?*" (laughs) I looked at him and said, "*I've got a thirteen-inch ponytail and a beard.*"

You know, everybody in the insurance business back then wore a suit and tie, and I didn't even *own* a suit and tie. He said, "*Well, here's the deal. How old are you?*" At the time I was 22. He says, "*If you get into the insurance industry and you survive until you're thirty, you'll be set for life.*" That really hit home with me, so I said, "*Okay.*"

So I asked him, "*How many insurance companies are there?*" He told me, and I remember the number distinctly ... 1,836. Keep in mind, he was the insurance commissioner. I said, "*I don't know anything about any of them, so if I interview at five or six a day, it's going to take me two years to interview at them all.*"

He said, "*No, no, no, no, no,*" and gave me a list of six companies. He says, "*You go interview at these six. These companies are known for their training. If you hook up with any of these six, just put the blinders on, learn the systems, and they'll teach you.*" Well, there was something about the way he said it and what he said. I admired him to no end.

So, a little bit of history here. My father was a doctor — a podiatrist — and his brother, my uncle, was a dentist. When they were growing up, the story in the area where they lived was that the Goodhart boys had you from head to toe. Now, my uncle's son, my cousin, became a dentist, and my father was grooming me to be the fourth Dr. Goodhart. However, I was not one for medicine, let alone med school. He was amazed that I even *went* to college.

So, at some point, I had to break the news to my father that I wasn't going to podiatry school. I remember that day. It was the worst day of my life. I was scared to death. Now, the year prior to that, my father had redone his offices and added an office for when his son — me — came in. I have to sit down with him and tell him that I wasn't going to be a doctor. And the worst part of this was, my father was actually a founder of the podiatry school in Philadelphia, so getting in was not the issue. It just wasn't for me. So I sat down with him. I said, "*Look, my goal is to be a lawyer. I'll be a Juris Doctor,*" which was the highest law degree you could get.

My father was okay with whatever I wanted to do. Well, the idea of being a lawyer sounded great, but when reality sank in and I thought about going to college for three more years, I knew it just wasn't for me. So this whole idea that Herb presented to me about the insurance industry began to sound really good. I interviewed with a few companies. The first company I went into, they almost threw me out. I walked in with the 13-inch pony tail. I wore a shirt, but no tie. They were just so blue-blood straight-cut. It just didn't work for me. The second company I went to was a company called The Equitable. I sat down with the people at The Equitable and, lo and behold, they actually hired me.

Now, I don't remember the details, but in the process, they told me that I had to cut my hair. Of course, I knew that. Later on, though, I learned that they hired me because my father was a doctor. You see, when you get started in the insurance business, it's who you know and contacts you've made. They jumped to some conclusions that my father would be there to help me get started. In their eyes, my father, being the prominent doctor that he was, would have thousands of contacts. We sat down and I got hired. You'll love this. I started April 1st, 1976, with a $500 a month salary — $250 on the 15th of the money, $250 on the last day of the month — plus half-commissions. And at the end of two years, if I would have made full commission, then I would get the difference. So I was hired on a $6,000 annual guarantee. I mean, that was crazy! Six thousand bucks guaranteed!

So, I started to learn the business. I took their course and I had to pass a test, so I put all the test information on flashcards, and the woman I was dating at that time — who later became my first wife — she would show me the flash cards. She'd say, *"What's indemnity,"* and I would give her the answer, et cetera, et cetera. I passed the test.

I started April 1st, 1976, so on March 31st at twelve noon, I got my hair cut. There was a hairstyle salon there in the area called The Mane Event, so I went in there to get my hair cut. Here I walk in and my hair was as straggly as it could be. I was on that chair for almost an hour. I walked out with my 13-inch ponytail hair in a bag, which I kept for about ten years until my wife at the time threw it out. I have a picture hanging on a wall of my office of me looking like Meat Loaf.

> Meat Loaf, born Marvin Lee Aday, was a hard rock/heavy metal singer and film actor.

Part of the deal with The Equitable was, when someone new started with the company, they would run one ad in one newspaper to announce their affiliation. There's a newspaper in Philly called the *Jewish Exponent*, so I figured I'd put the announcement in there so all my friends, family and neighbors would see it. That's the picture I had enlarged and hanging on the wall in my office.

I looked like Meat Loaf, but when I walked into the office on April 1st, my first day there, nobody knew who I was. My beard was trimmed, my hair was parted down the middle, and I actually went out and bought some sport jackets and suits. I did my training and went to work. It just felt right. As crazy as it sounds, I was walking around wearing a suit and carrying a briefcase, and somehow or another, I just felt ... you know, I felt legit. I felt like a businessman. I felt like I had achieved something. I hadn't achieved squat, but I had my suit and briefcase. It was just ... I don't know. It felt good.

SALES
We want you if you want independence, are willing to work hard & expect to be compensated accordingly. To the qualified applicant we offer an opportunity with unlimited income and permanent career with one of the largest financial planning corporations in the world. Salary plus comm basis.
    CALL MONDAY
Successful people have little time, I, Joel Goodhart, will be available Monday at 215-667-6115 (Bala Cynwyd)
    Equal Opportunity Employer

June 15, 1980

2  The Squared Circle

So, you're in the insurance business. When did wrestling come back into the picture?
All right. I'm thinking that year was 1985.
That's correct.
So, I'm in the insurance business, and during those nine years, I got myself established. I survived financially. I was making a good living ... real money. I was married at the time and I had built a relationship with some accountants who were starting to send me referrals. One day, one of them called me ... an accountant named Bruce Goldstein. He said, "*I have somebody I want you to talk to. I want you to meet him. He's an interesting guy and he and his wife need some life insurance. Can you go out to see him today?*"

Well, in those days, you went out to the client. I mean, today they all come to me, but in those days you went out to the client, so I drove over to their house. The first thing I realized was that they were in a neighborhood in the River Wards section of Philadelphia called Port Richmond, which today is very heavy blue-collar. Back in the day, I would say it was low to middle class. I walked into the house and, quite frankly, I didn't know what they wanted. Their names were Paul and Carmela Panfil. Now, Carmela will play a big role in this story, but we sat down and I started talking about life insurance. They were both ... I'll just say they were heavy. They weren't fat. They were heavy, so I knew they weren't going to qualify for the preferred rate. We discussed things and they decided to fill out and submit the applications. Back in the day, the applications were just two pages. It was simple. At the end of our meeting, Paul says to me, "*By the way, if you ever need tickets for any concerts, Broadway shows, or sporting events, let me know. I hawk tickets on the side and I can get you whatever you need.*"

I thought, "*Hey, this sounds good.*" It's great to be able to call somebody up and get front row seats to something. You pay extra, but you can at least get them. That was the end of that conversation. Two weeks later, I got the information for their life insurance, so I went back to see them. After I presented the insurance policy and all the accompanying literature, Paul says to me, "*By the way, are you doing anything Saturday night?*"

I said, "*Why?*" Now, keep in mind. I have kids at home, a wife at home, and he asks me if I'm doing anything Saturday night. I said, "*No.*"

He says, "*Well, I got front row seats to the wrestling matches. Do you wanna go?*"

Wow! So I said, "*Sure!*"

Now, this was when the NWA [National Wrestling Alliance] was coming to Philadelphia. I can probably confirm the year if I can talk to somebody who was in Crockett's office. Elliott Murnick was my contact, but he passed away a couple of years ago. Anyway, we go to the matches. Paul was able to get front-row seats because the NWA was fairly new to the area. There I am sitting on the front row with Paul ... and the matches were just awesome! I hadn't been to a wrestling show in 10 years, give or take, and I started going every month with Paul. Now

Carmela, like I said, really became a big part of the story because I would come to their house and we'd sit and talk wrestling all night. It was just ridiculous.

Your attendance at those shows led to an amazing time in your life, which we'll get to later. What did Paul do for a living?

Paul was in the metal business — iron, sheet metal, that kind of stuff — so he was a blue-collar kind of guy. Carmela was an at-home, Italian mom. And here's this Jewish kid hanging around with them. We had a connection because of the wrestling stuff. Well, Carmela had history. Bruno had stayed with her, Dominic DeNucci had stayed with her. She was friends with Ivan Putski. They used to go to the matches all the time. All of a sudden, I'm starting to get into this flavor of what professional wrestling had morphed into from what I knew in the past ... battling inside the ring, battling outside.

Friday, July 5, 1985 —
Squared Circle opened their doors, claiming to be the first shop selling merchandise specific to professional wrestling. They were located at the I-95 Marketplace on U.S. 1 and Route 413 (exit 24, I-95 north) in Levittown, Pennsylvania.

> **THE SQUARED CIRCLE wrestling paraphernalia**; I-95 Market Place, Routes 1 and 413, Levittown; Carmela F. Panfile.

Carmela and I, one day, were sitting around their table having a bite to eat. She used to cook phenomenally. She made the best chicken cutlets in the world ... unbelievable. One day, we looked at each other and said, "*You know, we need to do something in the wrestling business.*" That was when wrestling was starting to become more mainstream. The WWF was big-time. It was really taking off and Hulk Hogan was getting very popular. The NWA was also coming into the Northeast. So, we started to throw ideas around. I wasn't thinking about promoting wrestling, but I wanted to do something different from what I did every day. Out of the blue, Carmela and I came up with the idea of opening a wrestling store. I had never heard of anyone having a wrestling store. At the time, if you wanted any wrestling dolls, you had to go to Toys "R" Us. I mean, it was all mainstream stuff, but we wanted to get into the wrestling piece of this, so we decided to open a wrestling store called the Squared Circle. We came up with the name and actually trademarked it. Since I was still working full-time in my profession, and Paul was doing his thing full-time, and Carmela was raising a child — she was a full-time mom — we didn't want to do anything that was going to be open seven days a week. We wanted to maintain our regular schedules ... just kind of fill the weekend. Paul found a place called the I-95 Marketplace, which was open Thursdays through Sundays. The I-95 Marketplace was like a flea market.

Let's talk about the origins of the Squared Circle store. Were the start-up costs for the store very substantial?

It's been so long, but I think we earmarked $5,000 to start the store.

Was the start-up money a 50/50 split between you and the Panfils, or was it a three-way split.

That's something I've thought about since you sent me that list of questions. I'm pretty sure I put up $2,500 and Paul and Carmela put up $2,500. I don't think we were one-third partners ... me, Paul and Carmela. I think it was a 50/50 split.

One thing I do remember is having that conversation because, if Carmela and Paul each had 33 percent, I would be the minority partner ... and they were husband and wife! So I think it was 50/50.

One thing I do know that was an even split was that none of us had any retail experience. (laughs) We had to go find the companies who did the marketing, we had to figure out how to order the wrestling magazines, and then, we got in touch with the WWF and learned where they did their merchandising. And since we didn't have any background in retail, none of the production companies would give us consignment on their stuff, so when we bought the Hulk Hogan figures, we had to buy them outright. When we needed action figures of any wrestlers, we have to buy them. The companies all wanted their money up-front because we didn't have a track record or business credit. When we opened the store, though, we had a stocked store. The only thing we got on consignment was the magazines, but the reality was, people didn't come to our store to buy the magazines because they either subscribed to them or bought them in their local five-and-dime or grocery stores. We discounted the magazine in the hopes of enticing buyers, but we could only discount so much. That was a problem with all our merchandise. I mean, the Toys "R" Us stores of the world could certainly sell things cheaper than we could.

We opened the store [on July 5, 1985], which took up about 150 square feet in the Marketplace, and it was all wrestling stuff. Carmela and I had to go buy a cash register. We had no idea how to do all that stuff.

As I mentioned earlier, Carmela was friends with a number of the wrestlers, so at our grand opening, we had an autograph signing with Bruno Sammartino and Dominic DeNucci. That got the word out big-time. We had them sitting outside our store at a table.

It sounds like you got off to a good start.

We absolutely did ... well, sort of. People would get in line and ... well, the people who got in line for the autographs got the autographs, then they'd walk in the store and maybe they'd buy a shirt. Maybe they didn't. Again, we had such a small store that we didn't have Bruno and Dominic *in* the store. We had them *outside* the store, so people didn't even have to walk into the store to get the signatures.

You know, it would have been smart to figure out a way to put Bruno and Dominic in the back of the store because, that way, the people might buy something on their way through, but again, this goes back to that day, at that time, neither myself nor Carmela had any retail experience at all.

We had two regular televisions. Big high-def TVs weren't even a thing at that point, obviously, so we had wrestling running non-stop on two televisions. Fans would come in and watch Memphis and Japanese wrestling, as well as other stuff that tape traders sent around. We had a lot of customers — and I use that term loosely — who weren't happy with what the WWF was offering, so we looked for videos that might interest them. Slowly, but surely, the word got out that there was a wrestling store out in the middle of nowhere. When wrestling fans showed up for the first time, they'd drive up every weekend after that. We became the center of focus.

What ultimately happened, though, was that we had a large fan base that didn't buy anything. The only people who really got into what we were doing were the fans who were buying the VHS tapes at the time. We had some things that other stores didn't have, like specific t-shirts, but for the most part, most of the people who came to our store would spend all afternoon watching video tapes and buying sodas from the vendors next to us. Yeah, it was frustrating. It was a cool idea, but in the world of finance, it made no sense. As you said, though, it did give us a starting point and we were having a lot of fun.

Carmela once made a comment in a newspaper article that you had plans to open stores in other towns.
Yep, but we never did. You know, in the beginning, we realized we were the only game in town, so we thought we'd clean up. I always had this starry-eyed vision. I have to do the biggest thing, so why not open these things and make a chain out of it? You know, franchise them. Well, that's easier said than done. We never made money at that store, so it would have been hard to convince *anybody* to open one. So, yeah. That never happened.

Did it ever get to a point where you were at least covering your expenses?
Well, the answer to that is, yes ... our expenses. We did make a little money — very little — but that was only after we started promoting wrestling shows. I knew that even if the store closed, at least the shows would make money. I used to say we had built a kingdom. The truth is, though, that we never made any real money. In fact, when I shut down Tri-State, I calculated my losses ... and they came to $168,000. That was from 1985 until around '92, and at that time, $168,000 was a *lot* of money. Most of that fell on me. I was doing really well in the insurance and investment business, but I was funneling most of it into the wrestling business. However! I was a rock star! (laughs) The one thing you learn about the wrestling business is that it's hard to find a niche in the business where you can make money. I admired guys like Rob Feinstein, who's made money, and Meltzer obviously made a living. Guys like that, who were on the outside, but were able to make money, did what I couldn't do. You know, I blazed some trails for these guys, but the reality is that some people find a niche in the business and make a living doing it, while others, like myself, never did.

I'm sitting here listening to this and I'm stunned by the fact that you lost $168,000, and yet, it hasn't seemed to jade you against the wrestling business. No disrespect meant, but you really were what we call a money-mark. I mean, you just didn't seem to care. And even funnier than that, while I'm sitting here thinking, *"Why would he hang in there as long as he did when he wasn't making much, if any, money,"* I suddenly put myself in your place. I've either been in or around the wrestling business since 1968, and I spend four to six, often more, hours a day writing, researching, whatever. And yet, if I divided the money I've made by the hours I've put into what I do, I've made pocket change. But I think for both of us, it was — and is — a labor of love.
You are right on the money when you say I was a money-mark. There's no question about it. I just loved being the center of attention. I loved the fact that the wrestling fans saw me as their connection to the business. We'll get into this later, but I did the ring announcing for [Jim] Crockett's NWA shows when they were in town, and most nights, I'd go to the Airport Marriott after a show. (laughs) Now, I was one of those guys who thought, *"If I change my clothes after the show, nobody will know who the hell I am,"* so I would wear the tuxedo that I wore in the ring when I went to the Marriott. Right? (laughs) Well, when I walked into the Marriott, there would be 200 fans there and they'd ask for my autograph. That's was really cool. To me, it was a rush. I was a player. I was the center of the universe. (laughs) Oh, god. Back in the day when I was young, I was so stupid. I wouldn't do it now, but back then it was amazing ... absolutely amazing!

The wrestlers talked to me, too, because they knew who I was. I got to be friendly with a lot of them. I mean, the parties were notorious.

In the days when I first broke into the business, wrestling promoters had stores sell tickets. Did you ever approach the WWF or NWA about selling tickets for them through the Squared Circle?

Well, what ultimately happened is, we did sell tickets for WCW. As we got more and more involved with the store, we were able to get tickets to their house shows. They would give me a block of 50 to a hundred tickets to sell, and they would always be the first five rows of one section, so once people got to know us, they knew if they wanted good seats, they could get them from us. We had the best seats in the house to those shows. So, we made a couple of dollars on ticket sales. We weren't scalping because we actually got the tickets from WCW. The only time we ever did tickets for Vince was when they had a *SummerSlam* at The Spectrum in Philadelphia [Aug. 27, 1990] and a couple of big shows in Philly. We had enough traffic come into the store that we would get a block of a hundred tickets, you know, that kind of thing, but we never became a major ticket outlet. They never promoted us on their TV show as a ticket outlet, either.

In regards to merchandise, did you deal specifically with wholesalers, or did you also deal with the WWF?

We dealt with wholesalers. It was interesting. I got invited to one WWF party in New York and, supposedly, the wholesalers suggested that I be there. They were celebrating Hulk Hogan's birthday. Strangely enough, Hogan is eleven days older than me. He was born on August 17, 1953, I was born August 28, so he's eleven days older. Now, I've never been a fan of the WWF product. I couldn't stand Vince. I didn't like what he was doing to the sport, but I was smart enough to realize that I could make money off their fan base, so I made the trip to New York. I'm not an idiot. The party was at a swank little place in New York and the only guys I actually got to meet at the party were Hulk Hogan and Brutus Beefcake, but they wouldn't remember me from Adam. When I left, I felt like I had to take a shower. You know, the WWF just was not my cup of tea. The Vince boys just were not what I was into. I blasted Vince and the WWF on our radio show all the time, so I kind of felt like a traitor when I left the party. The one thing I did learn was, you have no idea just how big Hogan really is until you stand next to him. It was scary. I was happy that I went, but I was happier to get the hell out of there.

What was your best-selling item in the store?

(pause) Wow! I'd have to say VHS tapes. Yeah, I think the video tapes because they were hard to find. We had shows from Japan, the Pacific Northwest and World Class. Carmela and I contacted Memphis, so we had the Memphis TV shows. Yes, I think tapes were probably our number-one seller. I think we did okay on the magazines, and Hulk Hogan posters always sold well, but videotapes were probably the number-one stock item.

I once read that you owned the exclusive rights to sell the Puerto Rico wrestling tapes. Is that correct?

Well, I had the … it wasn't exclusive, but they gave me the rights. Abdullah the Butcher hooked me up with Carlos Colón. We had the Puerto Rico tapes at the store. Tape trading was not the art form at that time that it was later on, so I don't know who said exclusive rights. I mean, we didn't have exclusive rights. We weren't big enough to have exclusive rights. New Japan also worked with me and gave me rights to sell their tapes, but there was never exclusive anything.

Do you remember any specifics of the deal you had with New Japan or Carlos Colón?

The deal was simple. I bought the tapes from them and I sold them. They were originals.

Oh! I thought you bought one copy and made copies to sell.

Joel helps two customers at the Squared Circle

Oh, no. I wasn't selling copies of copies, or copies of copies of copies. If you bought tapes at the store, you were buying originals. We weren't selling copies.

Did you sell tapes from other promotions at the store?
Yeah. Memphis, WWF. Again, the WWF tapes we bought through a distributor, so they weren't copies. We sold NWA tapes, but they certainly didn't have as many. One of the things we decided early on was, we were not going to sell copies, so when people bought our tapes, they knew that a tape of Puerto Rico wrestling actually came from Puerto Rico. We just didn't sell bootleg copies. We weren't into that.

Was the deal with Memphis the same as it was with Puerto Rico and New Japan ... you bought and sold originals?
Yeah, it was that simple. The organizations made the tapes and we bought them directly. The Memphis tapes were only available in Memphis — you know, Jackson, Nashville, whatever — so them getting an outlet in Philadelphia was pretty cool. We wouldn't buy a lot of tapes ... maybe ten of each show. If we sold the ten, we'd buy ten more. But, yes, we were authorized, but it was never exclusive.

I don't think I ever heard about Memphis selling tapes to the public in the Memphis territory. Did they actually do that?
Yeah, they had tapes.

That's something I didn't know. That was after I got out of the business.
Yeah, we didn't have bootlegs. Some of the guys actually had their own tapes. Jimmy Valiant had a tape, Eddie Gilbert had tapes, Adrian Street had tapes. We would show them on our wrestling tours ... the videos in the buses.

And you had one playing all the time in the store.
Yes. When Jerry Lawler got his head shaved, they had an entire video on that feud. Memphis had one on the cage match. They had Paul E, they had Austin Idol, they had all the interviews. I mean, those tapes were hot sellers.

The hardcore fans did a lot of tape-trading, but most people didn't even know about that until years later.
Oh, yeah. Jerry Lawler's TV shows in Memphis [*The Jerry Lawler Show*] were weekly and we'd get them a few weeks after they aired. People liked them because Memphis had such a different style of wrestling. We eventually appeared on that show.

On Aug. 2, 1987, Paul & Carmela Panfil and Joel Goodhart appeared on Memphis TV on *The Jerry Lawler Show*.

There's an episode of *The Jerry Lawler Show* on YouTube with you, Paul and Carmela as guest.
We were on TV in Memphis twice actually. The first time on Lawler's show was Carmela, her husband Paul, and myself. [Aug. 2, 1987] After Lawler asked us questions about *Rasslin' Radio*, we gave him an award. Carmela was sitting in a chair opposite Jerry, while Paul and I stood behind him. I was wearing this stupid red jacket that had *Rasslin' Radio* embroidered on the back. I remember thinking to myself that, *"Nobody in Philadelphia will ever know this happened."* Now, the people who traded tapes saw it, but nobody else did.

Pepper Rodgers, the football coach, was also a guest on that show.
Yes, and 30 or 40 of the fans on the bus trip were in the audience. I got to talk a little — very little — but I don't remember Paul saying anything. He was really shy. At the end of the show, Carmela gave Jerry an acrylic brick that had something engraved on it.

"Rasslin' Radio and Philadelphia Loves Jerry the King and C.W.A."

How did you get "in" when it came to contacting the wrestlers?
Carmela had relationships with the wrestlers like nobody else. When she was growing up, the guys would come to her place at her mom's for dinner ... DeNucci, Bruno, Putski, Baron Mikel Scicluna. I used to kid her all the time, *"I'll bet there was a lot of sexual activity."*

"No, no, no."

And I'm sure there wasn't. Carmela was just a good person. Anyway, she knew the guys, so when we got involved, Carmela started making phone calls. That's how we got Bruno and Dominic to our grand opening. She also knew Jules Strongbow, who later appeared on the first wrestling card I ever promoted. She knew them all. She had the contacts, not me.

On Sunday, Dec. 22, 1985, Chief Jules Strongbow appeared at the Squared Circle from 1 p.m. to 4 p.m. to sign autographs.

Strongbow signed autographs at the store on Dec. 22, 1985. Were there other times when you had wrestlers sign autographs at the store?

Not officially, but Bruno and Dominic stopped by every time they came to the city. At the time, Dominic was still wrestling, but he also was training wrestlers and promoting. After one of the autograph sessions, we sat and had lunch — or dinner, or whatever it was — and he said to us — in his heavy Italian accent, of course, God bless him — and he said, "*Did you ever think about promoting.*" Carmela and I looked at each other like, we wouldn't even know where to get started. So Dominic said, "*Let's get started.*" So we made plans to book a show at Neshaminy High School in Langhorne, which was about 15 minutes from the I-95 Marketplace. But it's one of those high schools that, if you don't know how to get there, you can't find it. Well, we booked the matches, and obviously, Dominic knew a lot of the local talent. The main event was Dominic DeNucci — of course, he made himself the main event — against Mighty Igor.

It's strange that Dominic booked himself against Igor, another babyface.

Dominic was our booker, so he wanted to have his name at the top. We had a tight budget, and it was hard to draw many people to a high school show with local guys. Dominic had been a big name in the WWWF and the people knew him. I don't know what his connection was to Mighty Igor, although they did wrestle in the same era. I think it was just a matter of Igor being the most available. I seem to remember that we had a $1,000 budget and Dominic wanted to have six or seven matches on the card. Of course, I gave the $1,000 to Dominic and told him that he could keep whatever he didn't spend, so he spent as little as possible. I think Dominic wound up with a hundred bucks. Years ago, I saw Dominic here at a show of old-time stars and we talked for ten or 15 minutes while he signed autographs for the people. I reminded him about that match and he remembered the whole story.

Now, at the time, Mighty Igor was really over the hill. (laughs) I mean, he hadn't wrestled in a long time, but Dominic and Igor used to be friends, so we put them on the top match. Troy Martin, who later became Shane Douglas, was on my card. I had not met Cactus Jack yet. He hadn't yet started training with Dominic. Anyway, we had a good card. We had some local guys on the card, but I didn't know who the hell they were. We drew something like 200 people, but we made money. I think we walked away with 300 bucks ...something like that. You know, it's one of those things that, once you get the flavor of being in the back and being in the business and hawking the tickets — I helped set up the ring — it gets in your blood. You've heard this a million times, I'm sure. Everybody tells you the story that they got started by setting up the ring. Well, I set up the ring. I thought the matches were good, although in hindsight, they sucked, but they were fine for what it was. Dominic was past his prime, but Dominic became my real "in" in the business. The first big card I ever promoted, I had Bruno and Dominic on the card. I got Bruno, obviously, through Dominic. But, anyway, we did that show and that got my juices flowing.

Where did you first meet Paul E. [Paul Heyman] and how did he come into the picture?
You know something? That's a great question because I don't have a clue what the answer is. I don't remember how I met Paul. That's weird. I saw Paul E. in Dallas a few years ago when I went to a *RAW* taping. It was the first time I'd seen him since 1992. He walked over. I didn't realize he was a businessman on Long Island. He just did that shit on the side for Vince. I'm trying to remember. I think it was through Jerry Lawler, but I can't say for sure.

Carmela & Jeannie (Peletsky) Siciliano talk to a customer.

We haven't talked about the fan club tours yet, but Paul E had worked in Memphis by the time you were doing the tours?
Yeah, I think it was through Jerry. It's a great question because now I'm thinking about it. It had to be through Jerry.

It's interesting because Paul E. started to let his hair grow long and I sort of followed suit. At some point, I let my hair grow a lot longer than he did his, but he kind of got me headed in that direction. We used to have great conversations. Paul E. was originally a photographer, so when I had him managing guys — Tom Prichard, Austin Idol, Larry Zbyszko — he'd pose for photos with them.

> The items sold at the Squared Circle included likenesses of Hulk Hogan and Roddy Piper, t-shirts, posters, buttons, board games, jigsaw puzzles, beach towels, kites, tote bags, coloring books, videotapes, 3-D slide viewers, watches, erasers, robes, belts, school lunchboxes, record albums, notebooks, photo albums, dolls, sheets, pillowcases, and comforters.
>
> During an interview, Carmela revealed that they sold *"more bad-guy stuff than good-guy stuff."* She also said they planned to syndicate their radio show and sell merchandise through mail orders, and had a list of 2,200 *"hard-core clientele."* Joel also had plans to publish a wrestling newsletter that would sell for $2.

3 Watching a Radio Broadcast

You mentioned blasting Vince on a radio show. Let's discuss how you got into radio.

One day, we were at the store and a man walked in. We didn't know him and he asked to speak with the owners. It's funny that I can't remember whether it was me or Carmela who was there at the time, but I think it was me. You'd think I'd remember something like that. Anyway, the guys says he was from WTTM [920 AM, now WNJE] in Trenton, New Jersey, and wanted to know if we'd like to do a wrestling show on the radio station. We didn't know anything about radio, but we liked the idea and we started to research it a bit. The station charged $75 for the 30-minute program, so Carmela and I signed a contract and made plans to drive to the station the next Saturday morning. WTTM was about a 30-minute drive from the store and we had to be there very early because the show aired at 7:00 in the morning. From there, we drove back to Levittown and opened the store.

The first reference found to the radio show, which aired on WTTM 92.2 FM, appeared in the March 1, 1986, edition of the *Philadelphia Inquirer*. The show was originally called "Rasslin' Review" and the co-hosts were Joel Goodhart & Carmela Panfil.

> **Radio shows**
> Rasslin Revue, 1 p.m. (WTTM-92.2 FM)
> Sportsline with Jeff Asch, 5 p.m. (WCAU-1210)
> Sports Talk with Bill Lyon, 6 p.m. (WWDB-96.5 FM)

So here we were buying the time. Over the next couple of weeks, word really started to get out about the program and people started calling in with questions about the wrestlers, wrestling shows, and even specific matches. Again, there was no [Dave] Meltzer newsletter dirt-sheets at that time. There was no Internet. There was no cable. This is just pure radio. We called the show *Rasslin' Revue*, so ultimately, the man from the station who came into the store was responsible for bringing us a whole new audience. It's a shame I can't remember his name. I don't think I'd recognize the name if I heard it.

At some point, we talked to a fellow by the name of Roger Krone. Roger was an insurance client of mine and has since passed away, but Roger sold radio time for the WDVT-AM 900 station in Philadelphia. WDVT stood for Delaware Valley Talk. The station was owned by a guy by the name of Frank Ford. Frank was a Philadelphia icon at the time. WDVT was located smack-dab in the middle of Philadelphia and it was heard everywhere!

Ford bought WFLN-AM 900, a classical radio station, in early 1985 and changed the name to WDVT and the format to "all-talk". Branded as "Talk 900", the station was located in the basement of NewMarket at 2nd and Lombard streets. Joel and Carmela's first show on WDVT aired on Sept. 13, 1986, from 1-2 p.m. and was repeated on Sunday from noon to one.

> Noon-1 WDVT Rasslin' Radio
> Joel Goodhart & Carmela Panfil.
> 1-2 WDVT It's The Law Chuck Rabb, host.
> 2-3 WXPN Amazon Country
> 2-3 WDVT Let's Talk Real Estate
> Phil Mitsch.

When we first started on WDVT, the show aired on Saturday mornings at 11:00 a.m. and was rebroadcast on Sunday mornings. At some point, the show was moved to late Friday afternoon — 6:30 p.m. to 8:00 p.m. — and later to Sunday from noon to 1:00 p.m.

It was always give-and-take on Friday afternoons because the station was licensed for daytime operation only, so it went off the air at dusk to avoid interfering with stations in other parts of the country. The neat thing was that the radio station was in a glass-encased booth in a little shopping area, like an outdoor mall, in an area of Philadelphia called Society Hill. People would sit in the atrium and watch Carmela and I do the radio show. We started getting an audience for the radio show, especially wrestling fans because ... you know, if a wrestling fan comes once, they'll come every time. We could have sold tickets. We'd have 20 to 30 people there every Sunday to watch our radio show. I always thought that was funny because, if you know anything about radio, you know there's nothing to see. How boring is it to watch two people do a radio show? Well, it would be if we had been talking about anything other than wrestling. We *did* have the audio piped outside so people could hear the show.

When we moved to WDVT, we suddenly hit what I would call mainstream radio. We started getting ratings and the whole nine yards. We paid for the airtime and we tried to sell commercials to cover the costs. Well, Carmela and I had full-time jobs.

You said earlier that Carmela didn't work outside the home. So was she a stay-at-home mom who worked out of her home?

Yes. She wanted to be home with her child, so she did all the accounting and paperwork for her husband's business. She stayed busy 24/7.

Who had time to sell ads? In hindsight, we lost money almost every week, but we generated enough interest that the radio show later sort of became my television in promoting my shows. So, in essence, the growth of TWA — I know I'm jumping ahead, but we'll talk about TWA later — the growth of TWA was tied to the radio show. The promotion of TWA was based on nothing more than a radio show, and we drew two to 3,000 people.

In my research, I noticed that you didn't do newspaper ads, either.

No. And this was before cable, before Internet. I mean, can you imagine what we could have done if we had cable and Internet?

Was the radio show just you and Carmela, or did you have occasional live guests?

Every once in a while, we would have a guest come in. I remember Cornette doing a show with us, but for the most part, the guests called in. Of course, when we did the shows in the mornings, Carmela and I would go out to breakfast afterwards and the people [wrestling fans] would follow us because they wanted to hang out with us. Here we are, walking into a restaurant, with 20 people coming in behind us. We would fill up a diner. The people thought we were superstars. (laughs)

Jim Cornette joins Joel during a taping of Rasslin' Radio.

I'm getting ahead of myself, but [in July 1988], I get a phone call from Roger Krone telling me that Frank Ford was retiring. He was going out of business and he was selling the radio station. It was immediate. We didn't even have a chance to go on the air and say goodbye to our listeners. Roger said, "*We're going off the air tomorrow at sundown.*" We later learned that Frank Ford was losing money. The major talk stations in Philadelphia were WWDB-FM and WCAU-AM, and WDVT couldn't compete. Carmela and I sat down for lunch one day and discussed some options of what we should do. Do we want to pursue radio somewhere else or not? You know, every once in a while, things happen, and people say things happen for a reason, so I said we'll take one more shot.

In Philadelphia, there's a radio station — it's still around by the way — called WIP. [WIP-AM 610] It was the main sports-talk station in Philadelphia. There was somebody working at WIP who did the news spots on the radio that I went to high school with — and the name will come to me — Betty Bernaman. She had a name that nobody in the world had except her, so I knew that was her. I thought she might remember me and might be able to help me get on a major radio station in Philadelphia. In my mind, though, I really figured there was no shot in hell. Regardless, I called the radio station and I asked for her. It's killing me that I can't remember her name. I asked for her and the guy who answered the phone says to me, "*She's out sick today. Can I help you?*"

So I said, "*Well, yeah. My name is Joel Goodhart. I had a show on both WTTM and WDVT, but as you know, WDVT is going off the air. I'd like to talk with somebody at WIP about possibly getting a radio show.*"

The guy who answered the phone was a guy by the name of Tom Brookshier. Tom had been a starting defensive back for the Philadelphia Eagles, a TV sportscaster in Philly, and was a minority owner of WIP. So here I am, calling for this female who does the news, and the guy who owns the friggin' radio station answers the telephone. Then he says to me, "*I know who you are. I've listened to you a lot.*" Well, as it turned out, he was friends with Dusty Rhodes.

Small world.

Oh, it's unbelievable. So he says to me, "*Let's get together and let's talk about it when she comes to the offices.*" So I go to the offices and I'm nervous as hell. I mean, this is big-time radio. WIP was the major station for Philadelphia sports. I walk in and there's Tom Brookshier. Now, again, I was a mark for this guy because was a legend with the Eagles football team. He was top of the line.

We had the meeting and we wound up talking wrestling for ... I'll bet it was an hour. He told me stories about being on a plane with Dusty and how he got to know Dusty on a first-name basis. Dusty actually gave him permission to call him Virgil. At the end of the meeting, he says, "*Sure, we'll put you on the radio. I hope you realize, though, that our fees are higher than what you were paying at WDVT, so you'll have to make a decision about that.*" He says, "*Our fee is $750 an hour.*" Now, keep in mind, we had been paying $75 when we started on WTTM, and at WDVT, we were paying ... I think it was $250 at the end. I can't remember, but now we were looking at $750.

That's a huge jump.

Yeah! In my mind, though, I kept thinking, "*This is a major Philadelphia radio station,*" so there was no way we weren't going to do the radio show. Now, keep in mind. This was back in the '80s, and 750 was a huge number. Going in, we knew we would have to sell advertising, but we also knew we were going to lose money. That actually was the beginning of the end for Carmela because she had the baby and she was concerned about spending that kind of money. Now, time-wise, I don't remember how long she was on the air at WIP. I mean, we can call Carmela and get her involved in this conversation. I think she was involved in it for a while, but at some point, it became a monetary issue for her.

The program debuted on WIP on Sept. 3, 1988, and aired on Saturday mornings from 8 a.m. to 9 a.m.

RADIO

5:30 a.m. **WIP (610) Pro Football This Week**
8:00 a.m. **WIP (610) Rasslin' Radio** with Joel's Goodhart
9:00 a.m. **WIP (610) Scholastic Sports Spotlight**
    with Marc Narducci

Did you recoup any of that $750 a week from advertising?

Yeah, we found some advertisers, but we never brought in $750 of revenue. Now, just so you know, it was through advertising that I first met Tod Gordon, which I know is one of the questions you plan to ask. Tod was a Philadelphia businessman who owned a jewelry store called Carver W. Reed. He was listening to us on the radio one Saturday morning and he actually called me to ask about advertising on the program. We had a conversation and I sold the opportunity for him to become a sponsor.

Tod Gordon was the founder and promoter of Eastern Championship Wrestling, which later became Extreme Championship Wrestling.

Do you remember what you charged for advertising?

I think it was $75 a spot, so if I had ten minutes in an hour, I would get back my money.

So spots ran about 60 seconds?

Yeah ... 30 seconds to a minute. It depended. Carver W. Reed — and there was a White House Carpets — they each got a full minute because they were established, legitimate businesses. Then I had some guys who owned comic book stores and whatever, so I gave them 30 seconds or something like that. But I don't remember ever selling enough spots to where a show paid for itself.

Again, part of the reason we struggled to sell spots was because I didn't have anybody working for me. It was a one-man operation. Well, one man, one woman, because Carmela played a huge part in it all and I couldn't have done it — especially at the beginning — without her. You know, the nitty-gritty of a business is not as sexy as the big picture. I was making a nice living with my insurance and investment business, so I didn't spend the time needed to sell the ads. If I had downtime, I'd rather do downtime with the business that was making me money than the hobby.

Carmela hosted the radio show with you for a short time when you moved to WIP. The last reference I can find of Carmela co-hosting the show was in a Sept. 1, 1988, newspaper article.
That's longer than I remember. Carm and I were the best of friends. We never had any disagreements on the radio except those we did for fun, but when the business started getting really serious, and now we had a bigger financial commitment, I was willing to go down that road ... she wasn't. At some point, the monetary issue got in the way.

Did you ever consider finding another co-host?
No. I couldn't imagine anyone could have replaced Carmela. In hindsight, she made the right move, but at the time, there was no way I was walking away from doing that thing at WIP. We did the show for four years. There's something called a Q-Rating, or Q Score, that measures the popularity of a company, celebrities, or other entertainment venues. We had a Q-Rating of 22,000 listeners per quarter hour, and some Saturday mornings from eight to nine, when we were on WIP, we were the third-most-listened-to station in Philadelphia during my hour, only behind the all-news station and the number one rock-and-roll station. So we had listeners, you know. WIP put us in prominence. I mean, the signal was heard everywhere. When the word got out about the wrestling show on Saturday mornings, I had so many call-ins that it was just ridiculous. It was so popular that I began telling people that WIP stood for "wrestling in Philadelphia."

At various times, slogans used by WIP included "Wireless In Philadelphia," "We're In Philadelphia," and "Watch Its Progress."

Now that you were on such a high-profile station, your status must have grown considerably.
Oh, we very much became rock stars in the world of wrestling. When we went to the matches, people knew who we were. It was really interesting. When we walked into the Civic Center to see the Crockett shows, it was amazing. People came up, *"You're Joel Goodhart! I listen to you on Saturday mornings. It's nice to meet you."* It was funky. Later on — this was after I started promoting TWA — I went to a Crockett show at the Meadowlands. Here I am in North Jersey, a hundred miles away from home, and you would have thought I was part of Jim Crockett Promotions. I wore my TWA shirt that night and people knew who I was. The word was out that the guy from the Squared Circle was there.

Was anyone else doing radio at that time?
John Arezzi was ... up in New York. The radio shows were starting to take off. We were the trailblazers. I didn't realize it at the time, but we absolutely were trailblazers.

Teddy Long takes the mic from Joel at an NWA show.

I have several newspaper articles from the *Philadelphia Daily News* written by a guy named Dan Geringer. He really promoted you and your stuff.

Dan Geringer saw me as a personality and he wrote a couple of articles about us. One of them was titled, "The Gods Are Good to Goodhart". [*Philadelphia Daily News*, Oct. 25, 1989] That was when I got Bruno and Ric Flair together, but that's a whole 'nother story. There also was an article in the *Philadelphia Business Journal* — I still have the originals — titled "Goodhart by Night, Goodhart by Day." They ran a picture of me behind my desk in my insurance and investment business — Goodhart by day, of course — and another of me in my tuxedo in the ring doing ring announcing. That, of course, was Goodhart by night.

In Geringer's column on April 3, 1989, he made mention of you wearing snake-skin boots.

There was a place in Paris, Arkansas, called the B Bar A Boot Shop.

Bill Ash's dad.

Well, that's where I bought my snakeskins. I wasn't dressing like I was to be one of the boys because I was never a wrestler, as I've told you many times. I understand the difference between promoting and wrestling, but it was part of the persona I wanted to depict. In fact, Larry Gallone, who wrote my [arena] programs, actually created a set of legs wearing snakeskin boots resting on top of a desk. That, my long hair, and my sunglasses were my trademark. Keep in mind, I had to wear prescription sunglasses because I can't see without my glasses. The wrestlers had their gear and I had mine. Again, nobody wore that kind of stuff except the guys in the business. It's now 30 years later and I still have the boots. Those things last forever. I also bought a pair of ostrich boots. I don't wear them often, but when I do, it's like, "*Wow!*" But, yeah, that was my trademark.

Did you ever get any blowback from The Equitable over your connection to and participation in professional wrestling?

Are you kidding? That made me a superstar. What actually happened there was the publication of the article "Goodhart by Night, Goodhart by Day." The only blowback I got — and it really wasn't blowback — was when they told me, "*We're concerned that if you're spending time on wrestling, you're not focusing on your full-time career with Equitable.*"

I told them, "*I'll commit more than full-time to the company, and the minute you think I'm not doing what I should, you tell me, and I'll make changes.*" They never said another word. After all, the wrestling was on the weekends.

DAN GERINGER: Going to the Mat for a Dream

(excerpt) [Paul E.] Dangerously called Goodhart's radio show last Saturday and said: "Philadelphia stinks. It's the second worst city in Pennsylvania. The worst is Pittsburgh because that's where Bruno Sammartino lives."

Then he said, "Bruno's kid — this failure of a son who never won a world title like his father did — can't fill Bruno's galoshes."

Then Bruno Sammartino called in to warn Dangerously, "Stick your nose in and your nose is liable to go straight down your throat."

— *Philadelphia Daily News*: Wednesday, Jan. 17, 1990

When I started ring announcing, the first thing I thought about doing was dressing up. My father was a doctor and he *always* wore the doctor whites, so he couldn't wait for a wedding so he could wear a tuxedo. In fact, we buried my father in his tux. So I grew up in a household that looked at a tux as being something special, and I *always* wore it when I did the ring announcing.

You'll find this interesting, and I'll bet it's something you've never heard before. If you were going to be sitting ringside at one of my shows — the timekeeper, reporter, or whatever — I wanted you to wear a tuxedo. Yep! I didn't want the people associated with me at ringside to look like a bunch of schlubs. I wanted my promotion to have a first-class look to it.

If you watch videos of the matches from the '50s, you'll notice that all the men wore a suit and tie. Not just the ring announcers and timekeepers, but the fans! That was *my* little shtick. If you're gonna sit ringside, wear a tuxedo. In hindsight, it was ridiculous, but if I was going to introduce the people at ringside, I wanted them to look classy. (laughs) Of course, most of the time, whenever I introduced someone, my crowd booed them. Hey, what could I do? (laughs)

Did you ever get any blowback from WCW or WWE about the radio show?

I never had any reaction from the corporate offices, but I got reactions from the boys. They heard everything. They would listen to the radio show. In fact, at that time, not only did the hardcore fans trade wrestling tapes, but they traded tapes of my radio show.

When I promoted a few shows for the NWA, the Steiners got really pissed at me one time about something I said. I don't remember what it was, but at a show at the Philadelphia Civic Center, Ric Flair saw me headed backstage. He ran over and said, "*You don't wanna go back there. Just talk to the guys out here.*" He told me that the Steiners had threatened to hurt me. I don't think they would have done that, but if nothing else, they would have scared the hell out of me.

You see, I was anti-WWF and pro-NWA, but I realized at some point that I couldn't keep brown-nosing the NWA guys, so I found things to rip them for. That's probably what happened. I'm sure I must have criticized one of their matches or something. I saw Rick and Scott a few years ago and we laughed out it. So, yes. I heard from the boys, but I never heard anything from the corporate offices.

That brings me to another question. Several people wrote letters to the *Observer* about the radio show. One said you were "*pretending to be a wrestling journalist,*" but when people would ask you a question you didn't want to address, you'd cut them off. Others said you were constantly ragging on Vince.

Well, I constantly ragged on Vince. I couldn't stand the product Vince was putting out, but at the same time, I was trying to create a niche for my own product. So, yeah. I ragged on Vince all the time. In fact, what actually got me tuned to the direction I went with the TWA was that it became almost class warfare. You know, there were the hardcore wrestling fans who went to any match that was wrestling. If "wrestling" was on the marquee, they were there. Then there were those who said, "*I can't stand the WWF, but I love the new Crockett product.*" So Crockett built on that. And *I* built on what Crockett built on.

It's funny that you mention [Dave] Meltzer. I very rarely read his newsletters and I never had a subscription ... ever! People bring it up and I look at some of them, and they had great information, but I couldn't get past the fact that he exposed the business more than anybody in the world. I had no interest in exposing the business. Sure, questions would come up on the radio show now and then that would require us to break the [kayfabe] line, but as a rule, I tried to protect the business. To this day, when I go to these independent shows and I see the heel and the babyface drive up together, it drives me frickin' nuts. It even bothers me when they all come out of the same dressing room door for a match! I mean, how stupid can people be?

I find it interesting that people like you and me, who were *in* the business, but still somewhat on the fringes of the business, we were more protective of the business than the boys were.

Yeah, and you were in the business when *everybody* protected the business. Today, they don't care at all. I mean, they post stories on Facebook about things that happened in the locker room. Oh, my god!

Picture this scenario. We did a show in Maryland at the Cecil County Community College — the four Cs — and one of the top matches was Paul Orndorff against the Iron Sheik. Orndorff and Sheik were next-door neighbors in Atlanta, so they traveled on a plane together. They drove from the airport, but about three blocks from the building, Orndorff lets Sheik out of the car and Sheik has to walk three blocks to the college ... because we protected the business!

That's the difference between pro wrestling and every other sport. Charles Barkley once told me, when Dr. J and Larry Bird were on the court, they hated each other, but they could go to dinner together afterwards. They were just competitors on the court. In wrestling, if you're a babyface, you can't eat with a heel, because you can't separate reality from what goes on in the ring. Kayfabe was important in wrestling. I even had two separate dressing rooms in most of the buildings.

I flew Jerry Lawler and Kerry Von Erich in from Dallas for one of my shows. [TWA Spring Spectacular, March 31, 1990] They had wrestled for the belt the night before in the Sportatorium and Lawler was going to defend it against Kerry for us. They were on the same flight to Philadelphia, so I asked one of them to sit in the front, the other guy in the back. I had my brother-in-law — my ex-brother-in-law — pick one of them up at the airport. I had someone else pick up the other ... because I didn't want them in the same car. We protected the business.

4   Jim Cornette and the King of Prussia

You just mentioned being at one of Crockett's shows. You were involved with them at some point prior to promoting TWA. How did that come about?
One night, Paul and I went to Crockett's matches — this might have been the second, third, fourth time — and there's this guy walking around the ring before the show starts. Keep in mind, I'm on the front row. This guy looked important, and I'm obnoxious, so I just waved him over and said, "*You look important. Who are you?*"

He said, "*My name is Elliott Murnick. I'm with Crockett Promotions.*"

That's how I got to meet Elliott. I don't know if you knew Elliott, or knew who he was.

I sure did. Before he passed away, we had talked about me publishing a non-fiction book he wrote.
Cool. Well, Elliott was the promoter and he loved to be on his boat. Elliott never flew to Philadelphia, but he'd take his boat from North Carolina up to Delaware and come to the matches. So we met that night and we talked a few times after that.

One night at the matches, Elliott said, "*Why don't you come to the Airport Marriott after the matches and we'll sit down and have a drink.*"

Another side-note, I said to Elliott, "*Murnick ... you're Jewish.*"

He said, "*Yeah, I'm Jewish.*"

So the Jewish connection gave us something else in common. It was very weird. I said to Paul — because we had come in the same car — "*We need to go to the airport. Elliott wants us to have a drink.*"

We go to Airport Marriott and I'm like, "*What the hell's going on?*" The wrestlers were all there. They're partying their eyes out. The place was just popping. I sat there with Elliott and we talked and struck up a friendship. Again, we lived miles apart. There were no cell phones or anything back then. So every month or so, I'd see him around the ring. About six months after our first meeting, I get a phone call from Elliott. I had given him my business card. He calls me at my office and asks me a question that kicked off my wrestling career. He says, "*Crockett has some traveling dates available and they want to do a show during the week in the Philadelphia area. I can't get up there that often, so I was wondering if you would be my eyes and ears in Philadelphia.*"

That's almost a direct quote. That's the way I remember it, word for word, although I'm probably paraphrasing. But that's what got me into the wrestling business. Now I'm working with Murnick trying to find a venue. He introduced me to everybody. They didn't know me from Adam at the time, but Elliott would introduce me as his eyes and ears in Philadelphia.

Eventually, I booked a show for the Crocketts at the Sheraton Valley Forge in Philadelphia. Now again, I'm jumping ahead here because I had done a couple of small promotions on my own with Carmela before that happened, but I actually wound up promoting a few Crockett shows. That's when I got really tight with JJ

[Dillon], Jimmy Valiant, Tully Blanchard, Ricky Morton. I got tight with them because now I was actually in the back as Elliott's right-hand man. When Elliott came to Philadelphia, he brought me into the back. I was no longer first-row. I was in the back at the shows and I really got involved with (pause) ... I was never — to this day — I was never someone who was in awe of those guys. I didn't go up to them and bow to them. I looked at them as they were ... business people, you know? I know there's people that get involved in the business because they love a wrestler, or they love the business. I just got involved in it from a learning standpoint. I was there as the promoter, not as their friend. It is what it is. So, yeah. I actually wound up running a show for Crockett.

You say you weren't a mark for any of the wrestlers, but was there anybody at all that you had seen wrestle that you were somewhat in awe of?
Well (pause) ... yeah, I'd have to say JJ Dillon. Yeah, JJ. In terms of the wrestlers I had on that show that night, I had Midnight [Express] against Rock 'n' Roll. Talk about having the best of the best. I actually got tight with Tully for a bit, but JJ was the guy. He wore a suit and tie and stood outside the ring, and very rarely got involved in matches. Later on he did, but at that time, he was just the manager and advisor of the Horsemen. Again, I was into the suit-and-tie thing, and so was JJ, so I took a liking to him.

So after Murnick took you to the back, you were allowed in the dressing room and in the back when you were promoting the NWA shows?
Yes. Oh, yeah. In fact, at that point, I was Elliott Murnick's shadow.

So the boys didn't mind you being back there?
Nope, nope. In fact, JJ and I became friends and he introduced me to everybody in the dressing room. When you're with somebody like JJ, you're in! That's a sign to the guys that you're okay. Once I had Elliott and JJ on my side, it didn't take long to be accepted as one of the boys.

Do you have any interesting stories about any of those WCW shows at which you were the ring announcer?
Well, I got to announce the match where Tully and Arn lost the belts to Midnight just before they jumped over to Vince.

Did you know ahead of time that it was going to happen?
No. At that point, they didn't give me any finishes. Elliott was a smart businessman. He knew I had the radio show and, of course, I promoted the fact that I was doing the ring announcing. [Gary] Capetta, or whoever, had been doing the ring announcing, so when they quit, I took over. Elliott originally asked both me and Carmela to do it, but Carmela was never comfortable being out front, and she definitely didn't want to climb in and out of the ring.

To this day, I wouldn't mind doing ring announcing. It just worked for me. I have two photos from that time. One has me and Flair in the ring. Flair is in the corner and I'm in the center of the ring. Because of the angle the photo was taken, Flair looks half my size ... because he's further away. When I saw him a few years ago, I showed him that photo and kidded him about it. Then there's another shot of me and Black Bart, and Bart has a look on his face like he wants to kill me. So the ring announcing was fun. I got to meet the guys in the back because I had to get their weights. In that day, they never printed sheets of anything other than the lineup. Towards the end, they started telling me who was going over [winning], but when I first started, I wasn't told anything. In fact, the night of the Tully and Arn and Midnight match, according to the guys who were there, they made that decision that night in the dressing room because they had just signed the contract [with the WWF]. I don't know if even Crockett knew what was going on.

Did you realize something important and unexpected had taken place?
Oh, yeah. I went to the back after the show and thanked the guys. They were all buzzing about it. I don't think anybody there was aware that Tully and Arn were going to Vince until after the title switch took place. I'd bet Cornette and Midnight knew, though. I could be wrong about that, but everybody seemed to be surprised.

Take a look at your Facebook messages. I just sent you a lineup for the first show you mentioned.

King of Prussia, Pennsylvania: Feb. 19, 1986
WCW, Valley Forge Convention Center,
    att. 2,000
- Tully Blanchard beat Pez Whatley
- Ricky Morton & Robert Gibson beat
  Bobby Eaton & Dennis Condrey
- Ron Bass drew Black Bart
- Pez Whatley beat Teijo Khan
- Ivan Koloff, Barbarian &
  Baron Von Raschke beat
  Ron Garvin, Sam Houston &
  Manny Fernandez
- Jimmy Valiant beat Tully Blanchard
- U.S. title match
  Magnum TA* beat Nikita Koloff (dq)

Black Bart glares at Joel

Let's see. That's it! I have to tell you a funny story. Wait, wait! Oh, this is phenomenal! I can't believe that. Oh, my god. That's the first ... that's the first time I've seen this ... ever! You just went back to serious memories. Oh, my god! So wait, wait. Here's some stories. This show was so screwed up. I believe this was a Wednesday. We could look up the date. Oh, my god! I can't believe you found this! It's unbelievable. So, I get a phone call from JJ the day of the show and he tells me the guys were fogged-in in North Carolina and they don't know if they're going to be able to get to the show. Like I said, it was a Wednesday night, 2,000 attendance, and half of them were kids! The show started at seven o'clock because ... you know, the kids had to get home for school, et cetera, et cetera.

Long story short, JJ calls again and he says they're flying in, but they're going to be late. So I had to get in the ring and keep the crowd pacified. I got into my ring persona a little bit, but I was assuring the people that the wrestlers were on their way. They applauded each time. Now, I had arranged for a police escort to get the guys to the matches when they landed. Well, JJ, Tully and Pez Whatley were in the first car. Tully was a heel and Pez was a babyface, so they shouldn't have been riding together, but they didn't have a feud going at the time, so it wasn't a big deal. Pez said he'd wrestle in a warm-up against Tully to get the crowd going. The other guys were on buses. Tully and Pez changed in the car and walked into the arena in their gear. They got into the ring and wrestled until someone came out and told us the buses were in the parking lot. It was funny because Pez and Tully didn't know what to do [in their match] other than stretch it out until the bus showed up. Again, there was no cell phones, so once they were in the car, I had no communication at all.

The next time I saw Tully, I told him that he had been on my first [Crockett] card. He didn't remember me, obviously, but ... I can't believe you found this! This is great, great! You'll notice that Pez wrestled a second time — against Teijo Khan — and Tully wrestled later on against Jimmy Valiant, and those two guys were the stars of the show. Yeah, unbelievable. Unbelievable! You just made my day. This is great!

(laughs) Well, we'll be talking about a lot more things that you may have forgotten. Do you remember how long Pez and Tully wrestled?
Oh, ten or fifteen minutes.

That would have been a piece of cake for them because the guys did things on the fly pretty much every night back then.
Yeah, and they always produced. I remember it well. They got in the ring, JJ called the match from the outside a little bit ... Tully knew how to get heat. Tully worked for me later on my TWA shows and we talked about that. He said, "*Hey, I can get anybody pissed in ten seconds.*" They knew what to do. They fed the crowd and did a lot of out-of-the-ring stuff just to get the crowd going. The kids got into it big-time. But, yeah. Those guys actually did two matches that night. If I remember correctly, the show was scheduled for seven and it didn't start until about 8:15. I know it was more than an hour.

It was great for concessions, though, although I didn't have a part in that. The parents were getting concerned ... we're going to have to leave early, what do we do, how do we get our money back? I didn't have an answer. It wasn't my promotion. This was Crockett's promotion, so when they called me from the airport when they landed, I just kept the crowd going until someone showed up.

Now, when Tully and Pez finished their match, the crowd was really hungry. I mean, the crowd was waiting for something to happen. Well, nobody would put Rock 'n' Roll vs. Midnight in the opening match, but they brought them on early because they knew a lot of those kids would be leaving early.

I got tight with Jim Cornette. When he taped a television commercial for that show — which was in King of Prussia, Pennsylvania — he came out and said, "*Who is this King of Prussia? I want to meet this King of Prussia!*" I wish there was a copy of those promos because they were gold. Anyway, if you look through the matches ... I mean, I met Baron Von Raschke years later at the Cauliflower Alley Club.

Manny Fernandez and Joel backstage at an NWA show.

Regarding Crockett and Murnick, were they satisfied with the results of the show as far as attendance and the job you did?
They were more than satisfied. They told me that, at the time, they were only working the big cities, but they had found some opportunities to get the guys work on during-the-week shows. They didn't know how many of those shows they were going to do in Philly that year, but I was their eyes and ears. From that point forward, I was unofficially Crockett's promotion.

They had a show in Baltimore the next night. Did you have anything to do with that?
No, but they knew they were going to Baltimore, so they thought it was prudent to book the Valley Forge show the night before. They were just routing matches where they could to fill in the gaps.

Interesting. How long was it before they called you again? I haven't been able to find any other NWA shows in Valley Forge during that time.
No, that was it. The other Valley Forge matches, about four years later, were my promotion.

St. Marys, Pennsylvania: April 3, 1986
Jim Crockett Promotions
• Ricky Morton & Robert Gibson beat Bobby Eaton & Dennis Condrey (dq)

You once mentioned promoting a second show for Crockett in St. Marys, PA, and told me to ask you about it.
Yes. It was weird. Shortly after the first show for Crockett, Elliott called and said they wanted a show in another part of the state. Don't ask me how we wound up at St. Marys because I don't have a clue, but Carmela and I started to search for buildings and that's where we wound up.

That's weird because St. Marys was more than 250 miles from Philadelphia.
It's about two hours north of Pittsburgh and two hours south of Erie. It's in the middle of nowhere. But for whatever reason, we got the gym and booked the Crockett show. The main event was Rock 'n' Roll against the Midnight Express, so we brought in the A show. Of course, some people will tell me that if Flair wasn't there, it was the B show.

For a few weeks before the show, we promoted it on the radio. When we went up there on the day of the show, we rented a limo. It took us about five hours to get there, and it was a boring ride, so when we got there, I told Carmela that I would never *ride* to St. Marys again. Ride or drive, it wasn't going to happen. We had booked an appearance on one of the local radio stations ... not me and Carmela, but one of the boys. You have to picture this. We pull into St. Marys in this giant, white limousine. Well, of course, everybody thought we were the wrestlers. After the radio interview, we made an appearance at a supermarket with (pause) ... I'm trying to remember who it was. I don't recall which of the boys it was, but when we pulled into the supermarket parking lot, 50 kids must have run out to that limousine. They had heard us talking on the radio about the supermarket appearance. They were ready for us. That town was hopping. It must have been the biggest thing to hit St. Marys in decades, if not ever.

I remember the guys ... Ricky Morton, Bobby Eaton, Dennis Condrey, Robert Gibson ... saying they would never go back to St. Marys again. Clearly, it wasn't the biggest house they had ever wrestled in front of, but it was sold out, and it *was* a weeknight. It was a perfect add-on spot show, but Crockett never went back.

On the ride home, Carmela and I talked about how cool it was to have been treated like celebrities and how cool it was to be working with a big promotion.

Valley Forge, Pennsylvania: Nov. 17, 1986
Sheraton Valley Forge
• Bruiser Brody NC Abdullah the Butcher (double DQ)

Getting back to Valley Forge, after you promoted a show there for WCW, you promoted a show of your own.

Yes. I didn't want to run shows in high schools that nobody could find. I didn't like having 200 people in a high school gym. At the time, I didn't think that was what this business was about, although in reality, that's exactly what this business was about. But I liked doing the bigger shows in the nicer buildings. At the time, I had separated from my wife and I was dating the daughter of the CEO of the Sheraton Valley Forge. She introduced me to her dad and I talked to him about bringing matches to the hotel. The building was relatively new and they were looking for things to bring to the building. So he drew up a contract — you're gonna love this one — to bring matches to the Sheraton. It was an independent show.

So, who was my main event on that first show? Bruiser Brody against Abdullah the Butcher. Abby and I talk about that to this day. This must have been 1985 ... something like that.

November 17, 1986.

I'll defer to your records. Picture this ... Brody and Abby were my main event, so I'm in the back with them and they ask me, "*What do you want?*"!

What do I want? I didn't know anything! So, I told them, "*I want the classic Abby-Brody match. Just do your thing. Don't spend much time in the ring. Brawl all over the building.*"

Well, when you give Abby and Brody permission to do that, they're gonna take it to the nth degree ... and they did. They broke every table and chair they could find. They destroyed that hotel something fierce. The CEO sent me a bill for $2,350.

How did you get in touch with Brody and Abby?

I was afraid you were going to ask me that. I have no clue. I don't remember how I got them. I was talking to Elliott Murnick at the time because I got to know him a little bit, so he may have put me in touch with some of the talent. Carmela knew guys like Putski. I don't even remember the rest of the card. All I remember is Brody and Abby just destroying the place. No disrespect meant, but from that day on, there was no way that I was going to take a step back and promote a show with Dominic DeNucci against Mighty Igor again. It just wasn't going to happen.

TODAY

A Guide to What's Going On in and Around Philadelphia

By **JIM KNIGHT**
Daily News Staff Writer

Those grunts and groans emanating from the Valley Forge Convention and Exhibit Center, 1200 First Ave., King of Prussia, belong to some mighty big people, so be sure to preface any complaints about the noise with a most courteous, "Please." They are professional wrestlers putting on six matches beginning at 7:30 p.m. Among those going to the mat is Abdullah the Butcher (450 pounds), who is taking on Bruiser Body in the "Battle of the Titans." In a second main event, women's wrestling champ Wendy Richter lays her belt on the line. Tickets: $12 for reserved seats and $10 general admission. Info: 337-2000.

I heard your expenses for that show were around $18,000, and when it was all said and done, you profited $27. Does that sound correct?
That's very possible. I don't remember the figures, but I know I didn't make much. It was a true independent show. That was all my promotion. We didn't do any TV or radio, other than the commercials on our radio show. The commercials on the radio show weren't actually money out of our pocket, but that was an expense because we didn't sell those spots to anyone else. Talent, airfare and hotel for Brody and Abdullah, the building, security ... yeah, $18,000 is probably in that neighborhood. It wouldn't surprise me. The fee for the damages to the building, as I told you, came to $2,350. I would have made a profit if that hadn't happened.

I'm sure you had done well enough in your insurance business that you were able to cover the damages.
Oh, yeah. In hindsight, though, I must have been an idiot. I mean, I was laying out money to do shows. When I signed the contract with the Sheraton Valley Forge, they wanted a rental guarantee. Yeah, it was costing me money. To be honest, I was using the money that I should have been putting away for my kids' education to do those matches. Yep.

Did you have second thoughts at that point? Like, I don't know if promoting is for me.
I had second thoughts the day I did it ... before the show even started. (laughs) You know, it was strange. I always had this desire (pause) ... I'm a ham, so if I promoted a show, I made myself the ring announcer. Now I'm in the ring, now I'm in the back, and the guys are respecting me because I'm the guy with the pay envelope.

Valley Forge, Pennsylvania: Dec. 28, 1986
Sheraton Valley Forge
• Bruiser Brody vs. Abdullah the Butcher

There was another independent show in Valley Forge the following month ... December 28. Was that you, as well?
First of all, I wouldn't call my first show an "independent" show. It was just a one-off wrestling card. I didn't have an organized promotion. It was just a show we promoted off the radio show. But, yes. I had a second show (pause) ... I think it was five weeks later.

That would fit the timeframe of the two dates.

Joel Goodhart & Carmela Panfil, co-hosts of *Rasslin' Radio*, raised $1,427 in September to help pay hospital bills incurred by Michael Dopke, a nine-year-old wrestling fan who died of cancer. More than 130 people attended the benefit at Boulevard Lanes and a number of pro wrestlers called or visited Michael during his last days.
— *Philadelphia Daily News*: Oct. 9, 1987

What do you remember about the fund-raiser for 9-year-old Michael Dopke?
Yeah. Well, it's weird because I did *not* remember that until you sent me your email with that story in it. I do remember doing it. Carmela and I were so happy

that we were able to do something to help that boy's family. That was the first time we did anything like that and it gave us the sense that we could actually help people through what we were doing. The sad thing was, the boy died a week before the benefit, but we were doing it to help the parents with the hospital bills. There were hardcore wrestling fans out there who were so giving, and when push came to shove, they came through. It's funny when you look at that number ... $1,400. That's not a lot of money now, but in the '80s, that was a *huge* sum. We didn't have any $500 contributions, or even a hundred dollars. It was all a dollar, five dollars, ten dollars ... all small donations.

The benefit was held at Boulevard Lanes. Was it a dinner or something like a telethon?

What happened was, we had a lot of local guys — now, this was *before* we started Ringmaster's Wrestling School — so we put out the word to them. I basically told them, "*If you want to work on my shows, I need you to be at Boulevard Lanes.*" I wanted to have a wrestler on each bowling lane. You know, theoretically, we'd have one wrestler and three bowlers — hopefully wrestling fans — on each lane. Kids are funny. Kids just wanted to meet a wrestler. It didn't matter if they were well-known or if they were just occasional weekend warriors. The kids felt important because they met and talked to "a wrestler." Today, they don't want to meet just a wrestler. They want to meet someone like John Cena. But back then, if you were a wrestler, the kids held you in high esteem. They looked at the wrestlers as being big, tall, built, the whole nine yards. They didn't care who they were. Those local guys were *wrestlers* and kids wanted to meet them. We managed to get a wrestler on every lane, so it was a great time celebrating the life of that boy.

Several of the guys visited Michael before he died. I know Dominic, Larry Winters, and Ron Shaw all went to see him. That really made that boy's day.

We also held a miniature golf tournament one time. I think we had a wrestler at each hole. It was part of the branding we were doing, that we wanted for the promotion. We wanted the local guys to get some notoriety. Of course, to get a main-eventer to one of those things would have cost me a fortune, so that wasn't going to happen. In my view, the independent wrestling show is generally better than any WWE show. You get more wrestling, you get more emotion. I get it ... they're not six-four, blond hair, and built like Adonis. Even today, the local guys are undersized when it comes to professional wrestling standards, but many of them are top of the line. They either haven't been discovered or they have full-time jobs and don't want to make it a career.

On Saturday, Oct. 31, 1987, *Rasslin' Radio* hosted the *Rasslin' Radio Fan Club Halloween Party* from 1-4 p.m. at The Bus Stop.

On *Rasslin' Radio,* you promoted a Halloween party for the fan club. Was that the first fan club event you promoted?

I can't remember. I do remember having it at the Squared Circle. We asked people to come dressed as their favorite wrestler. I have a photo of me standing behind the cash register and dressed up like one of the Road Warriors ... face makeup and all. I looked like a complete moron.

I read a report that said the Halloween party was at The Bus Stop restaurant.

I think it was at the Squared Circle because I have that photo of me at the store in Road Warrior makeup.

Philadelphia, Pennsylvania: January 16, 1988
Arena, att. 7,500
Ring announcer Joel Goodhart, Timekeeper Carmella Panfil
• Dick Murdoch, Eddie Gilbert & Kevin Sullivan beat
    Sting, Ron Simmons & Kendall Windham
• Jimmy Garvin beat Black Bart
• Tully Blanchard drew Ron Garvin
• TV title match
    Nikita Koloff beat Mike Rotundo (dq, Kevin Sullivan interference)
• The Road Warriors NC Powers of Pain (double count-out)
• Dusty Rhodes beat Stan Lane
• Lex Luger beat Arn Anderson
• World heavyweight title match
    Ric Flair beat Michael Hayes

3 TITLES ON LINE AT CIVIC CENTER
by Rick Selvin
(excerpt) Saturday night's eight-match National Wrestling Alliance slugfest is being billed as "Rasslin' Radio Night," with show co-hosts Joel Goodhart and Carmela Panfil taking part in the ring duties — Goodhart as announcer, Panfil as timekeeper. In addition, members of the "Rasslin' Radio" Squared Circle Fan Club will watch the action from ringside seats. And Mary Galloway and Richard Hoscheid, winners of a "Rasslin' Radio" contest, will receive a bonus: backstage passes enabling them to talk with the wrestlers, get autographs, and pose for photos with their idols.
— *Philadelphia Daily News*, Friday, Jan. 15, 1988

On Jan. 16, 1988, two people — Mary Galloway and Richard Hoscheld, won backstage passes to an NWA show in a *Rasslin' Radio* contest.
One of the things I told Murnick was that we had to do some glad-handing for the fans. At the time, they had backstage passes, so we brought the winners to the back and they got to meet the wrestlers. They weren't in the dressing room — you know, the back-back — but they had seats on the stage. The wrestlers came out of the dressing rooms and everybody knew they were total marks. The heels didn't go up to them ... only the babyfaces. That was a time when we still protected the business.

The main event that night was cut short because there was an eleven o'clock curfew. Do you remember that?
Yeah. Keep in mind, in Philadelphia back then, there was a curfew for anyone under the age of 18, and obviously, we had a lot of people in our building who were 16 and 17. That had always been a thing with Vince, but even with Crockett, the shows had to end at eleven. The contract with the building stipulated that we had to be out of the building by twelve, so the show had to be over by 11:00. If they went over, they were charged an extra hour overtime at time-and-a-half. So those matches ended no later than 10:59:59. Crockett was starting to watch every dollar, so that was a strict rule.

I found an article about you having a second "Rasslin' Radio Night" seven months later. Was that something they did regularly?
I think we did the radio nights three times.

That's all I've been able to find. The second one was in August and the third in September.

Philadelphia, Pennsylvania: August 20, 1988
Rasslin' Radio Night, Civic Center, Ring announcer: Joel Goodhart
• Ron Simmons & Brad Armstrong drew Rick Steiner & Mike Rotundo
• Bobby Fulton & Tommy Rogers beat The Sheepherders
• Sting, Steve Williams, Ricky Morton & Brad Armstrong beat
   Al Perez, Larry Zbyszko, Arn Anderson & Tully Blanchard
• U.S. title match
   Barry Windham* beat Nikita Koloff (count-out)
• Dusty Rhodes beat The Russian Assassin
• U.S. tag team title match
   The Road Warriors beat Bobby Eaton & Stan Lane (dq)

On Aug. 21, 1988, *Rasslin' Radio* hosted a "Breakfast with Champions" featuring an all-you-can-eat buffet with Bobby Eaton, Stan Lane & Jim Cornette. The cost for members of the Squared Circle Fan Club was $20. The breakfast began at 9:00 a.m. at The Bus Stop.

With your ties to the NWA during that time, do you have any stories pertaining to the war between WCW and the WWF?
Well, I had involvement in one show for Vince. I actually ring announced two matches for them at the Spectrum. Not two shows ... two matches! And quite frankly, I'm sure I got it because they knew what I was doing with Crockett and they wanted the fans to see me doing a WWF show. The opening match was Nicolai Volkoff and the Iron Sheik, so I had to put over the Russian National Anthem gimmick. I didn't do anything else with them, although now and then I heard from guys who worked for Vince because — and I know I already told you this — I would blast Vince on the radio all the time. The only reason I was invited to the birthday party for Hogan was because of the Squared Circle. Anybody who was selling WWF merchandise was invited to the party, so it wasn't because I was a Crockett guy. It was because I sold their merchandise. I never tried to get involved with the WWF because ... you know, it's funny. I couldn't stand the product, so I ripped them all the time on the radio. If I hung around at a WWF show, I probably would have gotten my ass kicked. The only thing I remember about the night at the Spectrum — when I did the ring announcing — was Ultimate Warrior in the back with a huge bag of pills. If there wasn't a hundred pills in that bag, there wasn't two. He was just chugging them down. It was ridiculous.
Do you think it was steroids, painkillers, or what?
I have no idea. All I know is he was putting them down, and I know you don't take a hundred pain-killers, that's for sure.
(laughs) That's true.
The one thing I really remember is, he was built. Oh, my word. You know, I had been around Sting. I had been around Lex Luger. I had been around Sid Vicious. But there was something about Warrior that was just ... he was just cut. He was unbelievable.
Let's talk a little about the guys working for the NWA at that time. What do you remember about Sting?
He was another great guy. I always got the sense that Sting was ... what's the word I'm looking for (pause) ... he was a team player. It's very hard to be a team player in a sport where there's really no teams, but he was one of those guys. I mean, everybody recognized his talent, and the size and makeup added something

to it. Sting was the captain of the team. That may sound weird, but I always got that sense. He was never the booker. He was just a guy that attracted everybody. I remember watching a match with Sting and [Ric] Flair. Flair made everybody look good, but Sting could hold his own.

When Sting did that match [teaming with Flair against Great Muta and Terry Funk] at Halloween Havoc in Philly [Oct. 28, 1989], that I had some involvement with ... if you watch that match, you'll realize you're seeing a guy that understands the business. That's the one thing I saw from most of Crockett's people. They really knew the business. They had the psychology. They had the ring presence. They all had their little shtick. Back in those days, before TV was really big and the Internet came along, you pushed somebody like Sting, Luger, Nikita. They weren't great wrestlers. Those guys were all bodybuilders, but when it was time, they'd have a 35, 40-minute match.

In my opinion, Sting never really got the push he deserved. I think part of that was Sting, but Sting's fans wanted to see him. If he had been in Vince's world, he might have been a Hulk Hogan. I don't know that Sting could be the top guy. He may not have been able to carry it, but again, he was a team player.

Arn Anderson.
I admired the guy big-time. There were some people who thought I looked like Arn when I had my beard. (laughs) To me, Arn was the total package. Not the Lex Luger total package. Arn was a guy who looked normal. He wasn't a bodybuilder, but he looked solid. He looked like the average guy on the street ... until he got in the ring. Those guys could wrestle forever. We used to ask people on the radio, *"Who had the worst win-loss record in the history of professional wrestling?"* ... and the answer was the Four Horsemen. The Horsemen would lose every match except the ones that really mattered.

Arn could get into the ring with a non-wrestler and make him look like a world champion. He had that talent. Dennis Condrey had that talent. Flair certainly had that talent. Another one was Terry Funk. Jerry Lawler had that talent. Austin Idol had the talent. Tommy Rich. You go back to those guys that I dealt with.

There were times when I actually contemplated putting a name (pause) ... Tully Blanchard worked a couple shows for me. In my opinion, Tully was the glue that held the Four Horsemen together. Tully was the only guy from the Four Horsemen who worked for me in TWA. I never brought in Flair, JJ, Arn, or Ole Anderson. The only problem with Tully is that he was so busy that I couldn't get him booked out far enough to run an angle with him. I had Tully against Bam Bam in a cage match [March 31, 1990] and another time against Orndorff [June 9, 1990], but for no reason. There was no storyline.

If I could have gotten dates on Tully, I would have booked him on every show I did. Tully was one of those guys who never let his fame go to his head. If I had told him, *"Tully, I'm putting you in a title match against D.C. Drake and I need you to put him over,"* he would have done it, and he would have done it in such a way that he would have looked good doing it. I never asked him to do that. In fact, I *never* brought a name guy into my territory to put one of my local guys over. Look at my matches and you'll never see a match of a name versus a local. The name guys who were going to work for me were going to work against another name. I wasn't bringing them in to put over a guy who just started training at Ringmaster's wrestling school and needed a push. That just didn't happen. Never once did I do that.

Tully or Arn would have been the guys to do it, though. Now, Arn never worked for me because he had jumped to Vince and stayed with him, but the thing with

Arn is that he wasn't a guy who was going to draw by himself. No disrespect meant because he was a big draw as a tag team wrestler and I had a *lot* of respect for him.

Interaction with Jim Cornette and the Midnight Express?

Jimmy worked for me, as well. Back in the Crockett days, Jimmy and I sat in the back and talked. I wouldn't say we were friends, but we would talk. We developed a relationship. It was a natural relationship, so when I started running shows, Jimmy was on a lot of them. I actually had Jimmy wrestle one time as Stan Lane's tag team partner. [Philadelphia, Aug. 3, 1991] Jimmy was a guy who I'd tell what I needed and then I never had to have another conversation with him. I don't recall ever sitting down with him in the back and going over a match. We would have lunch, we would eat, we would sit and yak and chuckle, but when the lights went on in the arena, Jimmy became Jim Cornette. He wasn't Jim Cornette outside the ring. In the back, he was who he was — Jimmy Cornette — but *Jim* Cornette started when the matches started. He took his role seriously. He physically got involved in matches, which I think eventually really hurt him. His legs are all messed up and what have you, but the tennis racket gimmick was phenomenal. He was over. He was somebody the fans loved to hate. And those matches with Rock 'n' Roll ... I could watch those matches today over and over and over again. They are as enjoyable as hell because those guys knew the psychology of the match. I bring that up a lot because, in my opinion, there's much more to wrestling than the actual physicality. It's always the working with the crowd. It's the mindset, the mental part of it. I don't think the guys today get that. The ring entrance, the ring presence, was all there.

Any interaction with the Road Warriors at all?

Yeah. In fact, the Roadies were the only guys that ever ripped me off. (laughs) To the day he died, Animal insisted that it wasn't him. The Roadies were above and beyond everybody else. In terms of fan reaction in Philadelphia, when the music started, the place just exploded, and that happened everywhere! They clearly had the gimmick and the size, but when they got into the ring, they didn't sell for anybody. They were the original stiff guys.

Now, I got to know them because Animal was born in Philadelphia. He grew up in Minnesota, but originally, he was from Philly. I contacted them and got them and [Paul] Ellering to do an appearance for us. We rented a place in Philadelphia called the Woodhaven Sports Center [at the corner of Knights Road and Woodhaven Road]. Our deal was that they would sign autographs for an hour for $3,000 cash. Okay? So I started to promote it on the radio. I believe we charged $20 a person, but I may be wrong on that. That was on a Sunday and we were doing a show at the Civic Center on Saturday. So, on Saturday at the matches, I'm sitting down with Paul Ellering to make arrangements. We were going to have a limo pick them up. Paul says, "*The guys don't want to do it.*"

I said, "*What do you mean they don't want to do it? We've been promoting this thing forever.*"

We had a handshake, and a handshake worked for everybody with Crockett. I never had a signed contract with anybody. Paul said to me, "*Look, the guys just don't want to do it. Now, if you double it to $6,000, they'll do it.*"

Well, here I am, just hours before the show and we had a couple hundred people show up. Carmela and I were still working together at the time, so I asked what she thought we should do. We had no way to notify everybody. We wound up giving the Road Warriors $6,000, so they did the show, and all they had to do was sit at a table, answer some questions, and take pictures and autographs. It was a

Terry Funk clowns around with Joel at a luncheon.

typical luncheon that I used to pay the guys 500 or a thousand dollars, but they held me up for an additional three. In later years, Animal told me that he never got the extra money, so who knows the true story of where the money went. If Animal was lying about it, I can't imagine why he'd keep lying about it 30 years later. I never talked to Paul again, so I didn't have an opportunity to ask him about it, but they absolutely held us up for extra money the night before the show. That was the only time anybody had ever done that.

In my opinion, you were already overpaying a lot of those guys with your standard payoff of 500 to a thousand dollars.

Well, sure, but the Road Warriors took advantage of me. They did. They wound up getting another $3,000. Years later, interaction with Animal and Hawk was great. We never had any problems. I just put it in the past.

Ronnie Garvin.

Hands of Stone. Ronnie told me a story about the last year he wrestled. He only slept in his own bed seven days during that year. The guys were traveling constantly. When Ronnie came to the matches, if you weren't a wrestling fan, you'd never know that he was a wrestler. When he was dressed in street clothes, he didn't look the part. When he got dressed out, though, he looked every *bit* the part. And his handshake ... hurt! He got the name *hands of stone* for a reason.

Ronnie never worked any of my shows, but he was a pleasure to work with when I was with Crockett. He was a true professional. He worked hard every night. He never took a night off. Ronnie was a lot like Arn Anderson. He couldn't draw on top on his own, but he had great matches. His matches with Flair were fantastic and Flair put Ronnie over big-time. Ronnie was great working underneath

— semi-final or mid-card — and he deserved the push he got on top. I also got the impression that he was well-liked by all the other wrestlers. He was a true professional.

Was Ronnie being so busy the reason why you never booked him?
I never tried to book him. He never really did a lot of independent shows. I never saw him on an independent up here at all. I just think it was something he wasn't into. That being said, I don't think Ronnie Garvin would have sold me a single ticket. Ronnie just wasn't a guy who would sell tickets. If I had heard that he was drawing people for somebody else, I probably would have brought him in, but I don't know that he would have been a draw.

Barry Windham.
Interesting ... Barry ... a tall guy ... boy, oh boy. Barry was ... I'm gonna use the word distant. I got to meet him and talked to him a few times when I saw him in the back — all that kind of stuff — but he never worked for me in Tri-State. Yes, distant is the best word. He was polite, he was professional, and he did his thing, but I had very little interaction with him.

How about Dusty?
God bless Dusty. He was always ... I don't want to use the word *distant* again because I already used it, but you couldn't get to Dusty. He was always so freaking busy. He was always with the boys. He ran the back. We talked a few times, but he never worked for me, and none of his kids ever worked for me. Dusty was a guy who was larger than life. That's the right term for him.

Did you ever make an attempt to book him?
Nope, nope. Nope, I never did.

Mike Rotundo.
(pause) Quiet. I think we met two or three times. I don't know if some of those guys avoided me, as much as they avoided people period. Some guys just weren't people people. That's the best way to put it. That was Mike Rotundo. He was a very nice guy, was always professional, and did what he had to do, but he didn't search me out and I didn't search him out.

Lex Luger.
Luger and I got along real well. Luger did a luncheon for me at Champs. He said, "*Look, I'm into health food.*" We used to serve hot roast beef sandwiches, hot dogs, and all that kind of stuff. He says, "*Before we do the lunch, I want to go to lunch,*" which I thought was an unusual request, but okay. So, we went out to a Chinese restaurant that was about five miles from Champs. Now, I wasn't a little guy, but I was a midget compared to Luger, right? Luger ... God bless him, at the time, he looked the part. He dressed nice, he had the flowing blonde hair, he wore the cutoff shirts ... his arms were twice the size of a normal human being's. We sat down and had Chinese food. What did he order? Two bowls of rice. That's it. He orders two bowls of rice because he obviously ate a lot of carbs. I decided to get pepper steak with one kind of soup. He orders two bowls of rice. We sat there for about an hour and we talked. We got to know each other really well.

Afterwards, we went to the Champs thing, and again, everybody wanted to take a picture with him. Remember, back in the day, you didn't have cell phones, so everybody brought cameras. Luger proved to be a draw, not only at the luncheon, but everywhere he wrestled. Nobody could ever say that Luger was a great wrestler, but he *looked* like a great wrestler. Now, Luger and Sting were the guys that Crockett had at the time, and I think that if Vince had them at that time, with the TV and everything starting to come into play ... I always felt like Luger and

Sting never got to the level they could have. They had the persona. They had the look. The one downside to Luger was that he was not a great interview. Nikita became a great interview. Luger was never a great interview, but when Luger came into an arena, the people popped. He looked great in the ring. He was built like a brick shithouse. Two bowls of white rice. (laughs)

How about Paul Jones. He was managing at the time.
 He worked for me on the first major show I had at Temple University. I had Paul Jones against Junkyard Dog in a "dog collar" match. Nobody knew who Paul Jones was. He was another guy who didn't sell a ticket. I actually met Paul before Crockett started to use him as a manager. I saw Paul Jones and Junkyard Dog wrestle in Puerto Rico ... and they had a phenomenal match! I was so impressed that I *had* to have them on my show. To be honest, I put JYD on the card because he was black. Temple University was in a black neighborhood and I thought he might sell some tickets. And he did, but not a lot. Sylvester [Ritter, aka Junkyard Dog] was just a great guy. Paul was, too. Both of them ... "*Just tell us what you want us to do.*" Again, back in those days, if you were a heel, you didn't sign autographs. You didn't do any of that stuff, so Paul came to work, did his job, and he left. But again, my interaction with Paul was solely professional.

Ricky Morton.
 Oh, man. Ricky was a true, true, true professional. We got together a couple years ago when we went to one of those [Rob] Feinstein things. Ricky Morton ... now think about this. Rock 'n' Roll Express worked for me on the Crockett shows, but they never worked for me personally on one of my independents. They were never available. I couldn't get them. I had Midnight Express and the Fantastics, but I couldn't get Rock 'n' Roll. There were always busy.

 In my opinion, Ricky Morton is what made Crockett *Crockett*. Here was a guy who didn't have size, but the girls wanted a piece of him ... big-time. When Flair did the gimmick with the training bra, it was so legit that it was ridiculous because every teenage girl — from 13 years old and up — wanted to lose their virginity to Ricky Morton. (laughs) I laughed so hard when Flair gave Morton the bra because it was so true. If you were a 34-year-old woman, you didn't care for Ricky Morton, but if you were 15 years old, Ricky was going to be their first husband. The tickets they sold for Crockett was ridiculous. Ricky's partner, Robert Gibson, was a quiet guy, but Ricky was verbal. They were both true professionals. Cornette was the guy who first introduced me to them. Yes, Ricky was a great guy.

Do you remember anything about John Ayers in Philly as the special referee for a Ric Flair-Lex Luger match?
 Other than the fact that he was there, I don't have any memories of John Ayers at all. I do remember that night, though, because Midnight won the world tag belts from Arn and Tully. Tommy Young was the referee. Tommy came over to where I was sitting at the timekeeper's table, put his head through the ropes, and told me what to say when I announced the winners.

JJ Dillon.
 I loved JJ. To me, JJ was the epitome of what a wrestling manager should be. Vince put Lou Albano, Freddie Blassie and the Grand Wizard with guys who couldn't talk. They needed that verbal mouthpiece. JJ wasn't a verbal mouthpiece. He did talk now and then, but Ole, Arn and Flair didn't need anybody to talk for them. I think you could make a good argument that JJ was pretty quiet, and more than anyone else, he portrayed someone who actually "managed" his wrestlers in a business-sense. All JJ had to do was appear with them in his suit and display his arrogance. He didn't have to do much talking. He was an add-on who did a fabulous job of working the crowd. Cornette was another one who had working a

crowd down to a science. They both knew how to get heat, but they also knew that they were add-ons who weren't the entire reason for that heat. Some managers try to become the show. JJ didn't do that. Cornette didn't do that.

The managers today make themselves the show because the wrestlers can't get the heat. If a guy is in the ring, he should be able to draw heat, but they don't know how to do that, so the fans sit on their hands and don't boo.

Baron Von Raschke.

Baron was an interesting guy. Baron worked for me on my King of Prussia show. He was never over big in Philly, so I never used him later with TWA. He may have been out of the business by then, as well. But Baron was a really nice guy and a true professional. He played the hated German role in the building, but afterwards, you couldn't meet a nicer person. I've often thought that he was really too nice of a guy to be a Baron Von Raschke.

I always found the meanest heels to be the nicest guys outside the ring.

Absolutely. Abdullah was like that. When I booked Abby on my shows, he wanted to know what church to attend on Sunday. Inside the ring, Abby went wide open. Outside, he was just a gentle giant.

Any other memories of Abdullah?

You'll love this one. Abdullah beat the shit out of everybody he wrestled. Back then, he kayfabed *everybody* ... all the time. When he worked for me, he didn't say a word when he was around the fans. He kayfabed it the whole time ... except in the back. Well, I had him do a luncheon for me. Abby wore a suit, a tie, and a vest for the luncheon. I have a picture of that somewhere. He dropped the gimmick entirely. He answered questions in English and didn't play the gimmick at all ... and he was the star of a luncheon. The people loved him! Of course, back then, the boys weren't open with the fans like they are today. They tell everything about everything. Not back then, though, so go figure that one. Abby did a lot of shows for Feinstein. I had my picture taken with Abby. He points to me, I point to him. Now he doesn't kayfabe anything. He does all these interviews, he does all these wrestle cons.

Joel interviews Terry Taylor at an NWA event.

5  Autographed Underwear

Members of the Squared Circle Fan Club went on a bus trip to Atlantic City for *WrestleMania IV* on Sunday, March 27, 1988. The trip costs $45 for club members and $47 for non-members. The bus left the New Market (2nd and Lombard streets) headquarters of talk radio station WDVT (AM 900) at 1:00 p.m. and returned at 8:30 p.m.

The trip fee included a $25 wrestling ticket, round-trip transportation, $15 in "coin" from Trump Hotel and Casino (which hosted *WrestleMania IV*), and $2.50 in food coupons.

One of the things WCW and WWF did do was allow me to have some of their guys call into the radio show. I also promoted luncheons for the Squared Circle Fan Club. I'll tell you more about the fan club later, but I'd bring in some of the wrestlers for a lunch with the fans. I'd pay them 500 to a thousand dollars and we'd have 30 or 40 fans there. The guys would do an interview, have brunch, have their pictures taken with the fans, and just have fun socializing. I can give you a long list of people who did those lunches for me ... The Road Warriors, Cactus Jack, Ricky Steamboat, Sting, Luna Vachon. It was ridiculous. The one guy I never had do a luncheon was Dusty Rhodes. You can't get the guys to do that today. It's all corporate and you have to go through their agents.

A lot of the guys I had at the lunches called *me*. When they came to town with the NWA, they'd call and ask if I could make them some money. Typically, they came into town either the day before or the day after a show. The lunches were great and the guys were able to let their hair down a little and have fun with the fans. And they knew, "*I'm paying you five hundred dollars*" — or a thousand, or whatever — "*so here's the deal. You don't say no. If somebody wants to have their picture made with you, you have your picture made with them. If somebody want you to kiss them, you kiss them. If somebody wants you to sign their underwear, you sign their underwear. You're not here to say no.*" We had a little question-and-answer session and I told them not to give the client bullshit. "*Give them an answer. You can stay in gimmick if you want to stay in gimmick, but don't give them back,* 'No comment.'" No. So the guys would come and they actually had fun ... and at the end of the day they got paid.

I know Flair would have commanded a premium for the luncheons, but did you pay the rest of the guys a standard $500 payoff, or did it depend on their status in the business?

It depended on their status. In fact, I remember Lex Luger was a thousand. It didn't take long for the word to get around that there was a money mark waiting to book guys and overpay them. I *know* I did. If I said a thousand, they'd say, "*Okay,*" but if I said, "*Five hundred,*" they'd hem and haw. But I'd say most of the guys were $500 to a thousand.

If I remember correctly, Carmela charged $25 a head for the luncheon. That included a luncheon buffet, which was always the same — hot roast beef sandwiches, hot dogs ... you know, that kind of crap. There was a place in

Philadelphia called The Bus Stop. [Harbison and Torresdale avenues] That's where we held them. When The Bus Stop closed, we moved to a place called Champs on Roosevelt Blvd., which turned out to be a better spot because they had parking. Again, I promoted the luncheons on the radio show and the newspaper gave us a small mention. And I've always said, when I was promoting TWA, I had 22,000 listeners per quarter hour. If my listeners would have come to every one of my events, I could have been bigger than Vince, but I would have 22,000 listeners and only 2,000 people show up for my show after eight weeks of promotion. Okay? So there was a lot of people listening that didn't partake in any of the stuff I did.

The Squared Circle Fan Club had a Father's Day luncheon with Missy Hyatt on Sunday, June 19, 1988, from 2 to 5 p.m. at the Bus Stop. Club members paid $20, non-members $22.

One of the strangest luncheons I think you ever had was a "Father's Day Luncheon" with Missy Hyatt at the Bus Stop.
Yes! (laughs) In addition to that, at that point in time, Tod Gordon had become one of my advertisers. Not only did we have Missy at the Bus Stop, but she appeared at Tod's store to sell jewelry. It was kind of weird. I got really tight with Woman, Baby Doll, Madusa [Micelli], and Luna Vachon. The women who were in the sport were very outgoing, vivacious, and loud. They were women who would fit right in today, but back in those days, they were the exception to the rule. Yes, Missy did a luncheon for me. Preadolescent guys would come up for a picture and she would take a photo with them. She put that smile on and just pushed those tits right out there. When she did that thing at Tod's store, she wore jewelry and a low-cut blouse. She really looked good. She always made me crack up, too. She was really funny.

Those girls got a reputation in the wrestling world as being prima donnas. I never saw that. Missy never worked a show for me, but she was so gracious with the fans at the luncheon. Woman, Madusa and Luna all worked on my cards and I never had a bit of trouble from any of them.

There was one incident involving Missy at one of your events. Missy and Eddie Gilbert appeared at a Bowl-A-Thon and luncheon on May 12, 1991. It was reported that she got upset because a photographer was selling photos of her without her permission and the two of you got into a shouting match. Did that happen, and if so, do you have any memories of that?
I do remember that. Eddie and Missy were still an item at the time. I think that took place at Boulevard Lanes. I had a photographer named Pete. Pete has since passed away, but he used to take pictures. He was the photographer who got an okay from Crockett to sit in the first row and shoot pictures. What we would do was — and Elliott agreed to it because he thought it would help me make a few dollars — he let us put photos on buttons and sell them at Crockett's shows.

So, when I had Eddie and Missy, Pete made buttons and photos so he could sell them to fans who wanted Eddie and Missy's autographs. Well, Missy wasn't a big fan of that. I do remember them having words. I went over to her and asked her, "*What are you talking about? The agreement was that you would come here to do this. I told you we would have photos.*"

She said, "*I thought were going to be signing magazines and that kind of thing.*"

I said, "*No, this is what we do.*"

We had a conversation and it was really no big deal. There definitely wasn't any yelling. I don't know where that came from. Now, as I learned later, Eddie never gave her any of the money I gave him for the two of them. There you go. I was learning lessons about paying wrestlers. You don't give money to a wrestler and expect them to give it to someone else. You'd better pay the one wrestler and you'd better pay the other. I don't think Eddie was holding back on her. I had paid him earlier and I think he just hadn't told her. But it was no big deal.

What I heard was that the two of you started yelling and cursing at each other, with her finally saying she was "*out of here.*"

We had an exchange of words, but it wasn't loud, and there definitely wasn't any cursing. It was just a matter of her being surprised that we had all the pictures for sale and she wasn't getting a piece of it. But the longshot was, she didn't know she got paid because Eddie never gave her the money ... and she didn't leave early. Pete was the photographer for the Squared Circle.

Joe Zanolle was the official photographer for TWA, wasn't he.

Yeah. Well, actually, Joe evolved. He started out going on the Squared Circle trips with us, but when we were promoting TWA, he took pictures. At some point, Joe Zanolle went through our wrestling school and became a referee. Joe no longer referees, but he promotes ECWA [East Coast Wrestling Association] here in South Jersey. I don't know if Joe is a part-owner, but he does a lot of the booking, publicity, and still has his hand in some of the photography.

What was interesting about starting an independent in Philly is that both George Napolitano and Bill Apter both lived in Philly. They still live in the area. At the time, Bill lived about an hour from Philly. Bill introduced me to all the guys from *Pro Wrestling Illustrated* [PWI]. I gave all of the big photographers access to my shows. The only thing I asked of the guys was, if they used a picture from my shows, I wanted "TWA" mentioned in the article or the caption. Not "Photo by Bill Apter," but "Photo by Bill Apter, TWA Wrestling," or whatever. They all agreed to do that.

Speaking of photographers, when I had the New Japan match, I must have had 20 photographers. Mike Lano was on a podcast with me a few years ago. He was on for 30 minutes and he gave me some great endorsements. Mike was a great photographer. George Napolitano was at every show. They are as good as it gets. I must have had (pause) ... I'm going to say a dozen photographers at every show. Now, Joe Zanolle ... I don't know if you know Joe. He's a local guy.

I don't know him personally, but I know he refereed for you.

Yes. He was one of my referees and then became a booker for ECW, but before that he was a photographer. So, he was ringside at a lot of my shows. He has some great pictures. Mike Lano was from California. He worked for New Japan when I had Owen Hart and Takayuki Iizuka on my card. They flew him to Philly to shoot the match. Mike was a really good photographer.

Several times, you've mentioned a photographer named Pete. Do remember his last name?

No. He passed away, but I didn't even know about it until two years later. I'll tell you what happened with Pete. Pete was a guy who was always there. When we ran shows at the Civic Center, we sold buttons to raise money for Squared Circle. We had pictures of Ricky Morton, Robert Gibson, whoever. Pete took pictures, but he took them in the ring because he never got a pass to take photos in the back, so they were all action photos. Long story short, the fans loved the buttons. They were buying those buttons for a dollar, and back in the day, we made a profit selling them for a dollar. Today, there much more expensive. Pete lived in South Philly and was with us at every show ... the big shows, the little shows. God bless him. He was such a good guy. He just wanted to take pictures.

One of the reasons I got such good coverage from the magazines was because we were in Philly and so close to New York. The other thing was, I never hesitated to give photographers access to ringside to shoot to show. There's actually a video online from the time I created the TWA belt and there were photographers at ringside. As I left the ring and was walking away, one of the guys kind of motioned to me, as if to tell me he was going to recognize the TWA in *Pro Wrestling Illustrated*. Later, I actually announced that from the ring. They had that listing of promotions ... the NWA, WWF, Oregon, Memphis, and others, and Apter actually put my promotion in the listings. TWA was in the top ten, so having contact with those guys from the magazines was really cool. Of course, I was promoting in their back yard.

I didn't follow wrestling at that time and I never read the magazines, but I used to hear about the PWA ratings and how the wrestlers all wanted to get on that list. Why was that such a big deal?
The only way a local guy could get any notoriety outside of his community was to be mentioned in a national magazine. Well, D.C. Drake, Larry Winters, Johnny Hotbody, Rockin' Rebel, Jimmy Jannetty ... those guys started getting recognition in the magazine as being in the top 10 at TWA. That gave them some notoriety and they started getting bookings with other promoters. Back then, there really wasn't a way to promote themselves other than to get a reputation and get mentioned in either the magazines or the dirt-sheets.

Another benefit of the magazines was, when the independent guys started to realize that TWA matches were going to be main stories in *Pro Wrestling Illustrated* — Carmine [DeSpirito, editor of *Wrestling Eye* magazine] knew me, so he was 100 percent behind what I was doing, and other magazines got on the bandwagon with stories about my promotion — so those indy guys knew that if somebody took pictures of their match, that story had a good chance of getting into the magazines, and that was the only mainstream promotion they could get because the Internet was still years from being in everybody's home.

When Funk and Lawler wrestled, they would be in the magazine three months later ... and it would *always* be a bloody match. So, as a rule, the guys who worked for me never did a standard "*Fifteen minutes, I'm out of here, goodbye!*" match. And when I ran an angle with somebody, they realized I was going to book them for more than one shot. Those guys knew that I was going to promote big shows and that they might be on those shows with a nice payday. The biggest payoff that Cactus Jack and Eddie Gilbert had back in the day was the two-out-of-three-fall match they had in Philly. [Aug. 3, 1991]

On Saturday, Sept. 10, 1988, *Rasslin' Radio* debuted on WIP (610 AM). The show aired on Saturdays from 8 to 9 a.m.

You debuted on WIP in September '88.
Yeah. We went off the air Jan. 18, 1992, so if I started in Sept. '88 and it went off the air in Jan. '92, I was on the air for a little more than three years with WIP.
You taped a show every week, right?
Every Saturday morning.

Did you ever go on vacation and forgo doing a show, like during the summer or the Christmas holidays?
Nope, nope. I'm a workaholic. I'm one of those guys who, if I need a vacation, I'll do it during the week. I did do one show from Puerto Rico, the weekend of Hurricane Hugo.

No kidding?
I sure did. It was during a Squared Circle trip for the fans to Puerto Rico to see Carlos Colón's shows. Ten or eleven of us were going to the Saturday-night show in Bayamón. Abdullah [the Butcher] was scheduled to be on the card that night. The night before the show, we invited Abby to have dinner with us at the restaurant in a hotel called The Caribbean. As I'm sure you know, if you offer a wrestler a free dinner, they'll show up. Well, Abby was really funny and we were having a great time. Of course, the wrestling fans with me were ecstatic that Abdullah was having dinner with us.

On Saturday morning [Sept. 18, 1989], I did the radio show and it was sunny and beautiful. By two o'clock in the afternoon, the world came to an end. Hurricane Hugo rolled in and ravaged the island, including the hotel where we were staying. They lost a couple of floors and the power went out, but we were able to stay there. They had no food, though ... nothing! We saw a tree fly by our window during the height of the storm. We were stuck on the island for some time. I did shows live from Puerto Rico, one show live from the Great American Bash in Charlotte, a show from Memphis ... .no, I never took vacations per se. I'm one of these guys who can go on a business trip and make a vacation out of it.

So, Abdullah and I walked about two blocks to the Sands Hotel, which still had power, to play blackjack. The casino was open. What does Abby do? He takes a $25 chip and puts it in a groove in his forehead. (laughs) Everybody knew who Abby was because wrestling in Puerto Rico was big-time, and everybody in the casino must have come over to see him. I wish I had a camera with me that day. He just sat there with that $25 chip sticking out of his forehead.

One time (laughs) ... now, this is going back more than a decade ago. Abby still had his restaurant in Atlanta. There's an organization called the Million Dollar Roundtable, which is an international organization made up of the world's leading insurance and financial services professionals. I've been a member of that for more than 30 years. The conference that year was in Atlanta, so I called Abby's place and made a dinner reservation for eight people. Abby had told me he would be there, but he didn't show up.

Why wasn't Abby there?
He took a booking out of town. Yes, he was out of town. Here's what actually happened. I took a group of eight of us. I said, "*We have to go get ribs at Abdullah's place.*" They all knew my wrestling background, so we all went. We get to Abby's restaurant, we walk in, and we're the only ones there. I mean, literally, there was nobody else in the restaurant. So we walk in, we get a table for eight, and I ask the server if Abby was there. "*No, he's out of town. He couldn't make it. He told me you'd be here, though.*"

We sit down and eat ribs. They were so freaking good. You pick them up and you're going to taste them for a week in your fingernails. We got the ribs, the corn, the peas, the mashed potatoes. They fed us beyond belief. The bill was around $135, which was just ridiculous for the amount of food they served to the eight of us.

I see Abby now and then. We were in Atlantic City last summer when a group called GCW [Game Changer Wrestling, June 1, 2024] put him into their Hall of Fame.

Well, he's not in the best of health. I sat with him at his table for about two hours and I threw an idea by him. I said to Abby, "*Would you mind doing a foreword for me for my book?*" Now, of course he said yes, but he puts a price tag on everything. I'm not saying that's wrong. That's just how he is, and I understand that because, if he didn't, *everybody* would want him to do something for them for free. It's just like you told me not to give away free books. I remember the exact words you said. "*EVERYBODY will want to read your book ...*" and then you paused before you said, "*... if you give it to them for free.*" I understand that.

Abby and I have a great relationship, though, and he did tell me, "*Call me if you want me and we'll figure it out.*" I thought about bringing Abby to my "One and Done" show, but quite frankly, I don't know if Abby would be able to make it because I've heard that he's in bad health. If you see him today, he doesn't look like Abdullah the Butcher. He's 84 years old and he's lost a lot of weight.

THE GODS ARE GOOD TO GOODHART
by Dan Geringer
[excerpt] Yesterday, Goodhart met with the syndication guys to talk about going East Coast regional with Rasslin' Radio. If that happens, he figures his exclusive rights to distribute Caribbean wrestling tapes will pay off.

"If you're into gore," he explains, "there's more gore than in North America. You see heads busted wide open and stitched up on TV. Tables flying. Forks being used."

Forks?

"Forks," Goodhart says happily. "Forks."
— *Philadelphia Daily News*: Wednesday, Oct. 25, 1989

Did you ever consider doing, or talk to anyone about, national syndication of your radio show?
I had what I would call preliminary conversations. Of course, national syndication was always in the back of my mind. We didn't have the Internet, so I was always thinking, "*How can I market my radio show and promotion to a larger market?*" Now, we were struggling to pay the $750 a week, so we *never* would have been able to pay three or $4,000 for syndication. Hindsight's a great thing. If I knew then what I know now, I might have done that full-time and hired a marketing person who could have taken us to greater heights, but I didn't have the money to do that. Well, I might have had the money for a while, but I wasn't going to risk everything on a roll of the dice.

Another interesting side story to that, the one time I did talk to somebody about syndication, they told me that if I went national, Vince would do whatever he could to run me off the air and put me out of business ... and he would have!

Do you remember who said that?
No, I have no idea. I have no idea. I remember having those kinds of conversations with people, and at that time, Vince really was taking over the world. Even Crockett struggled when he came to Philly because this had been home territory for the WWWF/WWF forever. Crockett was looked at as the Carolinas coming into Philadelphia, coming into Baltimore, coming into Newark. You know, they were the outsiders trying to invade Vince's space. Crockett *never* would have done as well as he did if he hadn't had TV ... and I didn't have TV! I just had radio. So I've always been a marginal player. I didn't make all the right business decisions, and I obviously made some wrong ones, but at the time, I did the best

I could with the resources I had, the short pocketbook I had, and the limited space in Philly. I was fine with the little niche I carved out of the wrestling world pie. I was fine with it, but I'd be a liar if I didn't admit that there were times I wanted to do more. Yeah, I might have been able to branch out further if I had the right people in the business with me.

So how did the Squared Circle fan club and trips come about? Where did the idea come from?

I'm pretty sure that was my idea. We had people calling the radio show and I was just trying to figure out a way to bring some revenue into the store. If I remember correctly, dues [for the fan club] were $15 a year, for which I would send new members a business card that listed them as a member of the Squared Circle. Members got preferential treatment and discounts for tours and lunches. For example — and I'm not sure of the exact number — but lunches were $25 for members, $30 for non-members. It also was a way to generate a mailing list for the store and to encourage people to come to our wrestling shows. We published a newsletter for a short time to keep people in the loop of what we were doing, so members were always the first to know. They got the news before we went public on the radio.

How many members did you have at the max?

I would say a hundred and a quarter. It's cool because wrestling fans save stuff, and every once in a while, a Squared Circle membership card pops up on Facebook. They got discounts at our store, which really wasn't money out of our pocket because the fan club helped bring people into our store to buy something.

Listen To...

RASSLIN' RADIO

Every Saturday Morning
8 to 9 am
All-Sports Radio 610 WIP

Join the

SQUARED CIRCLE FAN CLUB

For more information call 215-745-8315
or write
Squared Circle Fan Club
PO Box 57068
Philadelphia, PA 19111

Ad from one of the TWA arena programs

If we had a special guest, we made sure they got an autograph. To get 125 people to join something like that back then was huge!

I ask that question because, in the old Observers, I read at least three times that the Squared Circle Fan Club had a thousand, 1,100 members. That surprised me because I had been in fan clubs, and I ran one in the early '70s, and I never heard of a fan club having that many members.

Yeah. There's no way I would've had a thousand people give me 15 bucks a year. I'd still be in the frigging business. No, there's no way.

I wonder where those figures came from because that was repeated two or three times over a few months' time. Is it possible you would have exaggerated the membership numbers to someone? I mean, you know how people do that, and after all, it is the wrestling business.

(laughs) Well, somewhere along the line, I very well *could* have said we had thousands of members. I wouldn't put it past me. I might have embellished it. First of all, though, even if I had a thousand members, how could I have given front-row seats and ticket discounts to a thousand members? I would have sold out the building every week. So, no. It was nowhere near a thousand.

Let's put it this way. If they were a member of the fan club, they got Joel and Carmela as their best friend ... and they saw us as a way to get to the wrestlers. They saw us as a way to get the better seats. I use a phrase that I stole from someone else many years ago. The phrase was, "*I'm a conduit because I can do it.*" Understand? I was the conduit for the fans who really wanted to get close to the wrestling business. You didn't go to Memphis if you weren't a member of the fan club. You got discounts on the bus tours. Picture this one ... all the people we took to Memphis got a tour of the dressing room.

I never heard that. That's awesome!

Yeah! When did you ever see 25 people from a bus tour go into a dressing room at the wrestling matches?

When did anyone ever see *one* person — not only from a bus tour, but *anyone* not connected to the wrestling business — get into the dressing room?

Exactly!

What a great idea! That would have been worth the price of the tour by itself to a wrestling fan.

Yes, it was.

And I understand you had wrestling videos playing on the bus.

Yes, we did. Back then, they had something called video buses. I'll give you an example. One time we went to an NWA show in Troy, New York, which was one of their TBS tapings. That was a great trip. It was the one where Flair and Terry Funk had the "I Quit" match. [*Clash of the Champions IX*, Nov. 15, 1989]

We sold out the bus and that was about a six-hour ride for us. We showed tapes from Japan, the Pacific Northwest, Florida, Georgia, World Class ... video the average wrestling fan *never* saw in Philadelphia. Again, the hardcore fans traded those tapes like crazy, but most fans didn't know about those tape traders. We were able to get those tapes. Jerry Lawler would send us tapes once a month with the four shows he ran. Our people were *not* WWF fans. They loved Crockett. On that particular trip, I brought along tapes of Ric Flair matches, Terry Funk matches, all leading up to the main event that our members were going to see at *Clash*. By the time of the Flair-Funk match, they were stoked!

It was funny because, typically, everybody is pulling into the arena parking lot and parking their cars. Well, here this bus pulls up! And we already had our tickets set aside at the Will-Call booth. In hindsight, I didn't charge enough for those tickets. What I would do (pause) ... I think the bus cost me $500, so there's $50 a seat, then the ticket price, and then I added $10 for profit. Those numbers worked ... but only if I sold out the bus. On some of those trips, I didn't sell out the bus, so I actually wound up losing money. That doesn't sound like much for someone to pay a hundred dollars for a bus trip, but back then, that was serious, serious money.

Your figures are pretty accurate. You also had shorter trips that cost less than that. On March 27, 1988, you sponsored a trip to Atlantic City for *Wrestlemania IV*. The cost for Squared Circle Fan Club members was $45 and $47 for non-members. That included a $25 ticket to the show, round-trip transportation, $15 in "coin" from Trump Hotel and Casino, and $2.50 in food coupons. What a deal! Any interesting memories from that trip?

No. I'm not sure why I put that trip together because I never did care much for Vince's product. It was funny because some of the people who went to the Crockett shows just refused to go to Vince shows. That's when I came to the realization that there are wrestling fans and then there are WWF fans. Today, the fans who follow WWE are not wrestling fans, because they're clearly not getting wrestling. They're into the showbiz, and that's fine, but they're not *wrestling* fans.

Back in the day, I used to compare wrestling to NASCAR. If you're a NASCAR fan, everybody who was a NASCAR fan was also either a Jeff Gordon fan or a Dale Earnhardt fan. They always took a liking to one of the drivers. The same thing with wrestling ... if you were a Crockett fan, you were either a heel fan or a babyface fan. You were one of the two. But then there were people who would cheer the Road Warriors when they came out — and the Road Warriors were heels at the time — and then they would cheer Rock 'n' Roll Express. The Crockett fans would cheer the match more than the individual wrestler. Now, with TV and everything else going on, it's just different. And the reason Crockett's not around anymore, quite frankly, is because the Crockett form no longer works. When TV took over, Hulk Hogan became the thing. You had to be Lex Luger. You had to be six-foot-four and built like a brick shithouse to make it on TV.

Years ago, WWWF TV matches were always seven minutes, and every match was a main eventer against a jobber ... and the matches sucked! But the matches were designed to put the main-event wrestlers over. Today, they're trying to do the matches with no jobbers and the matches are horrible. It's funny, but last night I was watching WAR a little bit. Now, I don't normally watch that stuff at all, but the Phillies were off, so I clicked through the stations and found RAW. It was horrible. I watched all of fifteen minutes. I mean, the wrestling was ridiculous. It's so obvious that the matches are scripted by Vince, or whoever, to a point that it's awful. I mean, the wrestlers can't even do believable interviews. Back in the day, that was the art of the business. If you couldn't talk, they gave you a manager — Grand Wizard, Lou Albano, Freddie Blassie. If a wrestler could do an interview — if they could talk — they didn't need a manager. That's what was so good about Flair and the Four Horsemen. They could all talk. They could all do a promo. JJ, Flair, Ole ... they did the best interviews in the world. And the NWA — Crockett — their interviews far surpassed the interviews by the WWF guys.

We loved it back in the day because they had 60-minute matches every night, six nights a week, and the guys had to drive from town to town. The guys today fly everywhere and they can't wrestle 20 minutes. The biggest difference between then and today is, in the NWA, Memphis, Portland, and even the WWF, the guys told a story in the ring! The stories today are nowhere to be found except in the script the guys are handed. The old guys learned the art of telling a story through a wrestling match. They knew how to keep the crowd involved. Okay, I'm off my soapbox ... well, at least for now. (laughs)

Thursday, Nov. 26, 1987 — *Rasslin' Radio* hosted a trip to *Starrcade '87*, which included a round-trip flight to Chicago, overnight accommodations at the Embassy Suites Hotel, buffet breakfast, cocktail party, poolside party, and ringside seats.

On Nov. 26, 1987, you took the group to Chicago for *Chi-Town Heat*, but instead of the bus, everyone flew on United Airlines. You only charged $289 a person, and that included airfare, hotel, a buffet breakfast, a cocktail party, a poolside party, and ringside seats. I don't see how you could have made any money at that price.

If I lost money, I didn't lose much. Back then, you could get a hotel room for fifty to $60, a flight for less than a hundred. I priced it right. I figured I'd make it up in volume. If I made $20 a head, I was happy. We flew whenever we were going to stay overnight, like when we went to Memphis.

How did the Memphis trips come about?

Carmela contacted Jerry Lawler. Carmela knew Jerry really well and he started to make appearances on our radio show. One day — on the air, mind you — he made the suggestion that we come down to Memphis. We were all for it, but again, we knew *nothing* about putting a trip together ... especially one with a lot of people. One of the guys I went to high school with owned a tour bus company. It was a guy named David Benedict and his company was called David Tours. He's big-time now. He runs his own buses. I called him and he put the tours together ... the fares, the hotels, the buses. Brian Heffron, The Blue Meanie, was on each of those tours. He was just Brian Heffron at the time ... a fan. I mean, when people see Blue Meanie, quite frankly, it all started with our Memphis bus tours.

How cool is that?

We had a hardcore group of ... I'm going to say 20 or 25 people. We did a longer tour of Memphis that included Memphis, Jackson, and Nashville. I think it cost the fan club members $400, or something like that. We were recognized at each of the shows as the group from Philadelphia. We also got to go to Jerry Lawler's softball games and meet his team, which was how I got to meet Sid Vicious. Everybody on that trip got really tight with Lawler and Jeff Jarrett, and that whole crew. Lance Russell came to one of our breakfasts. When we went down there, they gave us the red carpet treatment. The one downside is that it actually exposed the business, hardcore, for a lot of our people. The people on the Memphis trips who weren't the smart marks had their eyes opened real quick because we went to the show in Nashville, and they had the same matches that had been in Memphis a week or two before, and then they saw people who lost the titles in Memphis come out in Nashville with the title belts.

And lose them again.

And lose them again!

They promoted Jackson, Tennessee, at that time. The building they ran in was the coolest building I ever saw. For all intents and purposes, it was a bar, but it was three stories high with a big atrium and the ring was in the atrium ... and there was nobody sitting ringside. Everybody was standing first floor, second floor, third floor. That building was in my mind when I later came up with the idea for *Bar Wars*. The bottom line for this was, for every ying, there was a yang, and everything created something else. It was just very, very cool how things evolved for me.

Here's a good little story. Sid Vicious lived right outside Memphis in West Memphis, Arkansas. Sid asks me one day, "*Do you like dog racing?*"

I said, "*I don't know. We don't have dog racing in Pennsylvania.*"

He says, "*Come on. We'll go to the dog races.*"

We drive to the dog track and everybody knows Sid. I mean, come on! He's six-foot-nine, or whatever he was, and he lived there. Sid won, he lost, he won, he lost. I bet two dollars on every favorite to show and wound up with two dollars and forty cents ... but I spent a whole day at the track!

How open was Jerry Lawler with the fans on the tours? I mean, did he talk openly about the business, or was he pretty kayfabe?

He tried to keep kayfabe when he was with the group, when we were all together. One time, we all went to Church's Chicken for lunch and, for whatever reason, he was very open. One thing you learned about those guys back then ... kayfabe was the rule until they knew you were in the business. Just to sidetrack a little bit, one time, Nikita Koloff flew up to Philadelphia and we drove up to York [PA]. The funny thing was, during the trip, which was about 90 minutes from Philly, my windshield wipers died, and it was pouring rain. I could barely see the road in front of me. Nikita didn't really know me, so during that trip, he never dropped the Russian accent. On the ride back after the matches, the accent was gone. (laughs) Those guys kept kayfabe until they knew you were okay. Once they realized you were inside, they took the barriers down.

What helped a little bit was, the guys knew me as the ring announcer. I think that helped a little bit. The guys saw me in the back and, as crazy as it sounds, they talked to each other all the time, so word got out that I was okay. I'm not sure what year the trip with Nikita took place, but I was already doing lunches with the fans, so they had an idea that I knew what was going on. A lot of the fans on the trips were what we called smart marks, and those who weren't got somewhat smartened up while they were on the tour. For instance, the Great Muta always spoke Japanese, but there he was in the back speaking English. No, it didn't take long for people to tumble to the idea that things weren't quite as black and white as they appeared.

On one of the Memphis trips, Dave Brown gave everybody a speech about not cheering the heels. In Memphis, I'd have either Dave Brown or Lance Russell— sometimes both of them — come to the breakfast at the hotel. Again, I wanted to give the fans something different from an ordinary get-together. We'd eat breakfast and then we'd go to the TV taping that day. Well, Philly was a heel town, and they [Memphis] knew that ... and they didn't want the guys cheering the heels. That didn't work on television in Memphis. "*Boo the heels, cheer the babyfaces. You've gotta do that.*"

The first time we went to Jackson, they had a lot of people there, all of whom were booing Jerry Lawler's opponent ... and my people were cheering. So when we went to Nashville the next night, they told me they didn't want that. They told us that we needed to go with the flow.

Did your guys ever boo Lawler in the Mid-South Coliseum?

Well, by the time we got to Memphis, we had been in Jackson and we had been in Nashville, so we knew what we were expected to do at that point. Dave Brown was there, Lance Russell was there, Lawler was running things in the back. They gave us passes to the shows, so we had to do what they asked, and that's what I wanted, anyway. They were our hosts and I wanted to keep things kayfabe and the business protected.

Tell me more about Philadelphia being a heel town.

Philly's always been a heel town. In fact, the Flyer's hockey team was nicknamed the Broad Street Bullies. When they were first created, the powers-that-be realized that Philly was a heel town. Philly loved the bad guys. Vince never figured that out, and Vince always had Hogan on top ... a babyface! When Flair was at the top with Crockett, Crockett started drawing because Philly fans loved to hate. And in this city, the teams that people love to hate are over [popular]. I'm convinced that the Flyers, being the heels that they were back in the day when they were created, took on the persona of the city and the people loved it. When Dave Schultz would come out and beat the shit out of an opposing hockey player, that had nothing to do with hockey at all, but Flyers' fans ate it up.

I kind of figured that out when I started TWA. I pushed D.C. [Drake] as my champ because he was a heel. You'll find this really interesting. I remember having a conversation with Don Muraco. I brought him in one time for a match against Bob Orton at Temple University. [June 9, 1990] Muraco told me that night that he would do six- to eight-week tours of independent promotions. He would go into one town as a babyface. The next town he went to, for another promotion, he'd be a heel. He'd go from town to town changing from heel to face, which kept him fresh. If he went to a town where the champion was a babyface, he'd go in as a heel. He worked his way up to a title match, then he'd do a gimmick match, like loser leave town or something, and then he'd leave. Muraco made a living by changing his gimmick. Well, today you can't do that! You are what you are everywhere because everything gets reported on the Internet! You can't do the turns any more. You can barely run angles. It's very difficult. Whatever you do today, heel or babyface, you have to stay with it.

Again, back in the old days when Eddie Farhat was strong, what made him so strong? Well, he was the Sheik ... 24/7. He just had that attitude. The reverse of that is Abdullah. When he's in the dressing room, he's just so nice. He's just an old kid. Everybody knew what their role was, but some of them just lived it.

How much more difficult was it to arrange an overnight tour, as opposed to a one-day bus tour?

There was a lot more to the planning. With a bus tour, all I had to do was call David and tell him I needed a bus on a certain day.

The *Rasslin' Radio*/Squared Circle Fan Club took another trip, this time to Greensboro, North Carolina, on Saturday, April 23, 1988. The trip cost $270, which included round-trip airfare, hotel accommodations, two meals, and admission to the Crockett Cup finals.

You also made a trip to Greensboro for the April 23, 1988, Crockett Cup finals ... $270 for the same package.

The best part of that was getting the flavor of what wrestling was like down south. We did tours of Memphis, tours of the Carolinas, and even a tour of Atlanta to Crusher Blackwell's promotion. When you got out of the Philadelphia market, you realized that it was a whole different world. We were there when they were bringing the wrestlers in by helicopter. I was able to get backstage because I had worked with Crockett a little bit in King of Prussia. I wasn't well-known at that point, but the guys knew who I was.

On Saturday, May 21, 1988, wrestling fans gathered at the Airport Quality Inn from 9:30 a.m. until noon for a breakfast buffet with Johnny V. The cost was $20 for members, $22 for non-members. From 1:00 p.m. until 3:00 p.m., Captain Lou Albano, Joel Goodhart & Carmela Panfil made an appearance at The Comic Relief comic book store to raise funds for the National Multiple Sclerosis Society. Albano signed copies of *The Honeymooners* #7 comic book, which featured Albano teaching Jackie Gleason's character, Ralph Kramden, how to wrestle. Later that night, the WWF held a show at the Spectrum.

The following month, you hosted a breakfast buffet at the Airport Quality Inn on May 21 with Johnny Valiant, and later that afternoon, you, Carmela, and Lou Albano made an appearance at The Comic Relief comic book store to raise funds for multiple sclerosis.
I don't remember the Quality Inn, and I thought Lou Albano was at the Bus Stop.
It was just a fundraiser with Lou signing copies of his *Honeymooners* #7 comic book.
Oh, okay. Boy, oh, boy. Now you're bringing back memories. I forgot about that one completely. The funny thing about Lou was, Lou was from New York. I picked him up at the airport. Lou was the only wrestler I knew who never wore deodorant. I've gotta tell you, when he came off that plane, you knew right away that he didn't wear deodorant. It was unbelievable. Everybody was looking at us because Albano had the rubber bands in his cheeks. He was in full gimmick. I got to know Lou. I got to know Freddie Blassie. In fact, I still have one of Freddie's outfits. He autographed it for me. I never really got to know [The Grand] Wizard. For a time, it was in the back of my mind that being a manager was something I'd like to do. I knew I wasn't going to be a wrestler. Anyway, when Lou and I were in the car, we just talked wrestling. I drove him to the venue with the windows down. I'm telling you. That was the one thing I'll never forget about Lou Albano. He never wore deodorant. Oh, it was terrible.
Did he ask you why you had the windows down?
No. It was a nice day. Lou was a great guy.
I never heard about those fan trips until I started my research for the book. Of course, I was out of the business when you were doing them and I only followed the business a little through the *Observer*.
Here's another one. We had Tommy Rich on a bus trip with us. We had Buddy Landel on a trip. We did a tour of Georgia and I paid Tommy a hundred bucks to ride on the bus with the fans. Of course, I had to make sure the bus was stocked with beer. He drank, he had a ball, and I paid him a hundred dollars. Tommy got drunk and then had to go do a match. But it gave the fans an opportunity to be around those guys like friends, and not just a fan meeting a former NWA world heavyweight champion. And that's what really worked for us. We wanted the fans to see the wrestlers as a regular guy.
In July 1991, I put together a bus trip to Memphis, and while we were there, we went to a card in Jonesboro, Arkansas, which is on the other side of the Mississippi River, about an hour from Memphis. Jimmy Jannetty wrestled J.T. Smith in what was called "The Battle of Philadelphia indie wrestlers." [July 21, 1991] It was an add-on, so they didn't list it in the newspapers.

Jimmy shared the details about that match. *"Downtown Bruno was the referee. The match couldn't have been longer than five to six minutes. JT was the heel and was disqualified for throwing me over the top rope. Blue Meanie was there and videotaped the match."*

You had an employee at the Squared Circle named Jeannie Siciliano. Tell me a little about her.
Jeannie was a hardcore wrestling fan. Her last name was Peletsky then. To this day she's a hardcore wrestling fan. Jeanie went to all the matches, and I think she still does. I don't care who they were ... the WWF, independents, everything! In fact, her mom — who has since passed away — was a hardcore wrestling fan. Jeannie was a young kid at that time and she became my first and only employee. She actually worked at the store. That came about because, as time went on, I realized that I wanted to spend time with the fans watching the video tapes. I didn't want to be stuck behind the cash register, so we decided to bring Jeanie in. I don't remember what we paid her, but after we hired Jeannie, Carmela and I had more time to mingle with the fans. We didn't have to stand behind the register. It's hard to believe that Jeannie now has a son who is out of college. In the article you sent me from the *Philadelphia Inquirer*, I believe Jeannie's standing behind the cash register in the photo.

How long was the Squared Circle in business?
I'm going to say three or four years. We probably closed down in '89.

What was the lead-in to making that decision?
When I got to WIP ... and keep in mind, that show was Friday night and Sundays. It was clear that we couldn't continue to do both the show and the store, so I think there was an overlap. We tried to do both of them, but it became clear that the store wasn't going to make it. I'm sure Carmela can remember the dates better than me, but at some point, we just decided it was time to lock the doors.

What did Carmela do after she got out of the business?
Carmela still lives in South Jersey. She's not in the best of health. She's had her own issues. Carmela and Paul eventually got divorced. If you want, we can call Carmela and get some three-way calls going so you can get more information from her.

Did Carmela ever come to your TWA shows after you got things rolling?
No. Carmela never came to the TWA shows.

That's so strange. Was there a reason?
I found out later — much, much later — that she didn't know I was running shows. If you didn't listen to my radio show, you didn't know about them. That was our advertising.

So when Carmela got out, she got out cold turkey, like you did years later when you quit the business.
Correct. I didn't talk to Carmela for years. I had her phone number and she had mine, but we didn't call each other. Several years ago, she actually had a Squared Circle breakfast, a reunion, for about ten of the guys.

U.S.W.A. WRESTLING
JONESBORO, AR
EARL BELL COMMUNITY CENTER
BOX OFFICE OPENS 3 P.M.
ADVANCE TICKETS: FRONT PAGE CAFE
FOR INFORMATION CALL 932-8885 DAY OF MATCHS

SPECIAL NIGHT
SUNDAY, JULY 21 - 8:00 P.M.
PARADE OF CHAMPIONS

DOUBLE TITLE
WORLD TITLE-VS-SOU. TITLE
EDDIE MARLIN-SPECIAL REFEREE
JERRY LAWLER-VS-ERIC EMBRY

WORLD TAG TITLE
ROBERT FULLER AND JEFF JARRETT
-VS-
BAR ROOM BRAWLERS
BAR ROOM RULES

GRUDGE BILL DUNDEE -VS- LEATHERFOOT	TEXAS TITLE DIRTY WHITE BOYS -VS- TOM PRICHARD	OPENING MATCH ROB ZAKOWSKI -VS- SABU

Philadelphia, Pennsylvania: September 10, 1988
Rasslin' Radio Back to School Special, WCW, Civic Center
$1 for the first 500 kids who show up
- Ron Simmons beat Agent Steel
- Ricky Morton beat Curtis Thompson
- Brad Armstrong, Bobby Fulton & Tommy Rogers beat
  Rick Steiner, Larry Zbyzsko & Al Perez
- Dog collar match, Brad Armstrong handcuffed to Al Perez
  Dusty Rhodes beat Kevin Sullivan
- U.S. title match
  Sting beat Barry Windham (dq)
- The Road Warriors beat Rip Morgan & Russian Assassin #1 w/mgr. Paul Jones
- TV title match
  Mike Rotundo* beat Nikita Koloff (dq)
- U.S. tag team title match*, special referee John Ayres
  Bobby Eaton & Stan Lane beat Arn Anderson & Tully Blanchard
- NWA world title match
  Lex Luger beat Ric Flair w/mgr. J.J. Dillon (dq)

On Sept. 10, 1988, WCW promoted a show in Philly, another "Rasslin' Radio" night, this sone billed as "Rasslin Radio Back to School Special." That's pretty cool.

I was working closely with Elliott. The kids were going back to school around that time and Elliott was smart enough to realize that Carmela and I had the eyes and ears of a lot of kids through the radio show. Crockett's people were smart enough to realize that we were their Internet, even though nobody knew there was such a thing at the time. We made a few bucks at the store selling tickets. I think we sold 200 tickets, but I don't remember the exact number.

Springfield Skating Rink in Delaware County hosted a *Rasslin' Radio* party on March 31, 1989.

Did you ever promote a show in Allentown?

No, I didn't, but the NWA did a tour that included Allentown. I wasn't a promoter, but they asked for help, so I pitched in. I never personally promoted a show there. D.C. Drake promoted wrestling in Allentown — the Continental Wrestling Alliance — but that was in the early '80s, long before me.

If you're a wrestling fan 12 or under — and you can crawl out of bed early enough on Saturday morning — you might be able to see tomorrow night's National Wrestling Alliance card at the Civic Center for just $1.

That's the special deal being offered to the first 500 kids who show up at the box office when it opens at 10 a.m.

It's part of WIP's "Rasslin' Radio Back to School" special, which also includes a 7:30 p.m. autograph session with tennis-racket-wielding wrestling manager Jim Cornette and his United States Tag-Team Champions, Midnight Express (Stan Lane and Bobby Eaton).

Tickets for the evening's matches, $12 and $15, are are available at the Civic Center box office, all Ticketron locations and by phone from Teletron (1-800-233-4050). Youngsters under 12 who don't get in on the early morning $1 deal can buy $12 tickets for half price at the box office. Doors open at 7 p.m.; the matches begin at 8. Info: 823-7350/823-7400.

6  The Long-Haired, Snakeskin-Booted, Seriously Sunglassed, 36-year-old Insurance Salesman

Newark, Delaware: April 16, 1989
Newark High School, att. 1,100
Ticket prices $25 for golden circle (ringside), $13 reserved, $10 bleachers
- Bam Bam Bigelow NC Mystery Man (ddq)
- WWA heavyweight title match
  Tom Brandi beat Boy Gone Bad
- Indian strap match
  Chief Jules Strongbow vs.
    Tony (Hitman) Stetson
- Dog collar match
  Larry Winters vs. D.C. Drake
- Rocky Johnson & The Samoan vs.
    Cream Team
- Ladies
  Misty Blue & Heidi Lee Morgan vs.
    Kat Leroux & Linda Dallas
- AWF title match
  The Bounty Hunter* vs. King Kaluha
- David Schultz NC Magnificent Muraco (dq)

David Shults & Joel

The first show you promoted on your own took place on April 16, 1989, in Newark, Delaware. Your feature was Don Muraco vs. David Shults and it was promoted as a benefit card for the Newark High School baseball team.
 Back in the day, most of the independents promoted outside of Philly, so I had to get somebody to sell tickets. We'd rent a building and work with one of the student groups. Well, baseball teams had 20 or more young kids, plus fathers. It was never the band or orchestra. It was always a baseball or football team.

 And yes, I had Shults and Muraco. What I learned about the big names back then was that their value was not the match, but being able to put their name on the flier and in the newspaper write-ups. Their job was done before the show started.

Were you a bit intimidated by big-name talent like Shults and Muraco at that show?
 Before I talked to them I was, but when they got there, they came to me in the back and asked me what I wanted them to do. That put me ease, but I was smart enough to realize — and I told them this — *"Who am I to tell you what to do? You guys do this for a living, so I'll go with whatever you think is best. You can do a double DQ if you want. I just need 15 or 20 minutes and I want you to really work the crowd. I want the heel to be a nasty heel. I want the babyface to be a real babyface. Just go out and do your thing ... have fun."* I even told the guys, *"I'm probably overpaying you, so just give me my money's worth."* The guys respected that.

I saw David a few years ago at one of the wrestling reunions and he remembered the match. The one thing he actually said to me was that it was a joy working for me because I let them do their thing. There was no reason for me to tell them what to do in a match. It takes away from the art form. And David ... he was like the Sheik. He really worked his gimmick. He was a bad guy, and he had some notoriety from when he smacked John Stossel. Yeah, he was always a draw. Muraco was a draw, too. Later on, I had him in Philly against Bob Orton, Jr. They were never great matches, but those guys recognized that their job was done before the show started.

Now, even though I told the guys that they should do what they thought best, I also told them, "*I need eighteen to twenty minutes, and keep in mind, if you're going to give me your standard, every-day match, I don't need you again. If you want to work for me again, you guys do something extraordinary.*" I didn't care what the finish was.

From what I read, that first show at Newark High School was a benefit for both Newark and North East High School. A show at North East the year before sold out, so the baseball coach, someone named Mel Bacon, needed a bigger venue and decided to work together with the Newark coach.

I don't recall the name Mel Bacon at all. I do remember going to the high school. I just needed to get a ball team or some other organization involved because we needed locals to sell tickets. Later on, we did shows at local facilities hosted by youth organizations. I mean, if it was a benefit for someone or a charitable cause, people would come out to wrestling. Even if you had a little league team, if each kid sold four or five tickets, well, that was a hundred seats sold. We would sit down with the adult leaders and sell them a show. "*Okay, I'll be charging you X amount of dollars, so here's how many tickets you have to sell to generate Y. I'll promote it on the radio, but you have to do your part, which is to sell tickets.*" The radio promotion was part of the package. I'd tell them, "*Theoretically, you need to sell enough tickets to break even. At that point, all the people I bring in from the radio spots will be profit.*"

Did that usually work out well?

It usually worked out pretty well. However, once in a while, we'd get a little league team that just decided not to sell tickets, and it *didn't* work out too well. The bottom line was, when we drew up the contract, I didn't guarantee how many tickets we could sell, but I would ask them, "*How many main events do you want? The more main events, the more expensive the show.*" Back then, I knew what it would cost for the ring and what it would cost me for the local wrestlers. The only variables, quite frankly, were the main names.

Did you always have to reach out to teams and organizations, or did they sometimes call you?

Both. The ones who called us knew about us from the radio show. We'd meet with them and sell them on the idea. At the time, tickets were $10, $15, $20. Today, if you buy a show for $4,000, and you can't sell 300 tickets, you have a problem.

Who got the concessions?

Good question. They did, so they could make a profit on the food. And again, if they were proactive in selling tickets, they made money. The more tickets they sold, the more money they made, and the more tickets they sold, the more concessions they sold. On the flip side, if they weren't proactive in selling tickets, they either didn't make money or they lost money.

Did anyone ever get upset because they lost or didn't make money?

No, no. In fact, the ones who didn't make money realized they made the mistake. We explained all that when we first sat down with them. Now, the kicker was, the one thing that we always had to compete against was the cost of the show. They had to guarantee money to us before the show ever started, whereas they didn't have to invest anything for a bake sale or cookie sale, so we'd only go to the organizations that had a treasury and understood the risk. I'm proud to say that, more times than not, the organizations made money, although, at the end of the day, some would question whether it was worth all the work because, sometimes, they would make $800, and at others they wouldn't make much at all. And I'm being honest with you. There were easier ways out there for them to raise money. Wrestling was never something that was really, really profitable, because they couldn't get a thousand people to an independent show in a gym. It just didn't happen. However, everybody thinks they can sell out. *"Oh, every one of our kids can sell twenty tickets,"* and then, of course, they sell three.

I'm sure everybody thought wrestling drew on name-value alone and that it would be easy money.

Well, that's it. I remember having one ... and I can't remember which building it was, but I told the organization leaders, *"Here's what you do. You have twenty kids. The tickets are fifteen dollars each and each kids has to sell twenty tickets. So you say to the parents,* 'You owe us three hundred dollars whether you sell the tickets or not.'" Of course, nobody had the guts to do that, so the parents weren't on the hook, and as a result, the kids would sell three tickets ... to mom, dad, and the kid. They wouldn't get anybody else to come. It didn't take long before the organization realized they weren't getting a lot of outside dollars.

Back to the Newark show ... you sold something called Golden Circle tickets for $25, which was almost double the price of rows two and back. The first time I heard of anything like that was in 1972 when Eddie Graham promoted wrestling at the Bayfront Auditorium in St. Petersburg Florida.

People who bought Golden Circle tickets got to meet the wrestlers after the show for autographs and photos. Later on, that evolved into what I called "season tickets" for my big shows. One of the things I would tell the organizations was, we typically had 80 front-row seats. If they could sell those seats for $25 each, that was two grand ... just on those 80 seats. As a rule, shows back then cost four or $5,000, so half of their money was covered by the 80 front-row seats. The problem was, front-row wasn't enough, so we had to have an autograph signing in which they could actually meet and talk to the wrestlers. I didn't charge the organization extra for that. I just wanted to help generate them some additional dollars. And again, it was always that number. When we did our seating arrangement, it was always 20 seats per side, and those 80 seats were the easiest tickets to sell. Now, in hindsight, I could have charged a hundred dollars a ticket for those seats. Well, back then, $100 would have been a lot, but the people would have paid more than $25 for the front-row seats. You know, it's funny. At a lot of concerts, the front row seats are always sold, while the other seats may or may not sell. You've never seen an empty front and full back. People will pay for the front-row seats. My philosophy there was to give people a little bit more than just the front-row seat, and that was having, either before the matches or after, some kind of meet-and-greet.

Most people don't think about things like that. This gives readers sort of an insight into the things promoters have to think about.

Yeah. And the other thing ... when I started running the big shows at the Civic Center, I was contractually guaranteed to do four shows a year. So what I did was sell season tickets for the first three rows. If I remember correctly, those seats were $50 a show. That may be wrong. I don't recall the number, but let's assume it was $50. Well, again, the hardcores were gonna write a check for $200 ... and I sold them out. The good news was, I sold out the front row. The bad news was, nobody else had a chance to sit front-row because they didn't buy the season tickets. So, I mean, there was always a conflict, but I had to consider the revenue stream. And, you know, from a promoter's standpoint, the person who wants to sit on the front row, they're just gonna pay more.

Jumping ahead, one of the sayings I used to have about the TWA was that everybody in the building would have a front-seat at some point during the show. We wrestled the entire building. We had hardcore wrestling fans who would come because we would get wrestlers out into the crowd. That just built, built, built to a point where everybody knew that they were going to see some actual close-up action, no matter where they were sitting. Check it out on YouTube. You see the guys going all over the place. Of course, Eddie Gilbert and Cactus Jack were the leads on that. Those two guys just put their name tag on outside-the-ring action. Yes, people absolutely came to our shows because they knew there would be a lot of action, not only inside the ring, but outside, as well.

I've been unable to find any reference anywhere to your first show — the one in Newark with Shults and Muraco — being called Tri-State. It was almost nine months later before you held the first show billed as a Tri-State promotion.

That's correct. Tri-State was actually created when we started working the Temple University [McGonigle Hall] shows. When it became clear to me that I was on the verge of something big — the independent shows — I wanted to have a champion. When someone asked me what I was going to call the champion, I came up with the idea for TWA. That's when we started doing shows at Temple.

The night before your show in Newark, there was a show in York, Pennsylvania, and a lot of the same talent was on both shows. Did you promote the show in York, as well?

No, that was somebody else.

Do you remember who promoted it?

No. I knew you were going to ask that. I have no clue.

I want to ask you about some of the talent you had in Newark. Boy Gone Bad. Who was that?

Joe Daniels. As Boy Gone Bad, he was Larry Sharpe's champion. I don't know what happened to him. He was on one, maybe two, of my shows.

He wrestled Tom Brandi in Newark. I was going to ask you about Tom next.

Tom and I go back a long way. I booked him a few times. He was best friends with Mike Kaluha. Tom was one of those guys who had a great physique. The problem was, he wasn't a very good wrestler. He certainly had the look, especially when he wrestled as The Patriot, but everybody knew who he was because he had the same moves.

Chief Jules Strongbow. Was that the guy who teamed with Chief Jay Strongbow in the WWWF?

Yes. Jules and Jay were tag team champs. In my opinion, Jules made it because of Jay. He never made it on his own, and even though he had some background with a major promotion [the WWWF], which at that time meant something, I used him in one of the opening matches. I booked him in Philly one night against Randy "He-Man" Lewis, who had to be the worst wrestler in the world. Watch that match on YouTube. He was so bad that Jules wanted to kill him. It was just horrible. Jules was very supportive of what I was trying to do and he drove down from … I think he lived in Connecticut.

Rocky Johnson.
What?

Rocky Johnson. He and a Samoan — and I don't know which Samoan it was — were on the show in Newark and wrestled the Cream Team.
No way. Are you kidding me?

Nope.
That's funny because I don't recall Rocky Johnson being on my show. I absolutely don't. God, I hate this. You always bring up things that I don't remember and it pisses me off. (laughs) You know, I remember talking to Rocky and seeing him at shows, but I don't remember him being *on* one of my shows. You're saying it was Rocky and a Samoan?

Yep. He was teamed with someone billed simply as The Samoan against a team called the Cream Team.
I'm telling you, I don't remember ever — *ever* — paying Rocky Johnson a penny. I don't remember the Cream Team, either. I wish there was video of that show because it might bring back some memories.

I just sent you the newspaper write-up written by Dan Geringer.
Here it is. Bigelow against Mystery Man — no clue — Brandi beat Boy Gone Bad, Jules Strongbow vs. Stetson, Winters-Drake … holy shit! I don't remember Rocky at all! Well, Muraco-Schultz, I remember.

You also had the ladies in Newark … Misty Blue and Heidi Lee against Kat LeRoux and Linda Dallas. Were they all local girls?
They were all local … yeah, and they were wrestling long before I got into the business. When I say local, I mean they were all from the Northeast. Heidi still lives in the area, in South Jersey. She's still around and kicking. I have no idea what happened to the other three, but they were all local. If I remember correctly, Misty lived up in Connecticut, so she drove down. Misty's husband was the agent for female wrestlers, so I got Linda Dallas, Kat LeRoux, all those girls, through them. Misty booked all the girls' matches.

Did you have any problems with any of them?
No, none. I remember when I was booking them, everyone was telling me, "*They're nothing but prima donnas.*" The only problem I ever had when I had women on the card was making sure the places had separate dressing rooms for the guys and the girls. That was the trick, but they ran into that no matter where they went. I had zero issues with any of them. As I said, Misty booked the matches, and for the most part, it was all about putting Misty over. Misty always had the belts.

Back again to that first show in Newark … you had Bam Bam Bigelow against The Mystery Man that night. Who was The Mystery Man?
I don't remember that at all. I have no clue who that is. I don't recall ever doing a major name against a jobber. I had Bigelow against who?

The report said he went to a co-contest against Mystery Man, but the newspaper billed Bigelow's opponent as The Terminator.
Man, if Scotty [Bigelow] was alive today, I'd find out. I don't recall that. Where was that match-up?

Newark. It appears to have been your very first show.
No. Are you kidding me? I don't have a clue. I don't remember that one at all. Now, Scotty was local. He lived in North Jersey … Asbury Park. Here was a guy that was recognizable as hell. I told Scott he could be on every show I did. He's

another guy that was local and had built up enough of a name on television. And I loved his wife. His wife was dynamite. But I don't remember that match at all. The only guy that would have been The Terminator would have been the guy who used to wrestle as Bounty Hunter [Phil Livelsberger]. I used to use his ring, but I think that was Teddy's [Ted Petty] ring. So, no, man. I don't remember that at all. If it was a guy under a hood, why would I have it go to a double-disqualification? That's one where I would just have Scotty win it. That doesn't sound right.

From an April 3, 1989, newspaper article by Dan Geringer:
But Goodhart's obsession with wrestling has cost him dearly. *"Cost me 100 grand in lost compensation over the past four years,"* the long-haired, snakeskin-booted, seriously sunglassed, 36-year-old insurance salesman says, *"Cost me my marriage."*

About 13 days before the Newark show, Dan Geringer wrote an article about you, in which you were quoted as saying you had lost "100 grand" in four years. Now, that was *before* the show in Newark. Had you already lost that much money on the store and the radio program?
Yeah, that was a round number, but I was definitely in the hole. The key there wasn't lost money. It was lost compensation ... the lost money I would have made. There was a guy by the name of Larry Kayhan, a sponsor of the radio show, who owned a West Code video store in Philadelphia. I was still in the insurance business at the time. I had a client who wanted to see me, but Larry wanted to see me, as well, so I postponed the insurance clients to go see Larry. That pretty much became the norm. The insurance business was taking a second seat to wrestling, so I wasn't making anything near what I would have made with the insurance clients. I was getting more and more involved in wrestling and it was taking over my life. So I estimated, at the time, that I could have made 25 to 30 grand a year more if I would have focused on the insurance business. Now, in hindsight, I probably lost a lot more than that.

So what was your connection to Dan Geringer?
Dan was a staff writer for the *Philadelphia Daily News*. He took a liking to me and did an article for me almost every quarter ... maybe every five, six months. He would check in with me now and then and write an article. We would meet at his office and he would ... he'd do pretty much what you're doing right now. He would ask questions. I left the insurance business later that year on Dec. 1, 1989, so I was already of the mindset that I was going into the thing full-time. I just had to figure out the direction I was going. So, I hadn't lost any *real* money yet. I just lost wages.

On April 30, 1989, Ric Flair, voted "Wrestler of the Decade" by *Rasslin' Radio* listeners, was honored at a banquet held at the Civic Center Plaza Ballroom. Squared Circle Fan Club members paid $75 a seat, non-members $85.

Two weeks after your show in Newark, you put together a dinner for the Squared Circle Fan Club at the Civic Center Plaza Ballroom. You brought Ric Flair in as the special guest. You presented him with a title belt that night. Did you have that belt made? It was said to have cost $1,200.

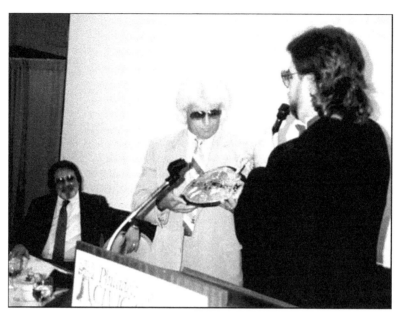

Joel presents the belt to Ric Flair; Elliott Murnick is seated on the left

I did have the belt made. We had a radio contest with listeners voting for the "Wrestler of the Decade" and Flair won. And before you ask, yes! It was a totally legit vote. It was not a work.

(laughs) That actually *was* my next question.
I actually had two belts made. Who knows if Flair still has it or not, but I have the other one. It's hanging on my wrestling room wall. The number was actually a thousand for *both* belts, not just the one. Flair told me that he hung it above his fireplace, but my gut tells me he either sold it or threw it out in the trash a long time ago. We actually have photos of him holding the belt.

Attendance for the Flair event was said to be 138 members paying $75. Does that sound accurate, and if that's the case, did you lose money?
I didn't lose money, and yes, that sounds about right. I charged $75 a head if you were a fan club member and $85 if you weren't a fan club member. I had to pay for the dinner and Flair's room, but I wound up making about a thousand bucks. Elliott Murnick helped me put it all together. Elliott, Flair, and Jim Ross were all at the dinner.

Did you have to pay Murnick to be there?
I didn't pay Murnick, didn't pay Ross ... and are you ready for this one?

Go.
I didn't pay Ric Flair.

You're kidding!
Nope. Flair did that for free. I didn't have to pay him a cent. Of course, I spent a lot on the belt, so he didn't walk away empty-handed. But, no. None of them got paid.

We'll get into how much *real* money you lost later on. So you were running the Squared Circle store, hosting *Rasslin' Radio* on the weekends, and now you were promoting shows. What led to your decision to quit your full-time job?

Long story long, when I first got involved in the business, I had every intention of keeping both careers going. I started in the financial services business back in 1976. By the time I got into wrestling in 1985, I had already built up a clientele. The thing about the insurance business, if you work hard and hold on for three or four years, you're usually over the hump, so I was able to maintain my practice and do the wrestling stuff on the weekends. The investments were my livelihood and wrestling was still just a hobby.

What started to happen was, I started to evolve. In the insurance business, I always wore a suit and tie. I was so straight-laced. With wrestling, you had to develop your gimmick — your shtick — and mine was to let my hair grow. I looked weird. I didn't look like somebody who was 30 years old and ten years into the insurance business, that's for sure. That was probably when the wrestling began to take over.

People would ask me, *"What's going on with the hair?"* Back then, there was no Internet, no Facebook, so nobody knew that I was involved with the wrestling stuff unless they were fans. What you come to find out, though, is that there were a *lot* of closet wrestling fans back in those days. They weren't necessarily ashamed of being a fan. It just wasn't something you talked about openly. If the subject of wrestling *did* come up in a conversation, people would usually mention the name Bruno Sammartino, and how they watched him on TV when they were kids, or how their father would take them to the matches. So at some point, you come to the realization that a lot of people you thought were straight-laced — like me — were actually fans of pro wrestling.

Anyway, as the business began to evolve, I would wake up in the morning and do something with the wrestling, rather than sell insurance and investments. What really helped me make the decision to go into wrestling full-time was a change of management in the insurance office. The new guy who came in demanded more of my time and he didn't like my long hair. He was a former football player, but he was *not* a wrestling fan. We butted heads a few times until I finally had enough, so on Dec. 1, 1989, I resigned my position in financial services. My full-time wrestling career went from that date until Jan. 18, 1992, the day the radio show went off the air.

Now, what's interesting is that I kept in touch with my clients. It wasn't like I just disappeared on them. I just didn't work at it. When I got back into the business, most of the clients that I had in '89 stayed with me, and I picked up where I left off. In fact, most of them listened to the radio show and were rooting for me. A few of them even came to the matches. The one thing I never did, though, was use one business to promote the other. I never called or wrote my clients to encourage them to come to my wrestling shows, and I didn't push insurance and investments on my wrestling contacts. I kept the two of them separate.

So at that time, you weren't partners in an insurance agency. You were just working for an insurance company.

Yes. I was a one-man operation. In the business at the time, you were either in the insurance business or the investment business. I was in the insurance business and dabbled in the investments on the side. Today, I do more investments than insurance. But back then, we were independent contractors.

Now, I also *was* a part of the management team, which meant I was somewhat of an employee of the agency, so I wasn't totally independent. I had to meet my numbers and typical management BS. I was in management for about nine years. As a manager, part of the deal was, if I hired you into the business, I had to be there to help you, and there were times when I wasn't there for the guys because

I was dabbling in my wrestling sidelines. Instead of taking vacations, I was going on wrestling trips. If I had an appointment to see a client, and an opportunity came up to talk with Ric Flair on the telephone, Ric Flair won. The wrestling connection was much more fun. And by that time, the store, the promotion, and radio show marketing was pretty much a full-time gig. Most of the promoters today don't promote full-time because they can't afford to do that. In hindsight, I realize that what I did was a pretty stupid thing to do, but for about three years, I lived in a world that was really cool.

So at the time, you were making really good money with the insurance business.

Oh, yeah. It was stupid. It was dumb. My decisions caused other problems, as well. I had separated from my first wife. But I had money in the bank, and when I started to dabble in this thing, I thought maybe I could make a go of it. I remember Yogi Berra once said, "*When you come to a fork in the road, take it.*" Well, I took it. I didn't know which road I was going down, but I took off on the journey and gave it a go.

Did your interest in wrestling play into the divorce?

Not really, but I'm sure it contributed. I've been divorced twice, but at that point, we were growing apart. I tried marriage twice, but I'm just not a marriage guy. My father told me that marriage was a 50/50 proposition, and I actually believed that, but in actuality, it's a 99/1 proposition. (laughs) Maybe that attitude is why I'm divorced. (laughs) I used to kid my father about that all the time.

Anyway, I was dabbling in wrestling while my wife was trying to raise a family. Now, when I took my kids to the matches when I got them on the weekends, they had a ball. They had a great time. They got to see their dad in action. However, as we all know, hindsight is always 20/20. I never really gave them what I would call "quality daddy time" because daddy was always busy handling the wrestling stuff. They would go on the bus tours, but again, I was busy doing my thing. It was never "*Let's go to the park*" or "*Let's play ball.*" It was more like, "*Daddy has a wrestling match tonight. Come with me.*" I'll never forget one of the bus tours. One of the women who went with us was gorgeous and she had a picture taken with my son. I have that picture somewhere of that gorgeous woman with this little kid. He talks about that to this day.

Did your wife have any interest in wrestling at all?

No, not at all, and that made things all the more complicated. Now, Marla, my second wife, loved the idea of me doing what I was doing. I met her during my evolution. She wasn't a wrestling fan when I met her, but she became one. She got into it and actually went to the wrestling matches with me a lot of times.

When I went to one of the parties at the Marriott after a show, she went with me. I told her, "*Here's the deal. If you want to bring a friend, that's fine, but when we get to the bar, that's work for me. I'm networking. I'm not there to spend time with you and drink with you. I'm there to network.*"

She really got off on the fact that when we walked into the hotel — of course, I was wearing my tuxedo — little kids walked up and asked for my autograph. True story, while I was networking, Ric Flair walked up and started hitting on her. Terry Taylor came over and said, "*Hey, that's Joel Goodhart's girl. Back off!*" She got a real kick out of the fact that some of the wrestlers were protecting her from getting hit on. (laughs)

How did you meet Marla?

It's funny, but when I met Marla, I was getting away from the insurance business. My secretary at the time — her name was Debbie Marinelli — Debbie sat down with me one day and she said, "*I have to ask you a question. What in the hell are you doing?*"

I said, "*What are you talking about?*"

Well, I don't remember who it was, but I had a female come to my office. She was tattooed from neck to toe. Back then, girls who had tattoos were considered to be sluts. (laughs) And she may have been! (laughs) Again, I don't remember who she was, but when she left, Debbie said to me, "*What are you doing? Why can't you just find a nice girl?*"

I said, "*Look, I'm just divorced. I don't want a nice girl. I'm getting involved in wrestling and I don't want any real connections.*"

She says, "*I have a girlfriend that you should talk to.*"

I told her I didn't want to be bothered. Well, she eventually set me up with Marla. She said, "*Here's Marla's phone number. She's expecting you to call her.*"

When I called her up, we talked for about five hours. Now, if you spend five hours on the phone with somebody, there's a connection. I eventually asked Marla out on a date. Marla was this straight-laced girl who worked in Center City, while I'm this guy with long, flowing hair. I asked her out for a Saturday night, and on Friday, I called her to cancel. She yelled at me, "*Why are you canceling?*"

I said, "*Well, something's come up and I have to be somewhere.*"

I had told her that weekends were really tough for me, so she said, "*Look, we've connected over the phone now for a long time. If you cancel our next date, it's over.*" Now mind you, it never even started (laughs), so I booked the next date for a weeknight because weekends were too unpredictable.

At the time, I had contacts in the limo business. I used to ask women to tell me what their idea of a first-date was. That gave me a pretty good sense of whether they were going to be expensive or not. When I asked Marla to tell me what her ideal first-date would be, she said, "*Getting picked up in a fire-engine-red Lamborghini, being driven to New York City to see a Broadway show, having dinner at Peter Luger's* [Steakhouse, in Brooklyn]*, and then driving home.*" Well, I had the feeling that this girl was going to be expensive and I wasn't sure I wanted to get involved with her.

Our conversation continued, and before I gave it any more thought, I called my limo guy and rented the limo for a Tuesday night. I wasn't taking her to New York City, though. I was taking her south of Baltimore for dinner at Sabatino's [Italian Restaurant] in Little Italy.

Marla lived in Northeast Philadelphia, in a small neighborhood of one-lane streets, so the limo could barely navigate the streets. I get to the front of her apartment and knock on the door. This is the first time I met her, right? I was wearing blue jeans, a blue shirt, jacket, cowboy boots — which were my trademark — sunglasses, and zubags, which I later realized was pretty stupid ... and I had the long hair.

When she opened the door, a bird flew out and landed on my head. It scared the hell out of me, but I thought it was cool. It was her pet pigeon. She says, "*You must be okay. If the bird likes you, you're okay.*" She put the bird back in the cage and we went out to the limo. Now, you have to picture this neighborhood. When word got out that there was a limousine on the street, the whole neighborhood was looking out their windows and doors. (laughs) We get into the limo and we talked during the entire trip. She had no idea where we were going, but she had faith that I was okay.

We drive to Baltimore and pull up in front of Sabatino's restaurant where I had made reservations. Back then, Sabatino's was the place to hang out after the wrestling matches. All the guys went there, so all the fans went, as well. The food there was phenomenal. When we got to Sab's, there must have been 50 people waiting outside. Everybody glared at us as we walked right past them and into the restaurant. The manager pulls everybody aside and says, "*I'll show you to your table.*" Marla got the impression that I was a superstar, so that was pretty cool. She loved the whole persona thing from the get-go. After dinner, we walked along the harbor for a bit and then rode home. Later on in the relationship, she told me that if I had made a move on her in the limo, I probably would have gotten laid. She was into the persona. Marla never knew me as a straight-laced insurance guy like my first wife did. She thought that's who I was.

One thing led to the other and we became a steady thing. We moved in together and the first office of the Squared Circle was in the den of our apartment. She would go to work in the day and I would go to work. At that point, I was full-time in the wrestling business.

Jumping ahead in time a few years, Marla got pregnant in 1991 and that's when reality hit me. The wrestling business was falling apart and we were losing money, so I knew that, with my third child on the way, I had to make some changes and bring in some income. I quit the wrestling business on Jan. 18, 1992, and my daughter was born on Feb. 5. Marla and I weren't married at the time, but we got married in December of that year, which has always allowed me to justify that we got married in the same year my daughter was born, although she was born ten months *before* we got married. (laughs)

As a side note, I had two sons from my first marriage. They thought I was a god because I knew wrestlers. One day, they had a day at the elementary school where the fathers came in to talk about their occupation. Of course, you had policemen, firemen, construction workers. Well, I didn't come in as the insurance guy. How boring was that? I came in as the wrestling guy. So, Larry Winters and I went to the school. I dressed in my *Rasslin' Radio* jacket, I had the long hair, and Larry came in wrestling gear. Here's Larry and I walking down the aisle to my son's classroom and everybody's starting to buzz. Larry looked like a wrestler. When we walked into the room, all the other fathers just stepped aside. (laughs) Well, the kids were just ecstatic. Of course, back then, very few people had cell phones, but if the kids would have had them then, they would have been taking pictures like crazy.

Great story.
Well, I don't know how I got off on that tangent.

I don't remember, either. Now, when you quit the insurance business, didn't you have renewals coming in for quite a while?
Yes, I did, but at that time, it was pocket change. Things are vastly different today, of course. If I retired tomorrow, I'd make more money than if I keep working. Despite my bad decisions, I've been very fortunate. I built up a very successful practice. My father told me many years ago that the definition of retirement was work because you want to, not because you have to. And I *could* retire, but I love working. I love doing what I'm doing. And quite frankly, I'm a boring guy, so what would I do if I retired? I live in a 55-plus community and I have an indoor pool and an outdoor pool. If I went to swim at the pool, I'd wind up talking to people, which is exactly what I do for a living. I'm not a world traveler and I'm not someone who likes vacations, so I just keep working. My father used to say, "*Work until the day the doctor says you can't work anymore,*" so that's what I'm going to do.

What was the reaction of your fellow insurance agents? Did they know how deeply you were involved in wrestling?

Oh, yeah. Of course, toward the end, they told me I was crazy to give up my business. Some of the guys really got into it, though. They saw the evolution, the haircut. A few of them actually came to the Crockett show at Valley Forge. One of the agents, who became a partner many years later, actually brought his kids to the matches, and he still talks about that. It's amazing that someone came go to an independent show in King of Prussia, and 30 years later, we're still talking about it.

The one thing you learn about wrestling is, people who are not into wrestling, and who don't know much about it, really get into the fact that you *are* into it, so the guys were supportive. On the other hand, they couldn't understand how I was doing it on the side, but those same guys had the time to play golf on Tuesdays.

From what I understand, you had a mobile telephone much earlier than most people.

There was a system called the PacBell [Pacific Bell] system and it was one of those phones that was drilled into the hump of your car. So picture this ... I had a white Cadillac. Now, this was back in those days where, if you had a Cadillac, you had made it. The sign of success wasn't an Audi. It was a Cadillac. That white Cadillac was big enough that I had a telephone installed into the car, and the PacBell system was the same system used on boats. You would dial a number, wait two or three minutes for the phone to find the signal and the satellite, and you'd be connected to the person you were calling. Again, hindsight being 20/20, I had a phone for the purpose of calling my clients during the course of the day. No, that's not what I did. I'd sit in the car and call all over the country to book talent for wrestling shows. If I had kept the invoices and bills from PacBell from 30 years ago, I would have all kinds of phone numbers. I took a *lot* of calls during the course of a day. It was cool.

Joel with his dad's Cadillac; note the Rasslin' Radio jacket

You eventually had to sell that Cadillac, didn't you?
My father was a doctor. This is a side story. My father's practice was in our basement and I lived upstairs with my sister and my mother, so we never had to drive very far. In fact, my father owned a Cadillac and he never bought tires. Whenever the tires would get 30,000 miles or so, he would sell the car and buy a new one. Well, one of those times, I bought the car from my father. That Cadillac had like 30,000 miles on it and I drove it into the ground. There are so many stories about the territory days, where the guys would drive four or 500 miles a day. I didn't drive that many, but it was no big deal for me to drive 250 miles every Saturday. I never bought another Cadillac after that one. In one of the stories Dan Geringer wrote about me, I talked about being divorced and in debt at age 36, and driving an '81 Buick LeSabre — one of those big tanks — that had a broken seat and was in the shop every other week.

What was your dad's reaction when you told him you were quitting your job?
Oh, he thought I was nuts. But again, my father is one of those guys who thought their son could do no wrong. My mother didn't think I could do right. (laughs) My father told me, "*You're a big boy now, so you have to make your own decisions.*" He was a big supporter. He listened to the radio show every Saturday morning, and when I came home after a wrestling show, he wanted me to tell him all the details of what went on.

Jerry Lawler clocks Joel with a title belt.

7 Tri-State Wrestling Alliance

I'd like to explore the early days of Tri-State Wrestling. How did you determine the style of wrestling you were going to present at TWA shows?

That goes back to the Squared Circle store. I had videotapes from all over the country ... all over the world. What I did was, I studied World Class, the Pacific Northwest, Georgia, Florida, Memphis, and I kind of blended them into what ultimately became the TWA. I mean, that's exactly what I did. I created a style for people who were tired of Vince's product. You know, Vince's matches were all the same. There wasn't much variety from one match to the next.

What led to you naming the promotion Tri-State Wrestling Alliance? I mean, I know you only promoted in three states ... Pennsylvania, Delaware and New Jersey. Where did the *origin* of that name come from?

Well, I always believed — and I actually said this on the radio show — I always believed in truth in advertising. One of the things that always bothered me was, you had the WWWF world heavyweight champion and *that* world heavyweight champion only wrestled in five states. Ric Flair was the NWA world heavyweight champion, and he wrestled in about nine states. They didn't wrestle all over the world.

So, my plan was to promote in Pennsylvania, New Jersey and Delaware. At the time, TWA — Trans World Airlines — was still a thing, and those initials just sounded good, so I came up with Tri-State Wrestling Alliance. (laughs) Of course, everybody told me it should be TSWA, but I just ran with TWA. I mean, TWA flowed a lot better than TSWA, and it worked.

Ultimately, I did matches in four states because I promoted a show in Maryland, but for the most part, I knew I would be limited to three states. So national syndication would only have worked if I was WWF-oriented or held more events, because I don't think what I was doing in Philadelphia would get over in Chicago. The one show I did in Maryland was at the Cecil County Community College in North East, Maryland. If you ever look on the map, North East is just over the border from Delaware, so it was the same market. I promoted in Pennsylvania, New Jersey, Delaware, and the one show in Maryland.

So, the initials worked. I came up with the name and stuck with it. It was truth in advertising. That's exactly what it was. Of course, when I ran the show in Maryland at Cecil County Community College, I started to reconsider. If I'm actually going to grow and promote outside the area, the name really doesn't work. My solution

was, if it ever got to the point where it became bigger, I'd change the name to Trans-America Wrestling Association, which would allow me to keep the initials. So, yeah. I liked truth in advertising, so we became Tri-State ... three states. We made no claims to being anything more. Our champion was *not* a world champion. He was a tri-state champion ... a *three-state* champion.

Did you have a physical office for your Tri-State promotion, or did you just work out of your home?

It was out of my home. It was an official office in the sense that I had one staff person who came to my house every morning and worked in my den. But, no. We never had an *office* office. And quite frankly, I swear, if we had an office office, it would have become a storefront, and if we would have had wrestling fans there, we wouldn't have been able to get work done.

Take me through the steps of securing a license to promote in Pennsylvania. I'm sure you must have needed a license of some kind.

Yeah, Pennsylvania had very strict rules. One thing was, we had to float a bond to protect the ticket holders, and at that time, getting a bond was difficult because I didn't have any employment, so I literally had to put up the full value — $10,000 — with the state of Pennsylvania for the quote-unquote bond. They also ran a credit check on me before they issued me my license. At that point, I was a legal promoter.

Do they still require that today?

Yes, but what happens is, those guys get a promoter's license and lease it out. They'll say, "*Give me five hundred bucks and you can use my license to promote your show.*" That's happening now as we speak. But back in the day, Pennsylvania had rules. One was to maintain a license. The second was that, at each show, you were required to have a doctor, and it had to be a doctor approved by the Pennsylvania Boxing Commission ... the state athletic commission. You didn't have to have an ambulance, but you had to have access to an ambulance organization in case you needed one. If I remember correctly, it was $300 for the doctor. Now, a lot of times, the doctors were wrestling fans, so they didn't mind coming to the matches. But, yeah. It was 300 bucks for the doctor back then ... and $400 for the ring. I used Ted Petty's ring and that included Ted working on the show. So, I had fixed expenses of $700 before we ever opened the doors! Then I had to get the insurance ... then I had to get the wrestlers. I mean, to promote shows properly today, you need tens of thousands of dollars. Back then, you didn't need tens of thousands, but you certainly needed more than I had. I was running on a shoestring.

I'm sure your outlay back then, in today's dollars, would be tens of thousands of dollars.

Oh, easy ... easy! And, you know. The good part was that I didn't need a lot of the money until the night of the show. The doctor got paid at the show. Petty got paid at the show. Even the wrestlers got paid the night of the show. So you crossed your fingers and hoped you had enough ticket sales to pay everybody.

Now, you know, I wasn't the best accountant in the world. I had money coming in and money going out, money going here and there, and it got tougher and tougher to keep track of where my money was going. But you know, when you did a show the way I did shows — and God knows, I overpaid and I had too many stars stacked up — my expenses would run $10,000. If I had 500 people at 20 bucks each, I barely broke even. If I drew 700 to a thousand, I made some money on a show ... and at times I *was* making money. You know, we had around a thousand people at Temple University, but the building held 1,400, so I would have four or 500 empty seats, which was lost revenue. Yeah, isn't that amazing? We were presenting some of the largest independent shows in the country, and I was barely breaking even.

It's funny because I didn't follow wrestling, other than reading the *Observer*, and even I remember reading about your shows. They sounded amazing, and even though I had worked in the wrestling business and had my fingers on the pulse of what it took to promote a show, it never crossed my mind that you were barely breaking even. You were promoting all those big names, so I thought you must be making big money.

Joel ring announcing

Well, you would think I was. I'll give you examples of, when you figure in all the expenses, I actually lost money. Now, keep in mind. At the time, I was paying $500 a week for my radio show. I would spend eight weeks promoting the card. Well, even though I was spending $4,000, it wasn't $4,000 for the wrestling show. It was $4,000 for the radio show. So, even if the show broke even through ticket sales, I lost 4,000 bucks. Okay? So when you start taking all that into account — and I didn't calculate how much it cost me to drive everywhere ... the cost of gas, highway tolls — when you start adding all that stuff up, then yeah! It really cost me $10,000 to run a $5,000 show.

So what did you do to promote your shows? Did you do window posters, newspaper ads, or fliers?

Well, we put fliers everywhere. We put posters everywhere ... those rainbow posters. We would put posters in storefront windows, on poles. Back then, you could put them on poles. Today, there are a lot of limitations to that.

Who took care of postering the towns?

Me. The promoter's job is to promote. Promoters today seem to think that if they pass fliers out, they're going above and beyond. No, that's what promoters do. Promoters promote! Steve Truitt helped now and then. He was my lighting and sound guy. Later on, he worked for Tod Gordon in ECW. Carmela helped early on, but for the most part, I was like a one-man band.

The radio show was my TV. You know, if you think about it, Crockett and Vince never, never put posters on poles, or hand out fliers. They had TV, so my radio was my TV. Hopefully, the local charities or Temple University promoted the shows. For the most part, though, it was word of mouth.

At one point, I hooked up with Ticketmaster and they sold my tickets, which helped because it gave me more of a national presence. We had guys coming in from California. We had people coming in from New York. They could go on Ticketmaster and buy my tickets. But the promotion was really the radio show. We did some local appearances that helped a little bit. My original hope was that the small shows I promoted, that drew two to 300 people, would ultimately feed the big shows, so at the local shows, I would give people fliers, which were discount coupons for tickets for the big shows. Then there was the hardcore, serious, what you would call smart-marks. They loved wrestling. They were always there. People who had never heard of TWA, but heard us on the radio, would come to the big shows. So we were able to draw a couple thousand people by using the little groups as feeders.

Did Ticketmaster keep you apprised of ticket sales during the days leading up to shows?

Oh, yeah. There was no going online at that time, so I would call the office and they would tell me how many tickets were sold. It was weird. They were closed on Saturday and Sunday, so I would call them on Monday. One time, I had the radio show on the weekend and a house show that Monday night. When I called on Monday, they had sold five tickets. That's when I started to realize that, if anybody was going to the show, they would have bought their tickets *before* my Saturday morning radio show.

The one problem that I did have — and I think all promoters have this problem — is that a lot of people don't care where they sit, so they just buy their tickets at the door. And I was my own worst enemy because I told everybody that *everybody* would have a front-row seat at some point during the show, so everybody knew they could have the worst seat in the house and still get to see some great action. Well, you don't have to buy the worst seat in the house in advance. You can wait and buy tickets on the day of the show. I had a lot of people do that. The good news was, I had nice walk-ups. The bad news was that I had no advance. The one thing that really helped was, the people who could afford to buy tickets up front do. I could charge anything I wanted for a front-row seat and they'd pay. The other seats, though, is where your profit is. But those people can wait until the day of the show to buy their tickets, so if it rains, they don't go. If it snows, they don't go. We always had to worry about the weather forecast, but there was no controlling that. Vince had it down to a science. He'd sell out a building within five minutes of announcing a show. I couldn't do that. My hardcores bought their tickets in advance, but most people waited until the day of the show.

Someone chartered buses from New York to your shows. Was that you?

No, it wasn't me. It was John Arezzi. John chartered the buses and brought people to Philly. When he was doing his radio show in New York, he would buy 40 tickets and bring a whole busload down from New York. John was smarter than me because he made tapes of his radio shows. From what I understand, he still sells them today.

Philadelphia, Pennsylvania: Jan. 27, 1990
Winter Challenge, McGonigle Hall, 1:00 p.m., att. 1,400
- Rockin' Rebel beat Joey Maggs
- Johnny Hotbody beat Tony Stetson (dq)
- Stretcher match
  Larry Winters beat D.C. Drake (balcony spot)
- Battle of the Bams Bams
  Bam Bam Bigelow NC Terry Gordy (both counted out of the ring)
- Dog collar match
  Junkyard Dog beat Paul Jones
- Nikita Koloff beat Manny Fernandez (dq)
- AWA world title match
  Larry Zbyszko* beat David Sammartino w/second Bruno Sammartino

Notes:
  McGonigle Hall was an athletic facility on the campus of Temple University.
  Johnny Hotbody was the WWA junior heavyweight champion.

Battle of the "Bam Bam's"

This is only the second time that "Bam Bam" Bigelow and Terry "Bam Bam" Gordy have met. The first match took place in Chicago and needless to say, nothing was settled. Both men want to be the only "Bam Bam" in professional wrestling. And anytime that personal pride is on the line, you can expect nothing less than a battle to the end.

WILL IT END HERE?

Do you want to be a wrestler???
Call the
ATILIS GYM
WRESTLING SCHOOL
215-449-5845 ask for Chuck
609-729-2050 ask for Joe

PROFESSIONAL WRESTLING AT ITS BEST
Sat., Jan. 27—1:00 P.M.
TEMPLE UNIVERSITY – McGONIGLE HALL
1800 N. Broad Street
745-8315 or 787-OWLS
Box Office Opens 11:30 A.M.
Doors Open at Noon
Come See: BRUNO SAMMARTINO · JUNKYARD DOG · BAM BAM BIGELOW · NIKITA KOLOFF · LARRY ZYBYSKO · AND OTHERS
7 MATCHES IN ALL
Ticket prices $13.00, $10.00
Listen to "RASSLIN' RADIO"
Every Saturday Morning
8:00-9:00 A.M.
ON 610 WIP

Okay. A period of almost nine months elapsed between your show in Newark and your second show ... which was your first show in Philadelphia and the first official TWA show. Why was there such a long period between the two?

It was a couple of things. One, most of those local shows were sold-shows, and doing a sold-show was really tricky. You had to find a school that had some money. And keep in mind, when I promoted the Newark show, I didn't have plans to be a full-time promoter. It just kind of happened. When I started to really get my teeth into it and started working it, my biggest concern was getting the right building. Quite frankly, I was a graduate at Temple, so I had some ins at the school. In fact, that first show at Temple [Jan. 27, 1990] was actually a benefit show for a group Tod Gordon got me involved with ... the Variety Club. That organization did wonderful things for handicapped children. Anyway, nobody was more surprised than I was when Temple agreed to let us hold our show there.

But McGonigle Hall was never a wrestling Mecca, you know. It was a building on campus that hosted college basketball and what have you. It was located on Broad Street in Philadelphia, and back in the day, Temple was not in the best neighborhood, so my shows were afternoon shows. They weren't night shows, and more times than not, they were on Saturday afternoons. In fact, I think they were all on Saturday afternoon. I'd be on the radio from seven to eight, or eight to nine, at the time, and then go right to Temple and do the show. However, there was a slight problem with holding shows on Saturdays. When I started using [Jerry] Lawler, Kerry Von Erich, and those guys, a lot of them were wrestling at the [Dallas] Sportatorium on Friday nights, so they were flying in on Saturday mornings, instead of Friday nights, which made it tricky. But all that being said, I was really gearing up to that big show at Temple, and like you, I was a one-man operation. So, yeah. If there was a nine-month lag between my first two shows — and I really don't remember for sure — it was nothing more than me not having the time to find another venue. If I was to make an educated guess as to the real reason behind the long period of time, it was probably the fact that I didn't know what the hell I was doing! (laughs) I didn't have a mentor ... someone to give me advice. I knew what I wanted to accomplish, but I just didn't know how to go about it.

Something else that you may not have thought about. Lawler flew from Memphis to Philly on Saturday mornings so he could be at my afternoon show, which meant he skipped Memphis television. He was almost always the main event at the big Memphis house show [on Monday nights], so it was important for him to be on TV [on Saturdays], but he wasn't going to turn down the $500 I was paying him. Now, I don't know about the numbers, but my gut tells me he wasn't making $500 doing Memphis television. Another thing that I thought was pretty cool was, when Jerry wrestled for me, they mentioned on the Memphis show that he would be defending his title in Philadelphia.

You had David Sammartino on that first card at McGonigle Hall. Did you have to go through Bruno to get David?

That's an interesting (pause) ... I don't recall now. I will tell you this. I tried to get Bruno to wrestle. Since Bruno was good friends with Carmela, I thought I could get him to do a ring appearance against Larry Zbyszko. He just didn't want to do it, but he went on to say, *"Why don't you use David?"* Now, the only reason David got booked anywhere was because he was Bruno's son. I don't think Vince would have given him a second-look if it weren't for Bruno. I don't know if you remember the match at the Spectrum with David against Ron Shaw. [Nov. 22, 1985]

You're talking about the "phantom submission match".

Yes. Now, keep in mind, Ron was one of the teachers of Ringmaster's wrestling school. Ron worked as a manager on several of my shows. In Philly for Vince, Ron wrestled David and Gorilla Monsoon was doing the announcing of the match, which was being aired on the PRISM Network. Obviously, Ron was doing the job for David. David, for whatever reason, just didn't want to wrestle that night. Just before they went to the ring, David says to Ron, *"I'm putting you over. Beat the shit out of me."*

Tell me what you know about it. This is a great story.

Yeah. When you get a chance, check it out on YouTube. Monsoon was told that Ron would do five minutes and then David would go over. Shaw beat the hell out of David, put him in a bear hug — which was Bruno's big finishing move — and

The "Phantom Submission Match" | Ron Shaw vs. David Sammartino

David submitted. The referee called for the bell and you can hear Monsoon's confusion. *"Wait a minute! What's happening?"* He even tried to deny that David had submitted, even though David had made it very clear that he was giving up. The only two guys involved in that match who knew what was going on was David and Ron. David was not a friendly guy and he wasn't happy with the way Vince was using him, but he worked the show.

Do you think David sold any tickets for you when you booked him against Zbyszko?

No. David didn't sell a single ticket. I know Bruno did ... just his appearance alone. Paul E. Dangerously was selling tickets at that time. I promoted it like hell on the radio and I think we had six or 700 people at the show.

It was more like fourteen hundred.

Was it really? Well, having 600 or fourteen hundred people come out for an independent show was a win. That was huge. I don't think any particular match sold the show. Having a minority like Junkyard Dog in a feature match may have helped, but David didn't sell a thing.

You booked David again 15 months later against Cactus Jack.

Yes, I did. I thought the Sammartino name would help, but what became really clear was that everybody knew he wasn't Bruno. I don't know how anybody could grow up in the shadow of Bruno. It was just too difficult. He worked a few shows for me and then disappeared. I don't know what he did after that.

Did David come across as being somewhat arrogant because he was Bruno's son?

I wouldn't say arrogant, but he expected to be treated differently. He was a Sammartino. I don't remember who I was talking to. It was someone from one of the magazines. I told them, *"He's not a Sammartino ... he's David."*

That really sums it up.

Bruno did something that night at Temple that just reverberated in the business — *my* business, in particular — and it was one of the most important things that ever happened to me during my time in the wrestling business.

At the time, I didn't realize the significance of what Bruno did, but he was on the card that night. Bruno was in David's corner and Paul E. Dangerously was in Zbyszko's corner. Now, if you remember, Bruno lived outside Pittsburgh, and when you ran shows at Temple University, you ran them in the afternoon because that neighborhood was not the place to go to at night. Bruno was the last match on the card. At the end of the match, I went to the back to thank everybody, and Bruno, right in front of all the boys — because everybody was hanging around

Larry Zbyszko at McGonigle Hall

waiting to get paid — Bruno says to me, "*Hey, Joel. Do me a favor. Mail me a check. I have to catch a plane."*

Well, when the guys in the dressing room heard Bruno tell me to mail him a check, they took that to mean their money was good. From that day forward, I never had an issue about money with *anyone* in any way, shape or form. And that word got out, and you know how everybody talks. They realized right away that Bruno left without getting paid and he knew I was good for it. That was the sign. A lot of little things like that happened along the way that helped build the TWA, and things like that were really important.

The reputation that I got in the business was that I *overpaid*, and more importantly, my checks cleared. And I never had a no-show ... ever, ever, ever. Part of that was the fact that I, A, overpaid, and B, they knew the money would be there and the checks would be good.

Tell me about Larry Zbyszko.
Larry was in the main event on that show against David Sammartino. Zbyszko played that heel role to perfection. Everybody up here in Philadelphia remembered — or at least knew about — the big feud Bruno had with Zbyszko. I saw Zbyszko's kid at a show a few years ago and the kid knew about that match. I haven't talked to Zbyszko in a very long time, but he was a true professional.

Two weeks before that show, both Paul E and Bruno called in to *Rasslin' Radio*. Do you remember that?
Yeah. I asked them to do that. I asked Bruno to call in because David was in the main event against Zbyszko. In Philly, the old-timers all remembered Zbyszko hitting Bruno with the chair. I was hoping to capitalize on that. I don't know if David wrestled Larry Zbyszko before or since, to be honest. Bruno was seconding his son and Paul E. was seconding Larry. It just had a natural feel to it. I seem to remember Larry and David not being available that day to do the radio show. Again, radio was my TV. Paul E. and I had a good relationship. He was on my show a number of times. I was paying Bruno to help me promote, and him being at the show was important. Paul E. did a *Danger Zone*, or whatever the hell it was called, with Bruno. That was all prearranged. I didn't know what they were going to say, but again, people listened to the radio show. Hopefully, it sold tickets. That was the idea.

Paul E. knew how to get heat, but in Philly, he started to get cheers. In fact, at one of my Temple shows, somebody brought a big sheet that said *I love you Paul E ...* or something like that. It was clear to me, though, that Paul E. was going places. I don't know how anybody couldn't have seen that. Paul E. is a really good, good guy. I'm glad he's made it.

Your first Tri-State card also had the *Battle of the Bam Bams* ... Terry Gordy vs. Bam Bam Bigelow. Who came up with the name "Battle of the Bam Bams."

That was me. The show didn't have a name like my shows did later on. I think I was the second person to feature a *Battle of the Bam Bams*. I don't know if it was Herb Abrams or somebody else. All I remember of that match was how big those two son-of-a-guns were. They were unbelievable. I never realized how big Bigelow was until I stood next to him. Then, when Gordy walked up, I felt like a midget. Gordy was so quiet. Gordy comes to the arenas, gets ready, does his match, and then goes back and takes a shower. You hardly hear a word from him. He was very quiet, very mellow. He was much more quiet than I expected. That night was when I got to know Scott [Bam Bam] really, really well. Scott was a major guy who was a draw for me.

D.C. Drake [Don Clyde Drake] and Larry Winters had a great series of matches against each other and then you put them together as a tag team. I know you first booked them against each other on your Newark show. There seemed to be great chemistry between them.

The Larry Winters/D.C. Drake series started way before me. They were wrestling together for the NWF.

Bam Bam Bigelow vs. Terry Gordy

For the first two years of his career, which began in 1980, Drake wrestled on the independent circuit. In 1982, he created the Continental Wrestling Alliance [CWA] promotion based in Allentown, PA. He sold the promotion in 1986 to a Robert Raskin, who renamed the promotion the National Wrestling Federation [NWF]. Drake remained onboard as the promotion's booker and TV producer until 1988.

Larry was a Philadelphia native who kicked off his wrestling career in 1982. In 1984, he made a shot with the WWF, losing a match to Ron Shaw (of the aforementioned "phantom submission match") in Reading, PA. Larry also worked for the AWA (MN), the AWA/NWA joint venture, Pro Wrestling USA, the NWA, Carlos Colón's World Wrestling Council in Puerto Rico, and short runs in New Brunswick, Buffalo, and Florida. Larry met Joel in 1989, while wrestling for Jim Crockett in Baltimore, and eventually hired on as Joel's booker with TWA and as the head trainer at the Ringmasters Wrestling School.

Larry and Don were on every card I booked and Larry was running my dressing room. Larry also was good friends with Bruno Sammartino. I think Don and Larry had wrestled on shows for Rob Russen's IWA promotion, so they had a feud going long before I came along. Larry and D.C. were top-of-the-card wrestlers who were over before they ever hooked up with me, and they were phenomenal. But it wasn't me who put them together. The difference for them with me, however, was that, instead of being the main event on an NWF card, they were now on the second or third match on a bigger card. The magazines were really into TWA, and Apter and Napolitano were taking pictures at the shows, so they got a lot of notoriety. I'll tell you what. Don and Larry *wrestled!* They set the bar for all the other independent guys. Tony Stetson and Johnny Hotbody took their cue and said, "*We've got to do better than them.*"

One of the best business moves I ever made was making Larry my booker. He also was a partner in the RingMasters wrestling school. Larry Winters and I hooked up very early on, and Larry kind of … I rode his coat tails, he rode my coat tails. He was in virtually everything.

How did you meet Larry?

Larry was friendly with Dominic DeNucci and he was on that show at Neshaminy High School. If you do any history of Dominic at all, Dominic was as cheap as you can get. He would have a fairly big main event, but everybody else on the card was local guys because he didn't want to pay for trans or hotel. And that was good business because there was a *lot* of local guys in the Philadelphia area. Like I said, on that Neshaminy card, the only out-of-towners were Igor, Dominic and Troy Martin, who was training with Dominic at that time. In fact, I saw Shane a couple years ago at one of Rob Feinstein's deals and I mentioned that, and Shane remembered the show. He probably knows more details about the show than I do.

What was your philosophy regarding finishes?

One of the problems with wrestling was, you have two guys. If one gets pinned, you have a winner and a loser. I mentioned this earlier … the Four Horsemen had the world's worst win-loss record, but they never — at least that I know of — won with a pinfall. There always won with some kind of a screw-job. Tommy Young would get knocked out or some similar storyline. My philosophy was, if I was bringing someone back, I'd be damned if I was going to have one of them get pinned, 1-2-3. I did what I called the "fuck-finish." I stole that term from somebody. I didn't come up with it myself.

Larry Winters was the guy who came up with the finishes. I would tell Larry, "*Look, here's what I need to happen. I need the heel to go over. I don't care how you do it. Come up with something, but I don't want it to be a clean pin.*" We needed to have the fuck-finish because I needed to keep the people coming back to see winners, not losers. I remember talking to Flair one time and he mentioned the fact that he was a 16-time world champion. Well, in order to be a 16-time champ, you had to lose the belt 16 times, and get pinned. But if you look back, how many of those pinfalls were totally clean pins? Just the other day, I watched his match with Sting that took place in Baltimore. Sting ran into the corner and hit the turnbuckle with his knee? Now, it didn't make sense for Sting to jump up so high that he hit the top turnbuckle with his knee, but that created the finish. Every finish had a storyline, and of the 16 times that Flair got pinned, I would guess that 14 of them had some kind of fuck-finish. That was my philosophy. I didn't want a clean finish. I wanted a storyline finish that would bring the people back to the next show.

The one problem we had in the wrestling world was, if you put a big-name against a local guy, common sense tells you that the local had to lose. I'm sure there were exceptions, but that was the standard. What I was doing was trying to move my locals higher up the card and not bury them, so I rarely had a main event with a name versus a local.

Larry Winters at the Original Sports Bar
Photo by Craig Prendergast

What was your deal with Larry Winters? Did you pay him a fee for booking?
Yes and no. He wrestled on every show and I paid him much better than anyone else. Well, anyone other than the big names I brought in. He was my highest paid independent guy. In fact, our deal was that he would be paid more than *any* other local guy who worked my shows. He knew what the other guys were being paid. He didn't have a clue about how much I was paying the major names, though. I would hope that nobody knew what somebody else was making. I'm sure Funk didn't know what I paid Lawler. The old-timers didn't share things like that with the other guys. Lawler didn't know what Austin Idol got paid. They were all independent contractors and they were paid the price they agreed to.

For the most part, the local guys were getting paid $75. Larry was getting an extra 50 bucks to book and run the dressing room ... sometimes more. And despite the fact that he was pretty much guaranteed more money, he was the hardest worker of all. Even more amazing, Larry was a wrestler, and at the same time, he was the booker who kept figuring out ways to put the other guys over.

That was always a problem in the old days when the booker was a wrestler. They almost always put themselves over stronger than anyone else, and it was usually to the detriment of the territory.
That's exactly right. Larry never wanted to be the champion. He had the tag team belts, but Larry was never the TWA champion. Larry was on every show I promoted. The only time he may have missed a show was if he was on vacation. He told me that he never took another booking because nobody would pay him as much as he was making with me.

The one thing I had to pay close attention to was making sure every match was different, because the hardcores came to every match. In the old days of the territories, every match could be the same in each city because they were working in front of different people. When you have an area like Tri-State, where the wrestling fans would come to every show that we did, every show had to have a stipulation. Every show had to have something a little different.

That's why we had "dog collar" matches, "pins count anywhere in the building" matches, the "steel cage" match. We never did a "loser leaves town" match because, quite frankly, we didn't want to lose anybody. We just had to keep creating the same storylines with different little stipulations.

Larry took care of the matches, but there must have been a hundred things that demanded your attention at every show. At what time would you arrive at the arena on the day of a show?

I used to get to the arena at one o'clock ... for no reason whatsoever. (laughs) You'll find this funny ... I always had the attitude — you mentioned my ego getting in the way — I'd get there at one because, my philosophy was, I'm gonna sit in the building. After all, I rented the damn thing. (laughs) Actually, the ring was supposed to show up around 2:30, and my philosophy has been, the promoter should be the first one in the building and the last one to leave. I got there so early that nobody *ever* got there before I did.

My schedule on Saturday was, after the radio show, I'd go home for a couple of hours to sit back and relax. I'd have a light lunch and then go to the building. I'd usually stand outside and work the crowd as they arrived. I'd welcome the wrestlers, especially the big main-eventers that came in. When a guy was there for the first time, I always wanted to sit down and talk with them a little bit. Not about their match. That was their playing field, but just to get to know them and let them get to know me. I'd tell them what kind of advance we had. I never talked numbers in terms of dollars, but tickets sold. *"We should have two thousand people here tonight."* Blah, blah, blah.

I always asked people about themselves. That puts people at ease and makes them feel important. I'd ask Jerry how Memphis did that week. I'd ask Austin Idol about whatever deal he was involved with in whatever territory he was working. I didn't have to ask some of the guys

Manny Fernandez backstage
Photo by Dr. Mike Lano

anything. They'd start talking and would carry on a one-sided conversation for 30 minutes. You could say hello to Manny Fernandez, sit down, and you wouldn't get a word in. I loved it, though, because he had such great stories. The best thing about Manny was, he never left anything on the table. He put his body on the line every night. Everybody knew that if they were booked against Manny, they were going to have a physical match. But getting back to your question, I just wanted to be there to make sure the ring showed up. Of course, it *always* showed up, but I also worried about what might happen if the ring *didn't* show and I had 3,000 people waiting for the show to start. That was scary. I mean, seriously! What if the ring truck broke down? What would I do?

Anyway, once the ring got there, I knew we were okay. Once the ring was set up, I'd sit back in the front row and just look at it and think about what we had planned that night. When the doors opened, people would come talk to me. I had a *lot* of people who wanted to talk to me, not necessarily because they liked me, but because they thought if they became my friend, they could get to the wrestlers. That goes back to the phrase I told you about earlier, "*I was a conduit because I can do it.*" I was the conduit to get to the boys, and if somebody wanted Eddie Gilbert's autograph, they thought if they got to me, they could get it.

I'd work the crowd until 40 minutes or so before bell-time and then I'd check with Steve Truitt, my sound guy, to be sure he had the sound system ready. He was my guy behind the scenes. There's a match on YouTube where Abdullah throws him against a wall and — supposedly — knocks him out. Truitt knew enough to stay down. (laughs) In fact, he knew more than Rockin' Rebel. (laughs) I'd hunt down Larry Gallone to see if he had the [arena] programs ready to sell. Then I'd go to the back to make sure everything was lined up, to make sure everybody was there. We'd go over the order of the matches. We never posted them on the wall with the finishes and the times like they do at independent shows today.

The lineup had the finishes and times on them?
Yes! The matches, the order, who's going over ... it's all right there on the wall! They circle the names of the guys going over. Chris Wylde, 12 minutes. That's no problem if the boys are the only people in the dressing room, but you always have janitors, building managers, and one of the wrestler's brother who accidentally wanders in. It's posted right there on the friggin' wall! They don't even attempt to hide anything anymore. I've even seen the finishes written on those sheets.

Did Larry Gallone get a cut of the program sales?
I don't think he got a nickel, but he put every one of them together. He just wanted to be involved. To be honest, if we sold 50 programs at a show, that was a lot. I think we were charging two bucks. After I paid for the printing, I doubt there was anything left. I had two people selling my programs at my shows ... my two sons. They were young and they were glad to be with their dad. But, no. There wasn't any profit to be split.

Who took the pictures for the programs?
That would have been Larry, but if I remember correctly, it was all drawings. I don't think there were any pictures in the programs. He drew everything. Larry lives across the street from my business partner. We stay in touch.

On the *Winter Challenge* show, D.C. and Larry went up into the balcony. What do you remember about that? Was that spot planned?
Yeah, that was planned. It was about a 20-foot drop. There were two matches. One where the balcony ... there was a crosswalk behind the baskets of the basketball court, and a lot of people would stand there rather than sit in their seats. Actually, it was Don Drake's idea to do that. They were standing up there on the crosswalk before the matches, talking and pointing. I just figured they were going to go up there during their match and brawl, and I remember thinking that it was a cool idea. What I didn't know was that they were talking about Don taking a bump from that second floor crosswalk onto the concrete below. Don told me later, "*Well, I'm about six foot tall. If I'm hanging, I'm only fourteen feet from the floor. As long as I roll when I hit the floor, I can break my fall.*" The other problem was that there was seats below the crosswalk, and Don was worried that he might land on them, which would definitely cause him injury.

Well, they didn't practice the drop. They decided to just go for it. God knows, I was worried for him, but I figured he'd break his fall. He might be sore the next day, but he'd be fine. In the back of my mind, I was afraid that he'd break something and I'd lose him. I have to admit that I was kind of being self-serving there. I didn't want to lose him.

Well, when he did it, everybody in the audience must have been thinking, "*Oh, my god!*" Nobody had ever seen anything like that! I don't know if anybody has seen anything like that since! If that happened today, a hundred cameras would have filmed it and it would be posted on YouTube and Facebook within minutes for the world to see. D.C. would have been propelled into instant stardom. It's hard to describe other than to say it was just amazing and the surprise of it was ridiculous. Nobody saw that coming.

He was a big guy, too.
Yeah. He wasn't tall, but he was solid. Don and Larry figured it out. It was incredible. Nobody expected it. There *is* a YouTube video of them battling in the rafters on the third level. That's like four stories up! Even today, when I watch that video, I'm like, "*Holy shit!*"

D.C. Drake hangs Larry Winters over the railing.

Did the boys know it was going to happen?
I have no idea. My suspicion is that they didn't know because, the way Temple was set up, there wasn't anywhere for the boys to sit and watch.

From what I understand, *Pro Wrestling Illustrated* did a big feature on that.
They were there. They were taking pictures. The biggest feature they did for us was the time we had Larry Winters pin Johnny Hotbody against the wall. That was a whole story ... *Was that a legitimate pin?* That was the big one.

What do you mean when you say Larry pinned Johnny against the wall?
It was a "pins count anywhere in the building" match, so I came up with this idea of having the pinfall take place on the wall. Sal Corrente was the referee. He remembers these things better than me and could tell you all about it. Before the match, I told Sal what we were going to do. What Larry did was hold Johnny against the wall while Sal counted 1-2-3. The stipulation was that a wrestler's shoulders had to be down for the count of three ... anywhere in the building! It doesn't say on the floor or in the ring. I seem to remember *Pro Wrestling Illustrated* featuring a story on the finish. "Was it legit? Was that a pin?" All of a sudden, it became the talk of the wrestling universe. Nobody had done that before and I don't know if it's been done since. It was unique. That was me. I always wanted to do something different. Yes, Sal could give you more details than I can.

Nikita Koloff was on the *Winter Challenge* show.
Great guy ... another true professional. Nikita did work some shows for me. The first time Nikita came in for me, he worked with Manny Fernandez. [Philadelphia, Jan. 27, 1990]

He also worked with Manny at your *Summer Sizzler* show on June 9, 1990.
That's right. Nikita was another guy who ... all I had to do was tell him how much time I wanted. He never bitched. He never moaned. When Nikita was in the ring, he was absolutely perfect for the role. The one thing about him that always impressed me was that he *was* Russian. By that, I mean, somebody gave Krusher Kruschev the Russian gimmick, but he was never a Russian. He was an American wearing a Russian gimmick. Nikita *was* Russian. Ivan *was* Russian. However they got their gimmicks, they were perfect for the roles. Ivan was another guy who worked for me. Ivan was phenomenal. When they went into the ring, I don't care if you were a smart mark or not, they were the bad guys. There were perfect together and they were perfect individually. Again, Nikita was a true professional.

8  Mr. Sandman Sleep Center

Cheetah Kid (Ted Petty) vs. Dr. Tom Pritchard

Philadelphia, Pennsylvania: March 31, 1990
Spring Spectacular, McGonigle Hall, att. 2,000
- Jules Strongbow beat Randy Lewis (dq)
- Rockin' Rebel beat CN Redd
- Taped fist first-blood match
  Johnny Hotbody NC Tony Stetson
- Tom Pritchard beat Cheetah Kid
- I Quit Match
  D.C. Drake beat Larry Winters
- Ladies
  Misty Blue Simmes beat Kat LeRoux
- Paul Orndorff beat Austin Idol
- Kerry Von Erich beat Jerry Lawler (dq)
- Steel cage match
  Tully Blanchard beat Bam Bam Bigelow

Jerry Lawler called me up when I had him against Kerry Von Erich and asked me, "*Would it be okay if I brought the fire?*"

I said, "*Sure. I don't think fire's ever been thrown in Philadelphia.*"

Jerry threw the fire and hit Kerry Von Erich. Again, I told the guys, "*Don't give me your standard match! I don't want you going through the motions. I can book a hundred guys who go through the standard motions.*" When I booked [Terry] Funk and Lawler, they could have done their typical shtick, but man, they went above and beyond!

What was the deal about paying Kerry Von Erich an extra $250 to make sure he got on the plane?

I wanted to have Jerry and Kerry on my show. Kerry had a horrendous reputation of doing no-shows. Long story short, I booked Jerry and Kerry. Jerry and I talked all the time. He told me that they would both be at the [Dallas] Sportatorium the night before. Jerry wasn't wrestling that night, but he would be there. They had to catch a flight after the show because my show was at one o'clock on Saturday afternoon. I told Jerry that Kerry had a bad reputation for no-shows and I was worried. I told Jerry, *"I'll give you an extra two-hundred-fifty if you'll take personal responsibility for getting him here."* It may have been a different number, but that's what I remember. *"Just make sure Kerry is on that plane because if Kerry isn't here, it will screw up the whole card."*

Jerry Lawler | March 31, 1990

Kayfabe was still a thing then, so Kerry sat in the front of the plane and Jerry sat in the back. We didn't have cell phones then, but I trusted my brother Scott to pick them up at the airport. The first thing Kerry said to my brother was, *"I'm starving. Can you take me to Pat's Steakhouse?"* He knew enough about Philly that he wanted to go to Pat's. Scott took him to Pat's and he ordered two steak sandwiches, which he ate in the car on the way to Temple. Now, most of the guys don't eat before a show.

It was the first time I ever met Kerry, although we had talked on the phone. This was the match where Jerry had asked me if he could use fire for the finish. Well, Kerry was spaced out. Now, I'll never accuse somebody of being drunk or stoned, but he was a space cadet. How he wrestled in the condition he was in is beyond me. I don't know how those guys did it. He came to the ring wearing one of the ugliest robes I had ever seen. It was a light green. One thing that surprised me about Kerry was that he was really shy, and he was shy about his body. I mean, that guy was built like a brick shithouse and he refused to take his robe off until the very last minute. Anyway, he got into the ring and goes up to the ring announcer and asks, *"What city am I in?"*

The ring announcer tells him Philadelphia. Here he is in Dallas ... he has a ticket to fly to Philly, has a three or four-hour flight to Philly, gets picked up in Philly, is taken to a Philadelphia steakhouse, comes to Temple University, gets into the ring — this was the eighth match of the night — and he wants to know what city he's in! Lawler always did mic work, so he got on the mic first. Kerry takes the microphone and says, *"You might be the king of Memphis, but I kick ass in Philadelphia"* ... or something like that. So he mentions Philadelphia. Of course, at the time, everybody knew about his foot.

They ring the bell and he takes the robe off. In the video, you get the sense that he wasn't comfortable with his body, which is unbelievable. Here's a guy who had all the ring presence in the world, who had the Von Erich name ... I never used him again. I used Kevin [Von Erich]. I used Chris Adams. But I never used Kerry again. I had no faith that he was going to show up or do what he had to do. Nobody was stupid enough to pay Kerry to come up to Philly except for me. For all I know, Jerry took the $250 and didn't do shit, but I do know that Kerry got on the plane and did the show. I didn't want a no-show.

Did Kerry get over with the Philly fans?
Oh, yeah. I had two kinds of fans. One was what we would call the "smart mark." That was the only way they were ever going to see Kerry Von Erich because they weren't going to make a trip to Texas just to see him wrestle. Kerry came out to a big pop. They applauded him. Then, when Lawler came out (pause) ... Lawler was a fan favorite here, so it was a face-face match. The wrestlers, a lot of times, never really knew how to react to the crowd. The biggest pop I ever got for a name was Paul Orndorff. He came out to Hogan's music. He would wait a minute, minute-and-a-half before he came out. The place exploded when he finally came out. When I used him at Temple, it was the biggest pop we ever got.

That's an amazing statement. You put Tully over Bigelow. Was there a reason you had Tully go over? It seems like Bam Bam would have been the guy to go over because you used him more often.
Here's the answer to that. It wasn't me. It was either Larry Winters or the two of them made the decision together. Yes, I used Bigelow a lot because he lived in North Jersey. He was a drive-down. I wanted him on every one of my cards. There were no transportation costs. I didn't have to pay for airfare. I had the same deal with Cactus Jack. He was on every show. He was from New York. But I don't know the reason behind the ending. That wasn't my call.

Of all the name talent you used that night, Paul Orndorff got the biggest pop.
It was at McGonigle Hall and it's on tape. It was louder than loud. He was over. It was the show we did for the Tabor Rams Youth Association. [Dec. 7, 1991] On those local shows, Vince's guys were over. He was fresh from WWF TV. I would have put him on every show. He worked with Austin Idol on the night of the Lawler-Kerry match. Idol was thoroughly exhausted, so they did arm-wrestling in the middle of the ring.

Bam Bam Bigelow backstage
Photo by Dr. Mike Lano

Lawler threw fire that night. I believe that was the first time fire was thrown in Philadelphia.
It was the first time I was aware of. That was Lawler's idea. He called me up and asked *"Can I do the fire finish?"* What was I going to say? I said, *"Sure."* I talked to Larry Sharpe now and then. I asked him, *"Did anybody ever throw fire in Philly?"*

"No." And Larry would have known. When Lawler threw it, Kerry sold it big-time. To this day, people remind me about the time Jerry threw fire at Kerry Von Erich ... and it was totally Lawler's idea.

Rob Feinstein was at that show. He said he went up and rang the bell — he was just being silly — so everybody thought intermission was over. You ran up and threw him against the wall and kicked him out.
Oh, yeah! I really roughed him up. I remember him doing that. Oh, I wanted to kill him. He was just a young, dumb kid, but I was really mad. It's funny. I'm not a fighter. I'm not physical. But I'm the kind of guy, if I was ever cornered, I would kill somebody. I would go down fighting. He was a kid, though. I threw him into

the wall and had him thrown out. I was pissed. Part of the deal with the building was, they wanted at least a 20-minute intermission to sell their concessions. He rings the bell, and all of a sudden, people are walking back to their seats. All I could think was, they're going to throw me out of the building! Rob had no idea of the ramifications. Even the boys in the dressing room were confused. They thought they had ten or 15 minutes, and then the bell rings. Oh, I just wanted to kill him.

Ringmasters Wrestling School was formed and a newspaper announcement was made on April 19, 1990. How did Ringmasters come about?

It was just a natural extension of what we were doing. Clearly, I didn't know what the hell I was doing, so I brought on two teachers, Larry Winters and Ron Shaw, as partners. Ron was a Philly boy who wrestled in preliminaries for the WWF. I never used Ron as a wrestler on my shows. I used him as a manager. He managed J.T. Smith. Larry was an established wrestler who had wrestled for several promotions in the U.S. and Canada. We found a facility in a gym on [7025] Frankford Ave. smack in the middle of Philadelphia. They had an area that had, quite frankly, nothing but mats on the floor, so we rented that space. My idea was to promote the school and create my own talent. Of course, everybody and their brother had the same idea at the time.

Our fee was $2,400, and we guaranteed that our graduates would earn at least that much on wrestling show appearances. What that meant to me was, if I was paying guys 50 to $75, I would have to book them on 40 or 50 shows for them to recoup their investment. My intent was to build my own circuit because using local guys was much cheaper than having to bring guys in from New York, New Jersey, or other parts of the country. Eventually, when we realized how much work was involved, we increased the fee to $3,000.

Ron was all about paydays. *"How much am I getting paid?"* He worked for the U.S. Postal Service. I don't know if he was a mailman or if he worked inside, but that was his full-time gig. I remember calling Ron and telling him I wanted him to manage J.T. When we got together, he worked at the wrestling school every night. I would love to talk to him if he's still alive.

The last I heard, he was in North Fort Myers, Florida. What was the deal between the three partners in the wrestling school?

> Notice is hereby given, pursuant to the provisions of Act of Assembly, No. 295, effective March 16, 1983, of the filing in the office of the Department of the State of the Commonwealth of Pennsylvania, at Harrisburg, PA, on March 15, 1990, an Application for the conduct of a business in Philadelphia County, Pennsylvania, under the assumed or fictitious name, style or designation of RINGMASTERS WRESTLING SCHOOL with its principal place of business at 7025 Frankford Avenue, Philadelphia, PA 19124.
>
> The names and address of the persons owning or interested in said business are: Joel Goodhart, 800 Cottman Avenue, Apt. 306A, Philadelphia, PA 19111, Ron Czaplicki a/k/a Ron Shaw, 4523 Convent Lane, Philadelphia, PA 19114, and John Charyszyn a/k/a Larry Winters, 9865 Bonner Street, Philadelphia, PA 19115.
>
> WEINSTEIN, GOSS, KATZENSTEIN & SCHLEIFER ASSOCIATES, P.C., Solicitors 1112 Avenue of the Arts Building Philadelphia, PA 19107

(above) Ringmasters Wrestling School notice

(below) New business listing

NEW BUSINESSES

Following is a list of companies that have indicated their intentions to provide goods and services to the general public in recent filings with the states of Pennsylvania, New Jersey and Delaware.

Philadelphia

MIKE'S AUTO GLASS 5922 Ditman St.; Michael Lipinski and Micfralip Inc.
S.H. CROSSROADS THRIFT STORE 2135-37 S. 61st St.; Spruce Hill Christian Thrift Shop.
FURNITURE CLASSICS refinishing; 213 W. Queen Lane, Anne McGuinness.
DEAN'S HEAD TO TOE beauty salon; 2947 W. Girard Ave.; Gertrude Dean Beauty Salon Inc.
COLEMAN INSURANCE SERVICE 5435 Chester Ave.; John P. Coleman
MIKE & KATE'S SPORT SHOPPE hunting and fishing gear; 7492 Oxford Ave.; Michael D. Panamarenko
SAFE & SECURE LOCKSMITH 11901 Alberta Dr.; Robert C. Buchys
HEADLINES HAIR STUDIO 4569 Cottman Ave.; Nancy Draber
FAIRMOUNT ELECTRIC SUPPLY CO. 3316 Fairmount Ave.; T. Earl Morley
M.D. PLUMBING 6055 Lawndale St.; Michael T. Ditty
PHILLY ROCK CAFE 718 Arch St.; Main Inc.
K.B.M. ASSOCIATES 7469 N. 20th St.; Deborah J. Mack and K. Benjamin Wilson
RINGMASTERS WRESTLING SCHOOL 7025 Frankford Ave.; Joel Goodhart, Ron Czaplicki and John Charyszyn

I don't remember the exact split, but my guts says it was equal shares. That would have been fair because those guys were doing all the work. I can look that up, but it's not like many of the trainees had $2,400, much less $3,000, to give me up-front in one lump sum. Glen Osbourne did. He paid us in cash and I paid Larry and Ron their portion immediately. I wasn't a guy who brought the money in and paid a monthly stipend. Whenever somebody gave me money, they got their share right away. Now, I would deduct the rent for the gym before I paid them, but that was the only thing that came out of the fees we were paid.

Larry and Ron were natural teachers. They committed to teaching our students every night, despite the fact that they both had full-time, nine-to-five jobs. I also committed to being at the school almost every night. I didn't have to be there. There was no reason for me to be there because Ron and Larry were doing the teaching. In fact, when I was there, I was probably in the way.

We paid rent to the gym owners and we bought a ring and put it inside the gym. I also was convinced that you had to see what you looked like in the ring, so I had the walls completely mirrored. Eventually, we booked wrestling birthday parties. We would get pizzas from the local pizza stand and the kids could come in and be in the ring with either Larry, Ron, or whatever other wrestlers might be there. The highlight was that the birthday boy got to pin the wrestlers. The kids had a great time and *we* had a lot of fun with it, as well. That tied up most of our Saturdays, but we made a couple hundred bucks.

That sounds like a cool idea.
It really worked out well. The kids knew who Hulk Hogan was, but they didn't care whether they were in the ring with Hogan or Larry Winters. Larry would be decked out in his ring gear when he came out. Other wrestlers, like Rockin' Rebel, did some of the birthday parties and the kids had their pictures taken with them. It was pretty neat. It was different. It was funny, but in many cases, it wasn't the kids who wanted the birthday parties. It was their parents. The parents loved it. A lot of them were wrestling fans, so they loved being around the wrestlers as much as their kids did.

I was on the radio from 7:00 to 8:00, or 8:00 to 9:00, every Saturday morning, and then I would head over to the gym for a birthday party at 12:00. I'm sure I looked like a complete idiot. I'd wear my Zubaz and *Rasslin' Radio* jacket and try to be my own persona, but the kids were there for the wrestlers. We had a great time, though.

I'm not sure how we came up with the Ringmasters name. I don't know if it was my idea, or Larry's, or Ron's. We formed a company and got a certified Pennsylvania license for Ringmasters Wrestling School. And it worked.

Quite frankly, of all the people who came out of that school, Sandman is probably the guy who made it the biggest. Sandman came to my school because he wanted to learn how to wrestle. Stevie Richards came out of that school. J.T Smith, Glen Osbourne, and Chubby Dudley [Bay Ragni] all came out of Ringmasters. Guys like Stetson and Hotbody, who were already established, hung out at the school. Everybody wanted to be a part of it, so it became a gathering place. By 6:00 p.m. every night, three or four local guys would be there. I remember sitting back and watching J.T. and Sandman wrestle as they were training. They were fun to watch because they were stiff as hell. The matches between Hack — Sandman's name is Jim Fullington, but everybody called him Hack — the matches between Hack and J.T. Smith [at Ringmasters] were matches I would have bought a ticket to see. They were great! Sandman was atypical of our students, and it was neat to see, from my perspective, people like Sandman come in off the street, and years later, see him packing houses. That was cool. There's something to be said about homegrown talent, no question.

Sandman really did make a name for himself in the days after TWA went out of business.

He sure did. I think he came to us through the Ringmasters Wrestling School commercials. He lived in a suburb out here called Havertown and he came to the matches with his wife. There are people who came to the school who had *the look*. If you saw them on the street, you'd think, "*That guy's a wrestler.*" Hack was one of those guys.

It's weird. Hindsight being what it is, when you bring guys into a wrestling school, you try to fit them into a role. Some guys look like heels, some guys like faces. You try to

Mr. Sandman

Photo by Craig Prendergast

find the right gimmick for some of the guys. For instance, Sandman. We couldn't figure out what to do with him. One day, I was driving down I-95 and I saw a billboard for a mattress company called Mr. Sandman Sleep Center. It hit me immediately. We'll call him Sandman. When I got back to the gym, I said, "*You know, I just had an idea. Think about this, Larry. Let's do a beach boy gimmick with Jim and call him Mr. Sandman.*" He later shortened it to Sandman, but at first, we called him *Mr.* Sandman. He had the blond hair and was the perfect fit for the gimmick. That's how that whole name came about.

When Tod [Gordon] got him, after I got out of the business ... well, I don't know if Tod made the change or if it was Paul E, but Sandman started wearing the Zubaz to the ring and drinking beer. In my opinion, he was Stone Cold before Stone Cold. Stone Cold Steve Austin stole that! I created the name Sandman, Sandman created the persona, and Stone Cold stole it. But that wasn't my idea. I'm not sure who came up with it, but it worked for him.

You mentioned Stevie Richards. He started training there, but the school closed before he had his first match.

Yeah. If we had stayed in business, there's no question that Ringmasters and Tri-State would have been a magnet to bring in a lot of local talent. Again, it was just a matter of timing and money. If I had unlimited money, or even a good money man, the school would still be there.

Was it a requirement for students to be 18 years old?

The law was very clear. You had to be 18 years old and drug-free. I honestly don't know if any of our students did drugs. We never tested, but that was a stipulation on the contract they signed. I used to tell people that we took some of the kids off the street, but I don't know if that was really the case. I had a feeling, though, that if it hadn't been for Ringmasters School, some of those guys would have turned out differently.

So you'd say Sandman was the most successful wrestler ever to come out of the school?

I think so, but you could make a good case for Stevie Richards.

One report I read said that J.T. Smith was one of the best workers in Tri-State. Do you agree with that?
Yeah, but I'm going to add to that. J.T. and Sandman was a better match than Drake and Winters. J.T. and Sandman was better than Stetson and Hotbody. Those two guys had some of the stiffest matches you've ever seen. They worked together at our school. J.T. grew into the role and did really well after that. I saw J.T. several years ago at one of Rob Feinstein's autograph deals. He has since retired from wrestling. He told me that he's had eleven concussions. He lives in Virginia and his doctor basically told him, "*There will not be a twelfth.*" At least, that's what J.T. told me. But I could book J.T. and Sandman every night and just tell them, "*Wing it! You win half, you win half. I don't care what you do tonight.*"

In hindsight, I had a troupe of talent. I could promote a card anywhere with JT/Sandman, Stetson/Hotbody, or Drake/Winters, and the people would get their money's worth and then some. When you add guys like Glen Osbourne — who really became something on his own — or CN Redd to the mix ... oh, my word. They could do it all. But those six wrestlers, those three matches, they were phenomenal. I must have seen Drake/Winters a hundred times. J.T. and Sandman were two guys created at my school, and every time I saw that match, I was amazed. Drake/Winters was around already. Stetson/Hotbody was around already. But J.T. and Sandman were right out of the school.

Did they do the same match all the time, or were they creative?
Oh, they were creative. I used to tell the guys, "*Fuck finish. Don't do any clean finishes because you guys are going to run every show.*" If you trained at RingMasters, part of the handshake agreement was, if you graduated, you would work on every show I had. Guys like Mike Bruno, Glen Osbourne, all those guys, they were on every show I did. That was my contract with them. Of course, that led to problems because I had a full show and it left no room for other independent talent! And there was no way that I, as a promoter, was going to tell Drake, or Winters, or Hotbody, or J.T., or Sandman, "*Take it easy because I've got names at the top* [the main event] *who might not ever come back.*" There was no way.

That's funny because that would never have gotten over in the old days.
No! I remember sitting down in my office one time and thinking that, at some point, I wouldn't need to bring in the major names again. That never happened, though. There was so much independent main event talent out there that I wanted someone on every show. However, I could have run a show with just my guys and we would have put on a great show. The problem is, it would have been in front of 75 people because most people want a name wrestler on the card. Today, there are shows being run in front of 75 people where the promoter actually makes a profit. Well, if you have seven matches on the card — two of them being tag matches — two referees, a ring announcer, you rent a building, sell tickets for $10, $15, and $20, and you draw 75 people and make money ... what does that tell you? You're paying everybody $15, $20. That wasn't my philosophy.

As I said earlier, a lot of the guys today don't understand that their job is to sell tickets. In today's world, the first match doesn't sell any tickets because the first match is probably two rookies just getting started. If you want to make it in this world today, those guys should be *personally* selling 25 tickets each. You put the guy who sold the most tickets over and you build them up.

When I go to these independent shows and the average show has 75 to 100 people, and 50 of those people are the exact same people every month and it doesn't grow, it's because your talent isn't producing the heat where people want to see them or the scuttlebutt. Nobody's talking to their friends. "*You've got to come to the show. This guy's absolutely amazing!*" That didn't happen with me.

Jimmy Jannetty
Photo by Craig Prendergast

They came to my shows and they saw ... I mean, basically, J.T. and Sandman were rookies performing in front of 2,000 people at the Civic Center. That doesn't happen in today's world!

Jimmy Jannetty ... You were his dad's insurance agent, right? Is that how you met Jimmy?

Yep. His father and his mother were clients of mine. One day, we sat down and he introduced me to his son, Jimmy. I'm not sure how the conversation started, but Jimmy wanted to be in the business. One thing led to another and he came in and trained. If you watch some of my early shows at Temple University, I had Jimmy working security. He'd lead guys like Lawler and Orndorff out through the crowd. What's amazing about the wrestling industry is that *everybody* helped put the ring together ... *everybody* set up the chairs. The guys who really understand the industry have done it all. They're not the prima donnas. Unless you're 6-foot-5, have blond hair, a tight butt, and washboard abs, you were expected to do everything. The guys who worked for me helped set up the buildings. They worked security before they started to wrestle. Jimmy was one of those guys. Jimmy could really work in the ring. He looked a lot like Marty Jannetty, so Larry saddled him with the name Jimmy Jannetty. As far as I know, he's still wrestling. I know he was working at Gangrel's wrestling school.

Ringmasters was in business from the day you opened until you shut down the promotion, wasn't it?

Yep.

At one of his shows in Stratford, New Jersey, Dennis Coralluzzo had a guy on his card named Al the Sledgehammer [Alfred Poling]. He wrestled in a handicap match against two masked men called The Ringmasters. Someone said their name was a knock on your wrestling school.

I'm sure it was. I don't remember that. I'm not sure I ever knew about it. Larry Sharpe and I always got along, but when Ringmasters opened up, he looked at us as almost direct competition to his Monster Factory. People don't realize this, but there was more competition between the wrestling schools than there was between the wrestling promotions! I never felt that way. All I wanted to do was create homegrown talent for my promotion. I wasn't looking to steal talent from Larry, and quite frankly I don't think Larry was trying to steal talent from me. What bothered him, I'm sure, is that guys, who might have signed up at Monster Factory, were signing up at my school. I think what we were doing made an impact on his bottom line. And, of course, I had the radio to promote Ringmasters. Larry never bought commercial time on Rasslin' Radio to promote Monster Factory and I certainly wasn't going to do it for free. But, again, there was more competition between the wrestling schools than the wrestling promotions.

What were some of the methods you used to teach the new local guys?

My business brain was always working. When I thought a guy was going to be a big star — Sandman was a good example — I created a VHS tape of him training, and growing, and evolving into his character. I did the same thing with the other guys. The tapes weren't for them to send out to other promoters to promote themselves, although they could have used them for that. They were for the guys to use to critique themselves, and maybe to make a buck or two selling them to the fans.

The guys could see things when they'd play a tape back that I missed completely. I wasn't a wrestler, so I didn't always see all the intricacies that the guys did, or that Ron and Larry did, but the tapes gave them the opportunity to study their moves and learn how to do things better.

One of the things that used to bother me when I watched the tapes was seeing a guy who threw a punch and missed by 12 inches. Jerry Lawler used to tell everybody, "*The one thing that exposes the business more than anything else is the punch.*" Lawler was the best puncher in the industry. If you ever watch his tapes, you'll notice that he does a *lot* of punching ... but he had it down to a science. You never see him miss. And yet, some guys would miss by six inches and the other guy would react. It's a sure bet that the people sitting in the front row saw it, and if those people were in *my* shows, they'd boo the hell out of you. If you're happen to miss, that's fine, but your opponent shouldn't react. But you've got to make some kind of contact.

Larry spent a lot of time watching the tapes. He'd study a match and then take the guys aside and tell them, "*Here's what you did right. Here's what you did wrong.*" He'd show them tapes of someone taking a bump that looked really good. It was art, but when he slowed it down, you could see that it didn't look like art at all. I always talked about the two components to a wrestling match ... the art and the science. The art is what Larry Winters taught the guys. I tried to teach them the science ... the storyline, the psychology, how to work a crowd. What moves can you make if you're a heel, if you're a face? Again, the thing that Rebel never learned — at least while he was working for me — Rebel would do heel moves ... when he was a *babyface*. He never really understood ring psychology.

Abdullah used to use a book as a reference to teach the guys about ring psychology. "*Do you read a book from the back to the front? The answer is no. You read it from the front to the back. The same goes for a wrestling match. You tell your story from front to back.*"

Terry Funk also talked about that a lot. "*Your match starts the moment you walk out of the dressing room door. As you're walking to the ring, you had better be in your persona. And when the match is over, you* stay *in your persona until you're behind closed doors.*" He talked about that a lot when he was in the dressing room with the young guys. I remember him telling them, "*Joel might be asking you for ten minutes, but you're really doing fifteen because the minutes walking to and from are important.*" Terry went above and beyond. I have to say, Terry, Lawler, Cactus, Eddie Gilbert — and there were others — they wanted to be successful, but they actually cared about *my* success, as well. At that point in their careers, Terry and Jerry were already there. In fact, you could argue that Terry Funk, at that point, was almost done. But they cared about my success. They realized that if I was successful, they would be making money. A lot of the wrestlers just didn't get that.

One of the big benefits for the local guys on your cards was getting the opportunity to rub shoulders with the veterans, like Terry Funk and Jerry

Lawler. Do you think the young talent learned from the time they were around them?

Oh, yeah. If they were smart, they would have kissed up to every guy I brought in and ask them about ring psychology. They didn't have the opportunity — at least, it didn't happen more than a time or two — to actually work with the main event talent. Quite frankly, that would be the death knell for a local guy. I always booked big-name veterans against big-name veterans, the local guys against local guys. But in the dressing room ... think about this. You're a rookie. You've been in the business for six months, or a year. And in the dressing room, you're sitting with Abdullah the Butcher, the original Sheik, Eddie Gilbert, Cactus Jack, Kevin Sullivan, Bam Bam Bigelow, Austin Idol. Oh, my god! What a thrill that must have been for them.

I wonder if the local talent ever came to the realization that the main event guys never talked through their match in the dressing room ... that they just winged it when they got into the ring.

I hope they noticed that. One of the things you *never* saw the veterans do was rehearse a match in the back. They called it in the ring. Local wrestlers today spend three hours going over their match ... move by move by move. The independent wrestler is very mechanical because they're new. They know what they like. I heard guys say, *"What moves do you like?"* and *"What moves don't you like?"* The established wrestlers didn't do that *ever*. Again, they called it in the ring. There was a reason for that. How do you know what's going to work and make the crowd pop until you do it?

I heard guys tell people, *"I was on Goodhart's big card in the Civic Center with Terry Funk and Jerry Lawler."* That put them up a notch. They couldn't say, *"I wrestled Terry Funk,"* so they'd get the rub from being *on* a card with Terry Funk, *on* a card with Jerry Lawler. Giving credit where it's due, my locals were a step above the local rookies and most locals from other promotions in the area.

Philadelphia, Pennsylvania: May 19, 1990
Police Administration Building, free show
• Johnny Hotbody vs. Tony (Hitman) Stetson
• Plus Larry Winters, Ron Shaw, Mr. Sandman, Jimmy Jannetty, J.T. Smith, Crybaby Waldo

Note: The May 19th card was part of the annual Police Department Open House. The outdoor venue was located at Eighth and Race Streets and carnival games and exhibits were featured throughout the day from 10:00 a.m. to 3:00 p.m. Admission was free with hot dogs, snacks and drinks available for 25¢. During the wrestling card, the police "cooperated" and put Johnny Hotbody in jail.

June 8, 1990 in Delaware
No match results available.

IF YOU GO

The annual Police Department Open House will take place from 10 a.m. to 3 p.m. tomorrow, rain or shine, at the Police Administration Building (the Roundhouse), Eighth and Race Streets. Carnival games and exhibits take place throughout the day. Motorcycle and horse rides begin at 1 p.m. Tri-State Wrestling Alliance exhibition runs 11 a.m.-1 p.m., featuring Johnny Hot Body vs. Tony "Hitman" Stetson, plus Larry Winters, Ron Shaw, Mr. Sandman, Jimmy Jannetty, J.T. Smith and the Great Waldo. Barney Battery smoke-detector skit starts at 1 p.m. Admission is free. Hot dogs, snacks and drinks available for 25 cents. Free parking available at Franklin Square. Information: 686-3380.

9  "For twenty-five dollars, she'll do anything!"

Philadelphia, Pennsylvania: June 9, 1990
Summer Sizzler, McGonigle Hall, att. 1,050
- Paddy O'Brien beat Boy Gone Bad
- Tom Brandi & Mike Kaluha NC American Pitbulls (double COR)
- American brass knuckles title match
  Cheetah Kid beat Tom Prichard
- Bob Orton Jr. beat Don Muraco
- J.T. Smith beat Mr. Sandman
- Jerry Lawler beat Austin Idol (dq)
- Russian chain match
  Nikita Koloff beat Manny Fernandez
- 6-man elimination tag team match
  Larry Winters, Rockin' Rebel & Tony Stetson beat
    D.C. Drake, Johnny Hotbody & Mondo Kleen
      Kleen beat Rebel
        Hotbody beat Stetson
          Winters beat Kleen
            Winters beat Hotbody
              Winters beat Drake
- Paul Orndorff beat Tully Blanchard

I was wondering about a couple of guys you had on the June 9 show at McGonigle. Paddy O'Brien.
  Boy, there's a name I don't remember. Nope ... nothing there.
The American Pit Bulls ... Gary Wolfe and Anthony Durante.
  The Pit Bulls were actually Larry Sharpe's guys. They were tag team champions later for ECW. They looked like wrestlers, whatever the hell that means. There's an interesting story there. When D.C. Drake started wearing the chain around his neck, a lot of people thought that was a take-off on the Pit Bulls, when the reality is, the Pit Bulls did it *after* Drake did it. Don E. Allen [Don Adelberg] came to the ring with the chain around Drake's neck. [Sept. 15, 1990]
These were the Pit Bulls who had a big run in ECW, correct?
  Yes. Gary Wolfe and Anthony Durante. Anthony passed away several years ago. Anthony was huge ... six-foot-something.
Just an FYI, Durante and his girlfriend overdosed in 2003. They had two small kids — a 21-month-old boy and an eight-month-old girl — and those children were alone in the house with the bodies for several days before someone found them.
  You see, it's that kind of stuff that bothers me. Once you have a family, you have to stop that shit. I never had any issues with Anthony, but how the hell do you do that?

Don E. Allen leads D.C. Drake to the ring.
Photo by Craig Prendergast

Madison, New Jersey: July 1, 1990
- Cheetah Kid & Tom Brandi beat King Kaluha & Ron Shaw (dq)
- Ladies
  Misty Blue Simmes beat Linda Dallas
- Larry Winters beat King Kaluha (dq)
- SD Jones beat Mike Sharpe

Philadelphia, Pennsylvania: July 21, 1990
Max Myers Playground
- Michael Bruno & Jimmy Jannetty beat Mr. Sandman & CN Redd
- D.C. Drake beat Larry Winters
- Jules Strongbow beat Mike Sharpe
- Midgets
  Little Louie beat Tiger Jackson
- Bob Orton, Jr. NC Ken Patera
- Johnny Hotbody NC Tony Stetson
- Ken Patera NC Kamala
- Battle royal, winner declared first Tri-State champion
  Winner: Rockin' Rebel
The title was immediately held up.

Tell me about Michael Bruno.
　Michael Bruno ... Michael Tartaglia. We talk at least once a month. Michael was a good little worker. I tagged him up with Tony Stetson as The Hitmen. They were both Italian, so it was somewhat legit. He was small, but a lot of the local guys who worked for me were small. One thing I can say about Michael is that he understood, early on, the psychology of wrestling. Wrestling is like anything else. There's the art and the science. The art is the physicality in the ring. The science is understanding what gets the fans out of their seats or back into the seats.

Speaking of small, you also booked two midgets ... Little Louie and Tiger Jackson.

Yes, I remember them. They were great. They worked for everybody, including Vince. The kids loved the midget matches. In some ways, they exposed the business because it was like a circus sideshow, but they were entertainers. I don't remember who put me in touch with them, but they worked the entire east coast. Everybody was using them.

Autumn Armageddon, **Sept. 15, 1990. Your semi-final was Abby against Manny Fernandez.**
I had them booked several weeks in advance. A few days before the show, Manny called and said he had an opportunity to do an afternoon show in New Jersey and he could drive down afterwards to my show. Again, professionalism. He asked me if that would be okay. I was smart enough to realize that he was

going to do it, anyway, and I'm sure he assumed I'd agree. I told him to go ahead and take the other payday. I don't know who it was for.

Philadelphia, Pennsylvania: Sept. 15, 1990
Autumn Armageddon 1990, Penn Hall, att. 1,500, gate $22,000
• Cactus Jack drew Eddie Gilbert
• Adrian Street w/valet Miss Linda beat Jimmy Valiant
• Tri-State Wrestling Alliance title match
   D.C. Drake (w/Woman) beat Rockin' Rebel w/Baby Doll
   — Drake won the title.
• Chris Adams & Kevin Von Erich NC Austin Idol & Al Perez (double cor)
• Sandman w/Peaches beat J.T. Smith
• Hair vs. Hair
   Tony Stetson beat Johnny Hotbody
• Abdullah the Butcher NC Manny Fernandez w/Cactus Jack (double dq)
• Jerry Lawler beat Terry Funk
• 22-man reverse steel cage battle royal
   Winner: Rockin' Rebel
Entrants: Chris Candido, Zebra Kid, Johnny Hotbody, Jimmy Jannetty, Glen Osbourne, John Osbourne, Rockin' Rebel, CN Red, Sandman, Ron Shaw, J.T. Smith, Tony Stetson, Tahitian Savage, Larry Winters, Bounty Hunter, Cheetah Kid, Crybaby Waldo, Ghetto Blaster, Top Gun, Triton, Larry Winters

---

(laughs) That's where I was headed with this. Actually, the other show was in Kingston, PA, about 112 miles away, and it wasn't an afternoon show. The show didn't start until 7:30 that night, which was the same time your show started. Manny wrestled Brian Blair and I'm sure the promoter put them on the first match so Manny could get on the road. They had newspaper ads in the Wilkes-Barre newspaper more than a week in advance.
   No kidding? That's something I never knew, but I'm not surprised because he showed up really late. In fact, he wasn't there when it was time for their match. Cactus Jack, who wrestled Eddie Gilbert earlier that night, told me, "*Don't worry. He's gonna show up. Manny is a man of his word.*" Well, he may have been a man of his word, but he sure stretched the truth a little. (laughs)
   Anyway, we didn't have cell phones, so I had no way to contact Manny to find out what was going on. Cactus, being the man he was — and Cactus had already showered and cleaned up after his match — stepped up to the plate and went out to the ring. That's one of the things that always amazed me. How a guy could wrestle, then shower and get dressed, and then wrestle again ... I don't know about you, but if I wrestled once, I'd be exhausted for three days. Cactus and Abby started beating the shit out of each other. They just winged it and the crowd got into it. Anyway, about five minutes into the match, Manny runs in and all three of them brawled all over the building. He had changed clothes during the drive down and literally ran into the arena and into the ring. Even the smart marks got into it. They knew everything and assumed it was all planned, but it was all ad lib.
On that same card, Rockin' Rebel [Chuck Williams] became the first TWA champion by winning the title in a battle royal.
   That's right, but on the next show, D.C. Drake beat him to win the belt. I put Rebel over at first because I didn't want the heel to get the belt from the get-go. My philosophy was that I had to be different. That's the night I had the pinfall take

place against the side wall. Again, that was a "falls count anywhere in the building" match.

So your intent all along was to give the title to Rebel and then move it to Drake.
That's right. Philly was a heel town, so I wanted to give it to the heel. Clearly, Drake was the guy who was going to get it, but I had to figure out how to get it on him, so we had a battle royal at the Max Myers Playground in Philly with the stipulation that the last man standing would be awarded the title. Oh, my word. It was 98 degrees outside. It was hot as hell. It was funny because one of the matches was Kamala against Ken Patera. Kamala lived in Mississippi and grew up in weather like that, but he couldn't breathe in 98 degree weather up here. (laughs) Not only that, but the ring mat was as hot as hell and Kamala wrestled barefoot. If you ever plan to promote wrestling, my advice is to do it indoors if you're going to use a guy who wrestles without shoes. (laughs) I was ring announcing and he's moving around. He tells me, "*I can't stand on this hot mat. What am I supposed to do?*"

"*Just keep moving around.*" (laughs) Kamala was a pussycat, though. I remember people telling me stories about him owning a 50-acre farm and that he worked that farm all day long. His Kamala gimmick was absolutely phenomenal, but it's sad that he got ripped off by so many promoters. There was nobody else who could have played the role of Kamala like he did. It's like Hulk Hogan ... nobody could have been Hulk Hogan other than Hogan. There were other Nature Boys, and Buddy Rogers was probably the best of the bunch, but Flair just ran with the concept.

Anyway, I didn't want Drake to win the TWA title on the playground show. I wanted him to win it at a big show. That was similar to what Crockett and Vince always did. The important title changes never took place at a local show. They were always at the big house where they drew the most money. So I thought, "*Okay, Drake has to win it from a babyface. Who can I use for that?*" Quite frankly, Rebel was my top baby, and Rebel looked the part. He looked like a wrestler. And it worked. I put all the locals in a battle royal at the playground show and I had Rebel win it. Technically, he was the first TWA champ.

Chuck [Rockin' Rebel] conducted himself in wrestling as a true professional, but his downside was that he just didn't understand ring psychology. Abdullah almost killed him one night. Rebel always had heat with Abdullah because, when Abdullah knocked Rebel down, he'd get right back up. Abby's gimmick was that he was a maniac, and when he knocks you down, you *stay* down. You don't get back up because you're making Abby look weak. If Sheik knocks you down, *stay* down! Rebel never understood that. Rebel would also do heel moves when he was a face.

Despite the fact that he never really understood the psychology, Chuck deserved to be the first champion, and he did sell tickets for me. I mean, he literally sold tickets. He did great sales. In fact, I used to pay him to sell tickets. I would give him 25 tickets and give him a percentage of each ticket he sold. And he sold them! He was one of the true independent wrestlers whose job was, not only to wrestle, but to sell tickets.

Someone once said, "*On a wrestling card, you have your two main events and you have the others. The others don't sell tickets.*" By that, I mean they don't draw people to the arena. The four names that you put on top of the card are what sell your tickets, so if you're an "other," you probably should pay your way. Today, it's very rare for a local wrestler to have a following. Chris Wylde is as good a wrestler as any independent I've ever worked with, but he had little following. That doesn't take away from his work ethic, but it's just the truth. Larry Winters and D.C. Drake were on all my posters because they had a following. Stetson and Hotbody had a following.

At that time, I asked the local wrestlers — the *other* wrestlers — to help sell tickets to the shows, and to Rebel's credit, he paid his way. The night he dropped the title to Drake, he sold almost a hundred tickets. What was I going to do? Bury him? No. I did a fuck-finish so he looked good in front of the hundred people who bought tickets from him!

I looked at it this way. If Rebel sold a hundred tickets and I drew 2,000 people, he was responsible for five percent of the house. He deserved his spot. I remember having the conversation before his match. *"Your job is to transfer the belt to Drake. We'll do a fuck-finish. I'm not gonna have you pinned clean in the ring."* Now, I could have put D.C. over really big by having him win cleanly, but Rebel was selling me tickets and doing everything that a local wrestler should do ... and he never once complained. He sold his way, made a couple of extra bucks, and got some paydays by proving to me that he could put asses in the seats.

Rebel told Dan Murphy, *"Joel was making a killing,"* **and went on to talk about how much extra money he made selling tickets.**

Oh, yeah. (laughs) I was making a killing. Yeah. Well, that obviously proved to be false. Those guys were used to wrestling in front of 60 people, so when they saw 2,000 people in the building, they immediately jumped to the conclusion that I was making a fortune, right? Meanwhile, they were driving nicer cars than I was. I mean, those guys would get a $75 payoff and walk away with $75. I sold $2,500 worth of tickets and walked away $125 in the hole. (laughs)

If I started a promotion today, it would have to be a two-way street between me and the local guys who work for me. *"Here's your pay, and you'd better make more than your pay by selling tickets. If I'm giving you fifty bucks and you don't sell me three tickets at twenty dollars, how does it benefit me to have you on the card?"* Most of them are great workers, but unless they're somebody who really has *it*, their talent can be replaced overnight. You know, I never wrestled. Those guys, to this day, put their bodies on the line for almost nothing because they love the sport. I loved the sport, too, but if a promoter can't make a buck, then those guys won't have a place to work.

You brought in Baby Doll to be Rockin' Rebel's manager that night. Tell me about that.

I was always trying to figure out an angle to book Baby Doll onto one of my cards because we had a little bit of history from when I was helping promote the Crockett shows. When we ran the angle with Rockin' Rebel and D.C. Drake, I had her manage Rebel, while Woman [Nancy Sullivan] managed Drake.

For the finish, Baby Doll turned on Rebel and threw powder into his face, which was something nobody expected her to do! That's how Drake won the belt. Again, a fuck-finish because I didn't want to bury Rebel. When was the last time you ever saw a match with two women managers? I don't think it had ever been done.

The only one I can think of would have been Precious with Jimmy Garvin and Sunshine with Chris Adams.

Okay, that's one time. (laughs)

Was there ever any talk of bringing the two girls back against each other?

No, never. At that point, Woman was pretty much done with wrestling. Baby Doll, in her own right, was a hell of a wrestler, but I couldn't get her! She was tough to book because everybody wanted to book her. I couldn't get her! It wasn't too long after that that I had my epiphany about who would and who wouldn't sell tickets. Baby Doll was great in the role she played in the NWA, but she wouldn't have sold me a single ticket.

I was going to ask you about Woman managing D.C. Drake. What was the story behind that?

I'll tell you exactly what it was. My mindset was, in order for my champion to have the most credibility, I had to find some kind of national connection. At the time, D.C. had been managed by either Don E. Allen or Tom Cusati. It's one thing when a wrestler is managed by a local manager, but bringing in somebody like Woman took D.C. and the title to the next level.

I crafted the idea because D.C. was a typical, bad-guy heel, and here comes Woman dressed in a black, really-sexy outfit. Of all the women who worked for me, to me, Woman was the most stunning. She was *gorgeous*! Her role as a manager was simply to strut her stuff. If you remember, D.C.'s entrance used to be about ten minutes long. He'd walk around the ring, over and over, and get as much heat as he could before he got *into* the ring. Well, the heat sure intensified when Woman strutted around the ring with him. It really worked well and brought the title to another level.

Rockin' Rebel won the belt in the battle royal on July 21st. Every reference to the TWA title that I've been able to find says the title was immediately held up after the match. What was the reasoning behind that?

I don't think it was. (pause) You know something … I hate it when you bring up this stuff because it makes me think. I do believe (pause) … I might be wrong, but I seem to remember Rebel coming out as the champion on the night he dropped the belt to D.C. You're making me think now. Damn, now I'm not sure. I thought Rebel came out with the belt, but if he didn't and we did hold it up, the answer to your question is … I don't have a clue. (laughs) That was 30-plus years ago.

You had another girl on that card … Peaches. She came in with Sandman.

That was Sandman's wife, Lori. Oh, she frustrated the hell out of me. Here we were building Sandman up. God bless him, he was a great worker. We figured we'd run the angle with Peaches. Peaches was cute and she had a nice body. I kept telling her, "*I need you to wear a bikini.*" You couldn't get away with wearing a thong like they did later on. She had a cute little body and would look great in a bikini. I wanted her at ringside to divert the attention of Jim's opponents.

Sandman & Peaches　　　　　　　　Photo by Craig Prendergast

Now, this was before political correctness was a thing, but I had to be careful because she was Sandman's wife. I told her, "*First of all, half the guys sitting at ringside will be drooling. Second, the photographers will take pictures and you'll be in all the magazines. I just want you to get up on the ring apron and strut your stuff.*" Well, she didn't want to do it. She wasn't comfortable with the idea at all. I think Jim was resistant at first, too, because it was his wife and they had a kid. She finally gave in for one match at Penn Hall when Sandman wrestled Tony Stetson. [Sept. 21, 1991] Sandman walked off and left her out there after the finish. Stetson put her over his knee and gave her a pat or two on the butt. Now that I think about it, that was the "last blood battle royal" and the fuck-finish was ketchup. Everybody used to think that wrestlers used ketchup to simulate bleeding, so the finish was a play on that. Tony and Sandman were the last two who hadn't bled, so she opened a ketchup packet and squirted it on Tony.

Other than that, Peaches was great. Her involvement didn't cost me anything because she was coming to the matches, anyway. Peaches was there only because Sandman was there, and she really didn't know what she was doing. She got into it, though, and she grew into the role.

Dan Murphy talked to Baby Doll about her time with your promotion. She said, "*At one point, his bag was stolen, and he showed up at the event without gear. That's how he started working in the wifebeater and the Zubaz.*" Do you remember that?
Vaguely. If she said that, I'll go with it. The one important lesson you should learn in the wrestling business is to always bring your gear. I always put my tuxedo in the trunk, just in case. You never know. But the other thing we taught the guys was to have more than one set of gear, and also to have more than one color. It just didn't look good when two guys got into the ring wearing the same color trunks. I used to have a pair of wrestling boots with JG on them. We kept them at the store in case anybody wanted to buy a pair of wrestling boots and wanted to see a sample. There was one time — and I don't remember who the hell it was — when somebody forgot their gear and they wore my boots. Well, I'm a 10½ and they wore a nine. It really looked bad because they kept tripping over them, and worse, they had JG on the side. But you make do with what you have.

The only heat I ever got over one of the girls was from Chris Candido. Chris brought his girl with him ... Tammy Sytch. I never liked Tammy. Never. I couldn't stand her attitude. Candido wanted me to use her. He even told me, "*For twenty-five dollars, she'll do anything.*" I just had no interest.

In Sunny's book *Shattered*, she said Chris wanted her to walk him to the ring and that was her debut into the business, even though you weren't going to pay her.
Chris was from the Monster Factory. He was a Larry Sharpe guy. I didn't want to use guys that were on other promotions unless we had some kind of agreement. It always went back to competing against each other. But Chris always wanted to work my shows. He was smart enough to see that, at that time, my shows were drawing bigger crowds. Yes, he did ask if Sunny could go to the ring.

Again, I think it was just her attitude that put me off. She was much sexier than Peaches and she was willing to do things that Peaches wouldn't. One of the things I never liked about Vince's shows was that everybody had a manager ... Albano, Blassie, the Grand Wizard. There were so many managers for such a long time that it got to where they no longer meant anything. God knows I'd never tell Vince how to run his shows. He made a billion dollars. But in my opinion, valets were in the same category as managers, and I didn't want to muddy up the waters — not to mention having to pay someone else — by having them on my shows. I had Woman managing Drake, and I had Baby Doll manage Rebel. I had no problem with the women being outside, but there was a point where it was just too much. There was a point where I had too many. Peaches was married to Hak [Sandman], and when she came in with him, she wanted to get paid. I mean, if I remember correctly, it was only $25, but why pay somebody $25 if they don't sell me a single ticket? The reality is, if I had known what I was doing, I would have put Sunny on every card. She would have done anything I wanted her to do.

Another thing about that ... whenever a wrestler comes to you with an idea, every idea they give you is an idea that put *them* over. As a promoter, you have to think, "*Wait a minute. I'm paying you to do what I need you to do, and you come to me and say* 'Let's run this angle,'" and every angle they give me puts them on top. When I learned that, I realized that most of the guys were self-promoting and self-serving ... and that's cool. They're independent contractors. They're looking to put themselves over. I remember eating a meal at a bar with Jeff Jarrett. He told me, "*A wrestler gets paid to make his opponent look great. Even if you're going to win, what makes you a better wrestler is making the other guy look so good, so that even though you're beating him, he looks better.*"

Flair was notorious for that. I had a conversation with Flair a few years ago. He talked about the first time he won the [NWA world heavyweight title] belt. He wasn't ready to be a champion. Back in the day when he wrestled in the different territories, he would wrestle for an hour every night against competition that was nowhere near his level. His job was to make the local champion look like a world-beater. If you've ever watched Flair's matches, every match is the same match, but when he would go to a territory, he would wind up losing ... and he made a living by losing. And yet, if you ask people who the greatest wrestler of all time was, most people will tell you Ric Flair. Again, we're back to the fact that Flair was a 16-time world champion, which means he *lost* the belt sixteen times. The guys who worked for Crockett — Rock 'n' Roll Express, Midnight Express, the Road Warriors — they didn't win every match! Rock 'n' Roll lost a shitload of matches with all the fuck-finishes. It was just amazing how the guys back then understood that, by losing, they were actually winning.

Any other memories of Chris Candido?
Only that he was a missed opportunity for me. In hindsight, Chris was a hell of a worker. I've seen videos of him working years after he worked for me ... and I missed it. I clearly missed it. The only time I ever had him work was in a battle royal-type situation. He was an add-on. I missed it. I used to see Sunny every once in a while at autograph shows and we'd talk and laugh about it. Yes, Candido and Sunny are two talents I missed for sure.

Unlike a lot of people, when you got out of the business, you got *out*. But did you have your ear to the ground and hear about all the deaths of young guys like Candido?
I was up on that only through the Internet. When I left the business, from Jan. 18, 1992, on, I didn't watch wrestling, I didn't attend wrestling, I didn't read the wrestling newsletters, I didn't read the wrestling magazines. I wasn't involved in any aspect of wrestling until 2009. During that 17-year period, I ignored it all. Now, I kept in tune enough to know when major things happened, like Owen Hart's death. I read about Candido and one of the Pitbulls [Anthony Durante], but I only learned about things like that through social media. I didn't talk to anyone and I didn't follow the business.

Johnny Hotbody lost a "hair vs. hair" match to Tony Stetson. Did Stetson plan to get his hair cut short anyway?

I'm not sure, but it was their idea. You know, the one thing that I took advantage of was the creativity of the local guys. They recognized that the programs had to end somewhere. They would end in a steel cage match, or an *I Quit* match... which I did with Drake and Winters one night at Temple University. [March 31, 1990] The one blow-off match I couldn't do was a "loser leave town" match. That used to work in Memphis all the time when a guy was leaving a territory ... and they *always* had guys leaving that territory. (laughs) Unless a wrestler was retiring — and my guys were all in their early 20s, so they weren't retiring — I couldn't do a loser-leave-town match because they lived and worked in Philly. I couldn't do it with the big names, either, because everybody knew they were only there for one night, or two at the most.

Did Stetson shave Hotbody's head, or did he just sort of hack it up?
He started to cut it, then we went into a fuck-finish.

You booked Kevin Von Erich just one time.
Yes. I had Kerry in before I had Kevin. When Kevin walked into the back, the first thing he said was, "*Kerry sends his regards.*" A few years ago, I met Kevin's kids, Ross and Marshall. The first thing *they* said to me was, "*Kevin says aloha from Hawaii.*" That was a cool moment. The three of us talked for a bit and then they called Kevin. Kevin actually remembered working at the Civic Center and remembered tagging with Chris Adams.

Who came up with the names for your shows?
That was me. When I decided to promote four major shows a year, I realized that they would be seasonal, so that's when I came up with Autumn Armageddon, Summer Sizzler, etc.

Did you read *Wrestling Observer Newsletter* at all?
After I got out of the business, never, but before that, yes. I don't remember *ever* paying for a subscription. Carmella did when we did the radio show. I haven't talked to Dave in more than 30 years, but I don't remember ever being a subscriber.

Did he ever print anything you didn't like?
Oh, all the time.

He would print TWA results, but most of the things written about you were letters sent in by readers. They either loved you or they hated you.
Yeah, I was polarizing, no question. Some of the guys loved me and thought I was the greatest thing since apple pie. I know there was a lot of scuttlebutt written about me when I left the business. My philosophy was, it didn't matter if people loved me or hated me. If they were writing about me, I was winning. I didn't care what people's opinions were. I certainly didn't change anything I was doing because of anyone's opinion, one way or the other.

Did I have an ego? Sure, I did. Did my ego get in my way? Yeah! Absolutely. No doubt about it ... because nobody was doing what I was doing. It wasn't until towards the end did I understand that I was trailblazing. I never watched a single ECW [Eastern/Extreme Championship Wrestling] show, but people tell me that ECW probably wouldn't have happened unless I had done what I did. Who knows, though? There were a lot of creative guys out there and Paul E may have hit on the idea himself. All I did was recognize the fact that independent promotions were all doing different things. I wanted to blend them all together, which is why, on my shows, you got a blend of this, that, and something else. I was just creating a little niche for myself.

I mean, people said there was too much action outside the ring, there was too much blood. I just kept telling myself, "*That's just one person complaining about the action outside the ring."* I probably could have found 900 other people to write letters telling Meltzer that TWA was the best thing on earth since apple pie. I had some people complain so much that I told them, *"If you don't like what I'm doing, don't buy a ticket."* Now, I do believe that if you bought a ticket, then you had the right to your opinion. I won't hold it against you. But if you don't like what I'm doing, then just don't buy a ticket.

Which brings up a topic I wanted to cover. In Wrestling Observer Newsletter, several letters appeared in "The Readers' Pages" column with people saying they liked your shows, but they didn't like the format because, as soon as the wrestlers got outside the ring, everybody stood up and the people in the back rows couldn't see what was going on.

Yep. We got that complaint a lot, and to be honest, I didn't care. What I learned — especially about Meltzer and his letters, or whatever — was that for every person that writes, there's a hundred that don't. People write about the negative, but they never write a letter saying, *"This was the best thing I've ever seen."* They're always going to pick on something they didn't like. In fact, they might like 95 percent of a show, but they'll write a letter that focuses on the five percent that they didn't like.

For example, I had a match with Jerry Lawler and Terry Funk, which was an audience participation lumberjack match. [March 2, 1991] We picked tickets out of a hat and we did a total shoot on that. I believe we had twelve fans who were selected to be lumberjacks. Well, that meant that 2,000 people *didn't* get selected, so the following week, I started getting phone calls to the radio show. They started right in ... *"That wasn't a shoot. You had the tickets you wanted to pick in the bottom corner of the hat."* Or whatever! The radio people told me that, for every phone call, there's a hundred who don't call, so if you get a phone call with somebody complaining, there's a hundred people who don't call to complain, and most of them must have thought the show was great. Sure enough, as time went by, we started getting way more of the positives than the negatives.

I have to admit, we also got complaints about being too violent. *"That's not a place for kids."* Okay. *"There was too much blood on your show."* Okay. *"There was too much violence outside the ring on your show."* Of course, my response to that was, a ring isn't going to hold a legitimate feud.

In other words, when I was on the radio, I always walked that fine line of kayfabe. I didn't want to expose the business, so I'd play stupid. *"How am I supposed to*

Terry Funk on the mic | Sept. 15, 1990   Photo by Dr. Mike Lano

confine guys to the ring? If they go out of the ring and I disqualify them, the matches will be over in no time." So, yeah. There were people who would complain. And keep in mind ... when we did our big shows at McGonigle Hall, there was no second story. Everything was on the first floor. There were risers, but when Eddie Gilbert and Cactus Jack would go out of the ring, the people on the other side really couldn't see what the hell was going on. So one of the things I did was, I told the wrestlers to work all four sides as much as they could. I had a show at Penn Hall [Aug. 3, 1991] with Buddy Landel against Austin Idol. I told them to do the whole match outside the ring, but I had them brawl all over the building so everybody had an opportunity to see the action up close.

We really didn't get a lot of complaints, but there was a *lot* of discussion on the radio about how the promotion was growing, and how we were being talked about by people nationwide. And the complaints never bothered me. I looked at it like, if that many people are talking about me, then that's a good thing. On the radio, I actually encouraged our listeners ... if you're concerned about bringing your child to a wrestling show where there's violence, don't bring 'em, and there were people who wouldn't bring them because of that. On the other hand, there were people who brought their kids *because* of that. The other thing is, back then, there was no Internet. There was no YouTube. If you wanted to see my show, you had to be there.

As a rule, wrestling fans were excited about the style of wrestling we presented. I knew from day one that we had to be completely different from the WWF ... and Crockett, for that matter. They had just phenomenal matches and I knew I couldn't compete with that, but the WWF or Crockett didn't have the brutal stuff we did. That's the one thing about professional wrestling. You always have to keep pushing the envelope.

Now, keep in mind, I was trying to establish myself at the same time that I was working *with* Crockett, and many of the boys at Crockett saw me as a meal ticket because I had all these lunches and I paid the guys cash. So, I was promoting the NWA at the same time that I was promoting what would eventually become TWA.

Did you ever get into an argument with a fan over anything specific?
No. The only complaints I ever got was because my shows were too long. I started at eight o'clock, when I probably should have started at seven or seven-thirty. My shows ran three hours and we had times when we were up against the curfew. So if there were any complaints, it was because I had too much talent on my show or it ran too long. And they were right.

Three hours is a long time to sit for anything.
Three hours was too long.

I'm surprised you never booked Bob Armstrong, or any of the Armstrongs, for that matter.
No, I never dealt with those guys. It was weird because they were great workers, but they (pause) ... again, I don't think they would have sold me a ticket. It's really weird because, back in the day, I was a frickin' mark. I brought in some of the guys because *I* wanted to see them. I had a match with Adrian Street and Jimmy Valiant, right? [Philadelphia, Sept. 15, 1990] Now, up here, nobody knew who the hell Adrian Street was. He never came north of the Mason-Dixon Line, but I liked Adrian. I wanted Adrian and Miss Linda on one of my shows.

Now, Adrian didn't want to work up here, so to get him to come up to Philly ... I found out that Adrian loved carousels. He collected carousels, and I knew a guy in Pittsburgh that was a big-time carousel collector. I'm talking about an actual carousel itself. I'm not talking about a toy. I got Adrian on the phone and told him

I wanted him to come up to the show. Before he could turn me down, I said, *"By the way, I also want to hook you up with a guy in Pittsburgh who collects carousels."*

Adrian went to Pittsburgh first and met with the guy. I don't know if he bought anything or not, but he came to my show afterwards. Well, by the time I got Adrian and Valiant, they were both over the hill. Jimmy's time was over and nobody except the real smart marks in the front row knew who Adrian was, so even though they were the third match on my [nine-match] card. Adrian came out to his music and the two old guys went at it ... and it was awful. It was awful! Adrian didn't sell me a single ticket. I didn't have one person say, *"Oh, wow! You're bringing Adrian Street in! I wanna see the show!"* But I got to meet Adrian and Linda. (laughs) Funny story, in the back before the match, Jimmy says to Adrian, *"Don't put me in a hold I can't get out of, okay?"* (laughs)

As far as the Armstrongs go, they just didn't appeal to me. I wasn't high on Jeff Jarrett, either. I knew Jeff really well from our Memphis trips, and I liked him, but I never had him come up to do a show. By late 1991, I cut back on the number of big-name talents I brought in because my guys were getting over. Where I had been having eight matches, with four of them being major matches and four local matches, I was doing eight matches with a main event and seven local matches. That's what I would do today, but back then, my super shows were exactly that — *super shows* — and I just didn't want to give the fans any less than that. That's the reason why guys like the Armstrongs just didn't appeal to me. I didn't think they could sell tickets.

Cactus Jack vs. J.T. Smith | Dec. 4, 1990
Photo by Craig Prendergast

Philadelphia, Pennsylvania: Dec. 4, 1990
Original Sports Bar
- CN Redd beat Johnny O
- Ghetto Blaster beat The Titan (kayo)
- Michael Bruno beat Glen Osbourne (dq)
- Mr. Sandman beat Wild Child
- D.C. Drake & Larry Winters beat Jimmy Jannetty & Rockin' Rebel
- Cactus Jack beat J.T. Smith
- Fall count anywhere
  Tony Stetson beat Johnny Hotbody

On Dec. 4, 1990, you promoted your first show at the Original Sports Bar. It was your first show with mostly locals on the card. The only big-name was Cactus Jack.

In theory, I was going to do well with that show because most of those guys were, basically, working for me for free because they were guys from the school. Everybody got something ... a few bucks. I had referees. I had a ring. I mean, it cost me money, but there were many different levels of experience on that card. And yet, people will say that those shows were phenomenal.

That seems to be the first time D.C. Drake and Larry Winters teamed up together at one of your shows. They had a long-standing feud before that. Explain how the transition came about.

The thought process was simple. We did everything we could with the two of them. There was nothing left to do, so Larry suggested that we put them together as a tag team. Larry was the head dog, and eventually it grew to include Johnny Hotbody and Don E. Allen. We called them "The Dog Pound." But it was simply done out of necessity. It was time ... and it worked! We did the Dog Pound similar to what the Freebirds used to do. We would use any combination of two out of the four.

The Dog Pound | Larry Winter, D.C. Drake & Johnny Hotbody

In January 1991, an independent promotion in Pittsburgh called themselves Tri-State Wrestling Federation. They used different talent. Did you know about that, and do you know if they were playing off of your name?

I never knew about them until you sent me your notes the other day. That's a good example of how things were back then. They were 280-some miles away and nobody outside of Pittsburgh even knew they existed. I remember going to the various towns in Memphis with Lawler, and the fans had no idea that they were seeing the same show that had been in another town the night before. There was no scuttlebutt, no social media, no video. You tell me there was another Tri-State promotion in Pittsburgh, and even *I* didn't know about it until now.

Regarding video, did Rob Feinstein sell videos of TWA matches at your shows?

No, he never sold them at my matches. He shot the matches with a handheld camera and sold videos later on, through the mail I guess, but I never saw a dime for them. Again, I wasn't savvy on the business aspect. I was a one-man show having a good time. Of course, Rob made a career out of that stuff.

I would guess it was because of you that he got his start in business.

Oh, yeah. In fact, I did a shoot interview for him a few years ago. I don't know if it did or didn't sell. Who am I? I also did a podcast a few years ago with Glen Osbourne, Bay Ragni — who was Chubby Dudley — and Dave Cujo, who wrestled as Cujo the Hellhound. They all told me that I was the guy who kicked off their careers. They all wrestled for 20 years or more and thanked me for being the motivation behind what they did.

Philadelphia, Pennsylvania: January 28, 1991
Original Sports Bar
- Johnny O beat Glen Osbourne (dq)
- CN Redd beat Wild Child
- J.T. Smith drew The Bounty Hunter
- Bam Bam Bigelow beat Mr. Sandman
- Taped fist match
  The Titan beat Ghetto Blaster
- Texas tornado match
  Rockin' Rebel & Jimmy Jannetty beat D.C. Drake & Larry Winters
- Stretcher match
  Johnny Hotbody beat Tony Stetson

Bam Bam Bigelow hits Mr. Sandman with a dropkick
Jan. 28, 1991
Photo by Craig Prendergast

Wild Child leapfrogs CN Redd at the Sports Bar
Jan. 28, 1991
Photo by Craig Prendergast

Mr. Sandman chokes Tony Stetson
Original Sports Bar | Feb. 24, 1991
Photo by Craig Prendergast

Philadelphia, Pennsylvania: February 24, 1991
Original Sports Bar
• Johnny Hotbody & CN Redd beat The Pitbulls
• Bam Bam Bigelow NC Crybaby Waldo (double dq)
• D.C. Drake beat Rockin' Rebel
• Glen Osbourne beat Johnny O
• Midgets
  Little Louie beat Pepe Gonzalez
• Tony Stetson beat Mr. Sandman (dq)
• The Bounty Hunter beat Michael Bruno
• Battle royal
  Winner: Larry Winters

Larry Winters pounds on Jimmy Jannetty
Original Sports Bar | Feb. 24, 1991
Photo by Craig Prendergast

10 TWA Phone Call from The Sheik

Philadelphia, Pennsylvania: March 2, 1991
Winter Challenge II, Pennsylvania Hall (Civic Center)
att. 1,735, gate $32,629
- Special attraction
  Al Perez beat Stan Lane
- Ringmaster Rumble, winner meets D.C. Drake
  for the TWA title
  Winner: J.T. Smith
  Other entrants: Don E. Allen, Bulldog Brower Jr., Michael Bruno, Cry Baby Waldo, Ghetto Blaster, Hoss, Jimmy Jannetty, Johnny O, Glen Osbourne, Rick Perez, CN Redd, Rockin' Rebel, John Rock, Sabu, Sandman, Wild Child & Larry Winters.
- Russian chain match
  Ivan Koloff beat Manny Fernandez
- Falls count anywhere in the building
  Cactus Jack beat Eddie Gilbert w/valet Veronica Lane
- Goodhart Delivers
  The Sheik w/mgr. Bulldog Brower NC Abdullah the Butcher (double count-out)
- Barbed wire match
  Tony Stetson beat Johnny Hotbody
- TWA title match
  J.T. Smith beat D.C. Drake w/Woman (dq)
- Fan participation lumberjack match for the USWA title
  Terry Funk* NC Jerry Lawler

Notes:

The $32,629 gate was one of the largest ever heard of for an independent show.

The main event didn't go on until after 11:00 p.m., so it was hard to get a reaction from the crowd, who had already seen everything from ref bumps, hotshot finishes, and juice in every match.

When the undercard wrestlers tried to pull them apart, Sheik (who had a blade on every finger) bladed each person one by one.

Drake was the Tri-State champion. Larry Winters ran in wearing a referee shirt and attacked Smith after a ref bump.

Goodhart knows wrestling

A regional wrestling fanatic, Joel Goodhart one day hopes to be known as "the Dr. Ruth of wrestling."

The 37-year-old Philadelphian has his own wrestling radio show, wrestling training school, wrestling league and wrestling fan club-travel agency.

Here is some of what he does:

Radio. Each Saturday from 8 to 9 a.m. Goodhart takes phone calls from fans on his "Rasslin' Radio" show on WIP (610/AM).

School. If you have $2,100 and pass your wrestling audition, Goodhart will train you at RingMasters Wrestling School. "We take one out of every eight who try out," he says.

Fan Club. For $19.95 a year you can become one of the 1,500 members of Goodhart's Squared Circle Fan Club. You get a membership card, button and invitations to luncheons honoring pro wrestlers. Eating at the luncheons is extra. Club members also can take bus trips to East Coast matches and other tours to see regional wrestling. Call (800) 272-7754 for information.

GOODHART

| Pro wrestling | Tri-State Wrestling Alliance's Winter Challenge II, Civic Center | 7:30 p.m. $12-$15 |

On March 2, 1991, you promoted a show with Terry Funk and Jerry Lawler on top. You drew a reported $32,629 gate, which was the largest gate ever heard of for an independent show. WCW promoted in Philly a month later and only drew 1,700 people. Do you remember anything about that?
  Absolutely. I had a super lineup that night and I expected a huge crowd, but it far surpassed my expectations. I really couldn't believe it. That was the night we had twelve fans as lumberjacks. Their job was to put Lawler and Funk back into the ring if they went out. Funk wanted to kill a couple of them. Those guys took the job real serious. It was a total shoot. Later, when WCW came in and drew about half of what I did, I was stunned because they had all that TV to promote their product. We drew almost double their gate on nothing more than radio and word of mouth.
  Now, the $32,000 gate was the good news. The bad news is that the show cost me $35,000. I actually lost money on that show. Meanwhile, Crockett drew 1,700 people and made a profit. What was happening at that point was — keep in mind that I was out of the business a year later — I was only beginning to understand what sold tickets. I was also getting concerned about the money drain. The more I spent, the more I lost. For all the people who give me so much credit for being a great promoter, the smaller, independent promotion that ran shows and drew 75 people ... they made money! They were a whole lot smarter than me. The lesson I had to learn was, you're in business to make a couple of dollars. Those guys were smarter when it came to business than I was. Yes, I beat Crockett, but Crockett's show that night wasn't that great, and beating Crockett didn't pay my bills.
  Back then, in the state of Pennsylvania, the athletic commission always published the gate, so Vince and Crockett knew I had a $32,000 gate. Neither of them called me, though, to tell me that I was hurting their business. I would almost bet that they knew my business would eventually implode. One of the things I had hoped for was for Crockett to call me and say, *"Let's do something together,"* but that never happened. At one point, I tried to get D.C. and Larry booked onto a Crockett show, but it never happened. Another time, I told Elliott Murnick, *"Look, you guys have eight matches. You provide the top four, I'll provide the bottom four."* I thought they were actually going to bite, but it never happened.

Did you ever hear anything from WCW or the WWF regarding your shows?
  No. WCW knew about us, obviously, because I was using their talent a lot. The boys never had a problem with us because I was booking them. Every time Crockett came to town, I had lunch with one of their guys. Back in those days, they didn't have agents, so it was all a bit easier. Again, I had been Crockett's eyes and ears in Philadelphia, so they didn't bother me. I never got heat from Vince or any of his guys, either. I heard stories all the time about Vince and this and that, but I never heard from any of those guys ... none of 'em! I never got heat from Vince. Now, I did have a few people who told me that Vince thought I was a problem in Philadelphia. On the other hand, Vince had me ring announce for him a few times because I was on the radio. I met Vince for all of two seconds one time, although he wouldn't remember me. Vince was the guy that I firmly believe ... look, Vince is a billionaire. He did something right. He knew that when I was badmouthing him on the radio, I was giving him free publicity. The answer to your question is, I had no heat with the big offices. Carmela and I actually flew down to North Carolina one time and met with Crockett. I had zero heat, and in hindsight, that's amazing because I was a problem.

Speaking of Carmela, did she ever come to your TWA shows?

No. What's interesting is, I saw her a few times after she got out of the business. She couldn't believe I brought in the talent I did and she knew a lot of the guys. But, no. She never came to the shows.

You would think she would have given how close you were with your business and everything.
You would think. Now, that being said, I also got the impression from Carmela that she wasn't there because, once she wasn't involved, she was now "a fan," and she didn't want to be the sitting-in-the-front-row kind of thing. No, she never came to a single match.

Did you ever have talent you wanted to bring in, but when you called them, they said Crockett or Vince had told them that they couldn't work for you?
Nope. At least not in the context of your question. I had Nikita on one of my shows after he signed [with WCW] and I had Cactus on a show after he signed [with WCW]. They both told me that their contracts forbid them to get into the ring because they could get hurt. They *were* allowed to do something *outside* the ring, so they did that. But the direct answer to your question is ... no.

Did you pay them less than what you normally would since they couldn't actually wrestle?
No. I paid them exactly what our agreement was. They were drawing cards.

Regarding local talent, you didn't promote weekly, so did *you* have any rules regarding wrestlers working for other promotions in the area in and around Philadelphia?
I used to tell the guys, "*If I don't have a show, go work!*" There was one thing I insisted on. If you wanted to work for me, and if I was going to guarantee you spots on my cards, then you had to let me know what you were doing with the other independent promotions.

It wasn't like the old days when promotions ran every night of the week and promoters could dictate that their talent couldn't work for another promotion.
No, it wasn't. I couldn't tell a guy that he couldn't work and make money. Other promoters may have done that, but nobody ever called me up and said, "*So-and-so promoter says I can't work your show.*"

So you had no problem with talent working for rival promotions in the area.
What I did was, I said, "*Here's the deal. If you're going to work my cards, there are two things I require. One, if there's a show running the same night my show is running, I win. Second, if you work somebody else's show, you've gotta protect what we're doing.*" In other words, if you're a heel with me, you can't be a babyface for the guy down the street. If you hold the belt with me, you can't get beat in the other promotion. You can do a double disqualification. That's fine, but you can't go lose in the other organization and then come back here as the champ. Of course, the nice thing back then was, Pittsburgh never knew what happened in Philly.

Other than the people who read the newsletters.
Well, yeah. That's correct. Another thing about Meltzer, he would take the PWI ratings and publish them in the *Observer*. So, on the good side, Meltzer gave us notoriety. On the bad side, he exposed the business more than anybody. The real key for us when it came to those ratings was, it gave us (pause) ... think about this. Picture a page in PWI. Bob Smith used to come to all our matches.

Who is Bob Smith?
Bob was a writer and editor of PWI. That one page in the PWI had the Top Ten of the WWF, the Top Ten of the NWA, Top Ten World Class, Top Ten Pacific

Northwest, Top Ten Memphis, Top Ten Florida, and Top Ten TWA. That put us on the same level with all the biggies ... and Bill Apter came to all my shows.

Anyway, those were the deals I had with the guys. I had my major shows and all the smaller shows. If you wanted to work every show, I'd put you on them, but you were expected to protect my end of the business.

I'll give you an example of the trust I had with my talent, and the trust they had with me. Mick Foley [as Cactus Jack] had an open contract — not a paper contract, but a handshake contract — for every show I promoted. Every show! Mick worked almost every show I had during my first year of promoting. In his book, *Have a Nice Day*, he mentioned my name on 12 pages. I mean, he saw me at the time as a big-time, independent promotion. Buddy Landel ... every show! Now, Buddy lived down south, so he couldn't come up to every show, but he knew that if he wanted to work any of my shows, the door was always open.

Judging by the lineup, I can understand why the March 2nd show cost you so much. You had a *lot* of top talent on that show.

When I got ahold of Eddie Farhat [The Sheik] and asked him if he would come in and work with Abdullah ... he was pretty much retired by then, you know, and I don't know if you know his story, but Eddie was never able to fly on airplanes. He got himself banned from every airline in the United States, so he had to drive. Sheik didn't like to drive, so he would have Sabu drive him. Sabu was his nephew. That's how Sabu came to work for me, because he was there anyway. The first night Eddie came in, we were sitting there in the back and Eddie and Abby asked me, "*What do you want?*"

I said, "*What do you mean what do I want?*" I said, "*I want you to give me the most violent match ever! The guys from the magazines will be here, so do your thing! I want it to be memorable.*" I didn't even tell them how much time I wanted. For the most part, with Abby and Sheik, their matches were eight minutes long and the post-match was 25 minutes.

It was funny because the fans were booing the match when Abby and Sheik were inside the ring, but as soon as they took it outside, they applauded. Not too long ago, one of the things I was talking with the boys in the back about was that I could never get enough stuff outside the ring, and I'm sure people say I overdid it. I get that, but I used to have this saying that everybody in the building will have a problem with seeing at some point during the show, so having the wrestlers go

The Sheik vs. Abdullah the Butcher

outside the ring and fighting all over the arenas, even the cheap seats got to see some action up close. Now again, in hindsight, I probably overdid it, but when people came to my show, they weren't sitting in their seats for long. Then they would go to Vince's show where everything was so damn sterile. I mean, it was just so obvious. I had to do something different.

That was the only time I got attacked by any of my wrestlers. You can see it on the video. Sheik was blown up and couldn't breathe, so he went back to the dressing room. Abby wanted to keep going, so he yelled for him to come back out. I went back to get Sheik, but he was done for the night. Abby wasn't through, though. When I came back to tell Abby that Sheik wasn't coming back out, he attacked me. He threw me to the ground, kicked me a few times, and gave me a head butt. It looked like I was getting mauled. I have to give props to Abby because I never felt a thing. I just played dead. The only thing I worried about was when Abby punched me and my glasses flew off. If my glasses got broke, I wouldn't have been able to find my way home. Luckily, I found them and grabbed them.

I always marveled at how the fans could ... what's the saying, suspend their disbelief? Years ago, Vince made himself the star of the show. Then Shane and Stephanie [McMahon] got involved as heels and people hated them. The fans all knew that the McMahons were controlling everything. They knew that Hunter, Steph and Vince were writing the checks to the talent. But for whatever reason, the fans could separate their minds from that and get into whatever storyline they were being fed.

That's one of the reasons why I never got involved as a talent. I was on the radio and everybody knew I was the guy who promoted the show. Everybody knew I was paying the guys. So what could I do? I couldn't be a heel in the ring and then a babyface the rest of the time. On the radio the weekend after Abby attacked me, I said he had been fined $5,000 by the state athletic commission. You would think that Abby would want to kill me the next time he saw me, but the next time I brought him back — and the people all knew that it was me who booked him — the next time I brought him back, I was the ring announcer and I stood next to him in the ring. Sure, my ego took over when I wanted to be a ring announcer, but I never wanted to get involved in the actual action.

Abby *always* gave the fans their money's worth. One night — and I always get the matches mixed up, so I'm not sure when this was — but Abby got onto the stage (pause) ... now I remember! That was the night Abby knocked Rebel down and Rebel kept getting up. Abby was pissed! Everybody was coming out to try to save Rebel and Abby was knocking *everybody* down. I'll bet he knocked down 15 of my guys. The smart ones didn't get up.

Think about this. It's weird because this has been coming up on the podcasts I do. Think about this one. I told Abby that I wanted the Sheik. Those guys don't give out phone numbers, so Abby calls the Sheik and the Sheik calls me for work. What are the odds of the original Sheik ever calling anybody?

I wouldn't bet on those odds.

Me, either, and yet, Sheik called *me*. I remember answering the phone. "*Hello?*"

"*Joel Goodhart.*"

"*Yes.*"

"*This is the Sheik.*" He didn't say, "*This is Eddie Farhat, the Sheik.*" He said, "*This is the Sheik.*"

Amazing.

He says, "*I understand from Abby that you wanted to find me. Well, now you found me. What's going on?*"

I told him, and he told me that he had heard about what I was doing. I said, "*I want to have an Abdullah-Sheik match.*" I did want that, but what I really wanted was a Bruiser Brody match, but he had passed by that time. Brody was on one of my first shows, but that was before TWA. I told Sheik that I wanted him to come in and he said, "*Fine, no problem.*" Then he added, "*Can you put Sabu on the card?*"

I had a battle royal, so I said, "*We'll put him in the battle royal.*"

What I didn't know at the time was that Sheik didn't fly, so he needed a driver to bring him to Philadelphia from Detroit. That's why he wanted me to book Sabu.

What do you remember about the Sheik being kicked off the airlines?

All I remember him telling me was that he had to drive from Detroit because — I believe it was United Airlines, but don't hold me to that — but when he got on an airplane, he was in character. He was a wild man and a heel. When he walked into the airport, he was a bad guy. When he got onto a plane, he was a bad guy. I remember him telling me that he had been banned from every airline in the United States, which was why Sabu was driving him from Detroit. Now, Sabu wasn't supposed to be on my card. I only booked him because he brought Sheik. I used him in the Ringmaster Rumble. It was the first time he worked heel. He also did a run-in to help separate Abby and Sheik. When he got into the ring, Sheik hit him in the face and the blood gushed. If you watch the video, Sabu flies into the ring, literally. He runs down and dives into the ring. It's classic stuff.

That match has legendary status. From what I understand, Sheik cut everybody who came into the ring.

You can see in the video, Sheik gigs Jimmy Jannetty. It was the first time Jimmy ever got cut. The one thing about Eddie, he kayfabed 24/7. I can't imagine him going into a restaurant and having dinner without gigging someone. (laughs) Oh, he played the part to the hilt.

When we first met, we shook hands. I'm sure you know the wrestling handshake, which is like a soft ...

We always called it the fish handshake.

Yeah. Today, nobody knows the fish handshake. To this day, when I meet someone, I'll give them a limp handshake because that's the way we always shook hands. Of course, they don't know I'm going to do that, so they give me a firm handshake and crack the bones in my hand. I don't know where all that started, but Sheik ... my god! Talk about a handshake. I didn't even feel it.

We used to call it "the office" because it let people know that you were smart to the business and worked loosely.

For a long time, I didn't understand why the guys shook hands so loosely, but over time, it dawned on me what that signified. It's like guys who scrape their shoes off before they get into the ring. There's no real need for that, but it's their way of showing that they respect the ring. It's traditions like that that keeps the old-school alive.

When it came to booking them, were Sheik and Sabu hard to deal with?

The answer is no and no. The Sheik was a pleasure! He gave me his price and I agreed to it. These guys were not idols to me, so I wasn't star struck or anything. When I called Eddie to book him, he knew who I was. Now, he knew of me through Abby, obviously. If you remember, Bulldog Brower worked some of my shows as a manager and he lived in Delaware. Brower had a real name in the Philly area because he wrestled Sammartino many times. Brower told Sheik about me, too. One of the things I used to do with guys — in this case it was Abby — was say, "*Look, I'm going to call Sheik to see if he'll appear on my show. Can you call him and grease my wheels?*" I did that with other guys, as well, so when I called them, they knew who I was and they knew a little about my background. Do you know what I called their match?

No.

Goodhart Delivers. It was the match that everybody wanted. One of the things I laugh about is, that was one of the matches that I got some notoriety for, but the only reason I got the notoriety is because I was stupid enough to pay them. I paid Eddie. I paid Abdullah. They did the match, but in reality, it was nothing special. Yeah, it was interesting, but both of those guys were more or less over the hill. Eddie was *really* over the hill. But I had no issues with either Eddie or Abby.

I don't think Larry [Winters] had trouble, either. He didn't have to give them a finish or anything other than how long he wanted them to go. Their matches always ended the same way. The match ends with a double disqualification or a double count-out, and when everybody boos because they think the match was too short, they go on 15 minutes longer doing their shit outside the ring.

Picture this ... I brought them back six months later in a barbed wire, cage match. We didn't *need* barbed wire. We just added that to make it sound good. They came out of the ring and outside the cage — and I don't remember the exact order — Terry Funk comes out, Kevin Sullivan comes out. They're out there with Abby and the Sheik. Are you kidding me? That was absolutely awesome! Terry and Kevin had already wrestled. I loved Kevin. Kevin comes out wearing my TWA shirt. On the back of the shirt was "We Wrestle. We Brawl. We Do It All." You can see it on the video. He's wearing my TWA shirt. It was classic. Cactus comes out, Sabu, my local guys. My plan was to bring Terry and Kevin back against Abby and Sheik. I went out of business before that could happen.

Where did the phrase *Goodhart Always Delivers* come from?
I wanted people to remember me as someone who always delivered what he promised. It's funny, but I've never gone by the name Joel. People just call me by my last name ... Goodhart. So, Goodhart Delivers. If you watch the video of Abby and Sheik on YouTube, you'll see the beginning of what I called Goodhart Delivers. It was just my way of saying that I deliver on all my promises.

How did Bulldog Brower come to work for you?
He got in touch with me. I grew up watching Bulldog Brower. When I met Bulldog for the first time, I was like a little kid. I had spent time with Bruno and now I was spending time with Bulldog Brower. Oh, my god! I was still a mark for some of those guys. Well, Bulldog had a son who was trying to get into the wrestling business. The kid didn't really look like a wrestler and I don't think he really wanted to be one. But Bulldog called and asked me to book the kid, so I put him in a couple of Ringmaster Rumbles. Bulldog came to a couple of shows, but I don't think I paid him a nickel. He just wanted to be

Johnny Hotbody & Bulldog Brower
Photo by Dr. Mike Lano

there. I had him come out with Funk. I had him come out with Sheik. Ninety percent of my fans had no idea who Bulldog Brower was, but it was a big deal to the ones who knew. He lived in Delaware, so it was a bit of a drive for him to come to my building. Sadly, I just couldn't figure out a way to get him involved in a match, so I never really utilized him the right way. Regardless, having Bulldog Brower on my shows was just ... when I think back it, I never really realized how much of an impact those guys had on me.

I know there have been times in our discussions when you mentioned that you weren't really a mark for the guys, but at other times, you definitely were. We all were at times.

The kicker is, I have no pictures of me and Bruno, no pictures of me and Bulldog, no pictures of me and Funk. I have one picture of me and Abby that was taken at Rob Feinstein's event several years ago. That's a shame because those guys were walking gods to me. But I was never a fan from that perspective. Growing up, Spiros Arion was my guy. I never met him, but if I had, I'm pretty sure I would have acted like a three-year-old. As a promoter, though, I wanted those guys to see me as a peer. Today, the wrestlers are having their pictures made with all the other wrestlers. The business has changed. I didn't want Jerry Lawler to see me as anything other than a guy who was in the business. I would go to Memphis and stand there talking to Lance Russell, Jerry Lawler, and Austin Idol ... and never had my picture made with them. It was amazing to me when I was in Vegas and Dr. D asked if he could have his picture taken with me! But, no. I was never a picture guy. They worked for me. I was their employer.

You brought Nikita back on March 2, 1991, but he didn't wrestle. What's was that all about?

That was when he signed with Crockett, and one of the deals was that he couldn't do anything in the ring. He was scheduled to do a tag match with Ivan on one of my shows. Nikita, obviously, didn't want to come to the show. Why come to the show if he wasn't wrestling? But I had never had a no-show, so I asked Nikita to come in street clothes. *"Don't bring your gimmick. Just show up in street clothes. If you want to get involved in the match outside the ring, fine, but at the very least, I need you to come out to the ring."* He actually came out to the ring and made an announcement. He got the microphone, thanked the fans, and walked out. Of course, he came back out during the match and got involved a little. Nikita was the guy I told you about who kept his accent with me all the way to one of the matches in York. On the way home he lost the accent. He really worked the kayfabe until he knew who and what you were.

One of the things that really jumped out at me regarding the March 2nd show is that you had Stan Lane and Al Perez on the opening match!

(laughs) That all started when they were guests on *Rasslin' Radio*. I don't remember whether it was Stan or Al — I'm pretty sure it was Al — but one of them said something to the effect of, *"We'd love to be the first match on the card."* I wasn't sure just how to respond to that because I didn't know where they were coming from. After a few seconds of silence, I said, *"I'll make that happen."* Well, Jim Cornette was at the Civic Center that night as Stan's manager and he was the first person to get into the ring. I had a big-time main event — Al Perez vs. Stan Lane — in my opening match. (laughs) You can see that match on YouTube.

That whole card was amazing.

I think that card was the pinnacle of my career. I mean, that show was absolutely stacked from top to bottom. Stan Lane was one of those guys who knew how to make the other guy look great. What's funny is that Stan was a much better wrestler than Al Perez, but he made Al look like the better wrestler.

One more question about March 2nd, Eddie Gilbert had a valet named Veronica Lane that night. Who was that?

I have no idea who she was. I know I didn't pay her. She got involved in the match. She threw her shoe into the ring or something, but I have no clue as to who she was.

Eddie and Missy were divorced by that time, so Veronica may have been his girlfriend.

I didn't know anything about the guys' social lives. I didn't *want* to know anything. I had enough trouble maintaining my own social life. (laughs) I was the employer, they were the employees, and I thought it was important to keep that separate.

That brings up another subject. Buddy Landel stayed in my apartment for a few days and Buddy would go out to Bennigan's, a restaurant near me. He'd get drunk as shit and he'd call me or Marla to come pick him up. I swear to God, he was drunk all the time. Buddy had the bleached, white hair, so people kind of knew who he was. Now, I don't know if Buddy was married at the time or not, but the one thing I realized was that wrestlers, when they were by themselves, they seemed to be very lonely people. They needed the attention of a crowd. When they went out to the ring, they took on their persona. They fed off of that. But when they were off by themselves, they were very lonely. I firmly believe the reason people get drunk, or high, is because they're lonely. Wrestlers felt alone because they saw themselves as either being used or noticed because of who they were. The well-known guys couldn't walk into a restaurant and just sit down for a nice dinner because fans would want to talk to them.

That's the downside to fame.

Absolutely. I could do the ring announcing and take off the tux ... and nobody knew who the hell I was. But if you were Andre the Giant, you couldn't walk into a restaurant and eat dinner. You can't go to the store. You can't go to church. Everywhere you go, people know who you are and they want to get to know you.

It's different today. Most of the wrestlers could go to a restaurant to eat and nobody would know who they were. Sure, they're on national TV, but how many people are wrestling fans? I mean, today, wrestling fans make up a tiny percentage of the population. In the old days, when people had fewer entertainment choices, pro wrestlers were celebrities, and everybody knew them. There *were* times when people would recognize me and would bother me while I was trying to eat, but I took it as an ego thing. I thought it was cool, so it didn't bother me. But I can't imagine being Ric Flair going to Applebee's for dinner in Charlotte. I seriously doubt that happens. Can you picture Ric Flair going to a movie? Again, that's why so many of those guys are lonely, not to mention the fact that some of them have to live their gimmick. Flair is a prime example of that. When he was on TV, he wore expensive suits, $600 crocodile shoes, and $13,000 Rolex watches. When he was away from the arenas, he was still dressed to the nines. He was always in character.

Now, guys like Arn Anderson and Tully Blanchard could go to a restaurant. Not in Charlotte, but they could go to a restaurant up here and most people wouldn't know who they were. When they were with Flair, though, everybody made the connection. JJ Dillon has that problem. Everywhere he goes in Delaware, everybody knows who he is.

I used to laugh when I thought about the guys back in the day when they traveled by car. Can you imagine Bruno Sammartino in a car with three or four other wrestlers and they pull into a tollbooth on the Pennsylvania Turnpike to pay a toll. What are the odds that the guy collecting the toll didn't know who they were? (laughs) Of course he did. The guys who had it made were the guys who wore the hoods [masks] or makeup. When they pulled away from the arena, they took off the hoods and nobody knew who they were. Bill Eadie, who wrestled under a hood as the Masked Superstar and under makeup as Demolition, could walk into any place he wanted and nobody would know who he was.

Dwayne Johnson would be having dinner somewhere and fans would walk up, pull up a chair, sit down, and start talking to him.

That's it ... but their fame also brought them a lot of perks. Many times, the restaurants would pick up the tab. Bernie Parent, who used to be the goalie for the Flyers, always talked about the fact that he hadn't bought dinner since 1975. Whenever he goes into a restaurant, somebody picks up the tab. Well, there's another side to that. When somebody picks up the tab, why don't you take a little time to talk with them?

Did you ever become good friends with any of the wrestling fans?
I don't know that I was *good* friends with anybody. I never went out for a beer with anybody because I didn't drink. I realized early on that people wanted to be my friend ... not because they *wanted* me as a friend, but because I could be the conduit to them getting to know the other guys. So, some of them used me. I get that, but at the same time, I used them.

Larry Winters and I were friends, and I became friends with most of the local guys because it was just natural. Of the main event guys, I would say I had a friend in Jerry Lawler, Austin Idol. I was friendly with Abby, but we never socialized. In my book, when you're true friends, you had a lot of contact outside the ring, away from the arenas, and based on that, the answer would be no.

Was there anybody you enjoyed hanging out with outside of the business?
A friend outside the business? No. Even to this day, I don't have any really tight, buddy kind of friend. That was just never me. If I'm home alone on Saturday night, I don't call somebody and say, "*Let's get together.*" No, the answer is no.

Looking back on all the guys you booked, which wrestler would you say you admired the most?
Terry Funk.

Why was that?
Terry was a professional. Now, again, part of that is due to the mark in me. The guy was a former NWA world heavyweight champion and now he's working for me. So, there I was again, with my ego getting in my way. When I booked Terry, I never had to worry about anything. I never had a concern that he wouldn't show, or that he wouldn't give me 110 percent. To me, Terry was the man.

Now, it's interesting because I had a couple of idols. Jerry Lawler, obviously. I don't know how many times he worked for me, but to me, Jerry was one of the easiest guys to work with.

I'd like to go one step further. Terry Funk was 1-a, Jerry was 1-b, Abdullah was 1-c, Cactus Jack was 1-d, Buddy Landel was 1-e. I have too many number ones, and the difference between 1-a and 1-b is so infinitesimal that I can't really say that I favor one over the other. However, however small the gap, Funk, to me, was the top of the top.

I looked at them all as my friends. I don't know if it was a two-way street with some of them. I'm sure some of them just looked at me as a good payday. But I do know that Kevin Sullivan was a two-way street. He even mentioned me in one of the shoot interviews he did. Eddie Gilbert did the same thing. I honestly think Funk, Lawler and Abby were two-way streets. I'll never know for sure. All I know is that I was blessed to have been surrounded by such great talent.

Langhorne, Pennsylvania: April 12, 1991
Neshaminy High School gym
- Bob Orton Jr. vs. Paul Orndorff
- Bam Bam Bigelow vs. Buddy Landel

Cactus Jack | 1991

Newark, Delaware: May 4, 1991
Police Athletic League benefit, att. 300
- Abdullah the Butcher NC Bam Bam Bigelow (double dq)
- Eddie Gilbert beat Buddy Landel
- Tri-State title match
  D.C. Drake* vs. J.T. Smith (dq)

Originally scheduled as:
- Bam Bam Bigelow vs. Buddy Landel
- Terry Funk vs. Eddie Gilbert
  Terry missed the show due to an injury (legit)
- The Sheik vs. Abdullah the Butcher
  The Sheik worked a show in Euclid, Ohio.

Note: Terry Funk injured his back in Osaka, Japan, on April 6.

When you were promoting, did you have many opportunities to do charity work or visit hospital patients with the local boys?

We tied every one of the big shows into Variety Club. Every one of those shows was a fundraiser for them. I used their insurance, so it was a two-way street type thing. Crockett's guys visited the Children's Hospital, which was right across the street from the Civic Center. Every once in a while, if we got there early and everything was set up, we'd go over and see some of the kids. Some of the local guys did that on their own. One time, the Variety Club Muscular Dystrophy telethon aired at the same time we were wrestling, so we asked some of the guys go over to the TV taping and make an appearance. I helped out with that telethon almost every year. We did some small fundraising things, like a bowl-a-thon and a mini-golf tournament.

North East, Maryland: May 10, 1991
att. 600
- Tri-State title match
  D.C. Drake beat J.T. Smith (dq)
- Honkytonk Man beat Paul Orndorff
- Cactus Jack beat David Sammartino
- Bam Bam Bigelow NC Abdullah the Butcher (double dq)

Philadelphia, Pennsylvania: May 11, 1991
St. John Neumann High School, 26th & Moore Streets
Tickets $11 to $15
- J.T. Smith beat The Sandman
- Larry Winters beat Jimmy Jannetty
- Johnny Hotbody & CN Redd beat Pitbull #1 and Pitbull #2
- Dog Collar match
  D.C. Drake w/Woman beat Tony Stetson
- David Sammartino beat Cactus Jack
- Paul Orndorff beat Honkytonk Man
- Abdullah the Butcher NC Bam Bam Bigelow (double dq)

Pro wrestling	Tri-State Wrestling matches, St. John Neumann High School, 26th and Moore Streets	8 p.m. $11-$15

On May 11, 1991, Herb Abrams had Cactus, Bam Bam and Paul Orndorff booked on a TV taping. During the negotiations, they had told him that they were booked that night on your card in Philly. He told them he would start the show at 7:00 p.m. and put them on early so they could get to your show in plenty of time. Well, the show didn't start until 8:00, so Orndorff and Cactus both left after having a heated argument with Abrams. Do you remember that?

I do recall something along those lines. It was interesting because Herb was trying to do what I did, but he had a lot of money behind him. He also had TV. I always told people that I was, at the time, the second-largest independent promoter in the country, and I always thought of Herb as being the first. But Herb and I never spoke and we never had any history. There were no telephone calls, no meetings at a convention. I never spoke to Herb, never had a meeting with him. The one story that came back to me was that Herb didn't pay what I paid, so I think when there were joint bookings, I tended to win out because of the payoffs. Yes, I do remember something to that effect, but I don't remember the details. Herb and I never, *ever* spoke.

What was your method of making payoffs? Did you send their money ahead of time, or did the guys trust you and wait to get paid at the shows?

I don't remember paying anybody in advance. Very often, I didn't have the cash until the night of the show. When I had the super cards and Ticketmaster was handling my ticket sales, they didn't settle up until three days after a show, so there were a lot of times when I had to pull money from my personal account and get reimbursed three days later. Again, guys like Bruno really helped make my reputation as an honest businessman. When he told me to send him his check, in front of all the boys, that really put me in good standing with everyone else ... and trust me, the word got around. A handshake agreement, even over the telephone, was all they needed.

One of the things you mentioned the other day was that you made payoff checks to the working name of the wrestlers.

Oh, yeah. I didn't write a check payable to Scott Bigelow. It was payable to Bam Bam Bigelow. Yes, I kayfabed it all the way through. I didn't write checks payable to John Charyszyn. I wrote it to Larry Winters.

Didn't they have problems cashing the checks?

No. I never had one person tell me that they had a problem cashing a check. Nope, not one. I think the guys were trademarking their names by then. I'm sure that Mick Foley was able to cash checks made out to Cactus Jack. Now that I think about, someone did tell me that the Iron Sheik had issues with that, but he never complained to me.

Johnny Hotbody & Larry Winters wear the Tri-States tag team title belts

Philadelphia, Pennsylvania: May 18, 1991
Spring Spectacular, Pennsylvania Hall (Civic Center), att. 1,253, gate $22,311
Tickets $12 to $25
• Tri-State title match
  D.C. Drake* beat J.T. Smith
• Winners to be first Tri-State tag team champions
  Johnny Hotbody & Larry Winters beat Jimmy Jannetty & Rockin' Rebel
• Al Perez & Buddy Landel beat
  Stan Lane & Steve Keirn w/mgr. Jim Cornette (reversed decision)
• Ringmaster rumble
  Winner: Pitbull Spike
Also: Bulldog Brower Jr., Michael Bruno, Cry Baby Waldo, Delaware Dynamo, Johnny O, Glen Osbourne, Rick Perez, Pitbull Rex, CN Redd, John Rock, Sandman, and Tony Stetson
• Terry Funk vs. Dick Murdoch
  Funk was injured. Joel got Dory to replace him, but Murdoch missed his flight.
• USWA unified world heavyweight title match
  Jerry Lawler beat Honkytonk Man (dq)
  Dory Funk Jr. interfered.
• Jeff Jarrett vs. Eric Embry (canceled, working in Nashville that night)
• Barbed wire match
  Cactus Jack NC Eddie Gilbert
This was said to have been the best match on the card. Cactus' fiancé came down to ringside to check on him since his face was caught in the barbed wire and they had problems getting him loose.
• Paul Orndorff beat Rick Rude (dq)

You've mentioned a few times that you never had a no-show, but I found a few shows where it looks like you did. At Pennsylvania Hall on May 18, 1991, Al Perez and Austin Idol were supposed to wrestle Stan Lane and Steve Keirn. Austin didn't show, so Buddy Landel took his place.

I don't remember that, but I'll make a note to check it. I keep writing these little notes because you keep bringing up shit I don't remember. I don't recall that one at all, but I'll check it out. It's funny, but I don't remember Steve Keirn ever working for me.

I don't know if this jogs your memory, but it was reported that Perez refused to do a job that night.

No kidding? I swear to God, you just totally befuddled me. I don't ever remember meeting Steve Keirn. Holy shit. You're telling me I used Al Perez twice. I know I had him once, but I don't remember having him twice.

You booked Perez three times ... on Sept. 15, 1990, and March 2 and May 18, 1991.

You just shocked the hell out of me. I don't remember that at all. Al was inexpensive. He came in from Florida. One of the times he was with me, one of my advertisers wanted him for an appearance. Again, hindsight's 20/20, but if I had been able to get enough dates out of him, which was tough to do, I would have put Al over.

May 18 wasn't a good night. You also had Terry Funk booked against Dick Murdoch. Terry was injured in Osaka on April 6 and was out with a back injury for more than two months. You brought Dory in to take his place, but then Murdoch missed his flight. Dory didn't have anybody to wrestle, so he

just did a run-in on Lawler's match with Honky Tonk Man. And finally, you had Jeff Jarrett on the card against Eric Embry, but they didn't show up because they were working in Nashville that night.

No way. I've always told everyone I never had a no-show because that's what I remember. And I don't remember *ever* booking Dick Murdoch. Did all come from Meltzer?

Yes. It was all tied in with the story about the disagreement between you and Missy.

While I don't remember booking Murdoch, I'll go one better. I don't recall ever meeting him and I don't remember talking to Murdoch about anything. I have to look at the notes on all that. I'm really curious about it. I'd love to see the information you have on that. Again, one of the things I was most proud of was that nobody ever did a no-show on me. That story about Murdoch just doesn't resonate.

We'll work on that and maybe we can figure out exactly what happened. There was a report after that show about Buddy Landel being fired after an incident at a hotel bar. Do you remember anything about that?

No! (laughs) Every day, you bring up something I don't remember. I don't recall ever having an issue with Buddy Landel. Buddy Landel first worked for me in Newark, Delaware. [May 4, 1991]

It had something to do with a girl arguing with Buddy. Apparently, she was drunk and hit him with one of her shoes. In return, he blew his nose on her.

Well, that would be Buddy. That I could actually believe, but I don't remember it at all.

Someone wrote a letter to the *Observer* and criticized you for hanging up on callers to *Ringside Radio*. One caller asked about Bobby Heenan's arrest, to which you said, *"Why discuss it?"* and hung up on them. On the same show, you hung up on another person who asked about a WWF card in Japan.

(laughs) There was a radio personality on WMMR-FM by the name of Howard Eskin. He shot from the cuff and didn't shy away from controversial statements. I tried to copy him a little, but it didn't work for me. The thing is, there are questions that lead to nothing but boring answers. Regarding the question about the WWF, I made no bones about the fact that I was *not* a fan of the WWF, and half of the people who asked questions about the WWF were just asking them to piss me off so I would climb their ass on the radio. They got into me chewing them out over the air.

J.T. Smith takes a powernap before his match.

Photo by Dr. Mike Lano

11 — The Biggest Payday / The Smallest Gate

Philadelphia, Pennsylvania: Aug. 3, 1991
Summer Sizzler II, Penn Hall, att. 562
- Sandman beat Rockin' Rebel (8:26).
- Falls count anywhere
  Cactus Jack beat Eddie Gilbert (16:13, 1st of 3 falls)
- Ladies
  Luna Vachon beat Madusa Micelli (dq)
- Stretcher match
  Eddie Gilbert beat Cactus Jack (9:50, 2nd of 3 falls)
- Handicap match
  Cry Baby Waldo beat The Spoiler & Rick Perez (4:23)
- Buddy Landel DDQ Austin Idol (12:17)
- The Fantastics (Rogers & Fulton) beat Stan Lane & Jim Cornette (14:33)
- Elimination match, TWA title at stake, special referee Bam Bam Bigelow
  Larry Winters, D.C. Drake, & Johnny Hotbody beat
    J.T. Smith, Tony Stetson, & CN Redd (35:03)
Drake beat Redd, Smith pinned Drake to win the TWA title, Smith was counted out, Winters pinned Stetson
- Steel cage match
  Eddie Gilbert DDQ Cactus Jack (3rd of 3 falls)

I've held off on asking about the Cactus/Gilbert feud until now, but I'd like to really get into it ... in particular, the barbed wire match. How did you come up with the idea for that match?

I was really creative, but all three of us had input in that. The first time I put Cactus and Eddie together [Philadelphia, Sept. 15, 1990], they were actually the first match on the card.

That's correct.

If you watch that match, I think you'll agree with me that it sucked. Gilbert very much wanted to be a heel. Cactus was the face. When they came to the ring, they tried to work the crowd, but they couldn't make it work. Other promoters might have watched that match and not brought it back, but it was clear to me that they had fantastic chemistry. When I first put them together, I didn't realize that. Part of it was the fact that Cactus was really *over* up this way. He was *crazy* over. If you told Cactus, "*Give me twenty-two minutes,*" he gave you 22 minutes and he put it all on the line. He did moves for me that, to this day, when I watch the video, I sit back and say, "*Oh, my God!*" He put his body on the line. From what I understand, he has a lot of physical problems now, and I have no doubt that part of it came from him giving me his all.

I loved the idea of building a program because that was the method used by the old-school territories. They'd bring two guys in and built up their feud week after week after week. I didn't have the luxury of having them wrestle each other every week because I didn't promote that often, but I eventually brought them back.

Five months later, March 2, 1991, *falls count anywhere in the building* match.

Yes. Even though their first match sucked, the best part of the match was when they were fighting outside the ring, and that's what led to the *falls count anywhere in the building* match. I'm dead certain Philadelphia had ever seen anything like that, and again, watch the video and you'll see almost 2,000 people who never sat down. They followed Eddie and Cactus around the building. To be honest, it was a real safety hazard because some of the fans got *way* too close to the action. I had eight matches on that card and it was fourth from the bottom. Can you imagine a match like that being fourth from the bottom! When the match was over, I just *knew* those two guys had to come back in a main event.

And that's what they did two months later ... May 18, 1991. That was the barbed wire match.

Yes. The premise to the barbed wire was to keep them in the ring.

That was the night that Cactus got his head caught in the barbed wire.

I want people to realize that nobody — *NOBODY* — not even Larry, ever told Cactus to get hung up in the barbed wire. It was wrapped around his throat and he was having trouble breathing. Of course, the crowd was cheering because they thought it was all part of the show. While that was going on, Eddie piledrove referee Joe Zanolle to the mat and knocked him for a loop. He had to be carried out by the EMTs. Joe was okay, but he didn't want to admit that to the EMTs because it would kill the piledriver gimmick and possibly smarten them up. I'm not sure if Joe knew how to take a piledriver, but I do know that nobody will ever use a piledriver on me in a million years. No way! Sure, most of the guys are professionals and know what they're doing, but if they screw up one time, you're paralyzed from the neck down ... or worse! Joe's action says a lot about kayfabe back then. That was the rule we lived by. It just was. Today, it's gone. It no longer matters. But to Joe, it was always about the show.

In the back after the match, I told Cactus that I wanted to bring him and Eddie back again, and for whatever reason, the idea of a two-out-of-three-fall match kept coming up. In the process, Cactus came up with the idea of each fall having a different stipulation.

That match took place ten weeks later on August 3rd.

The first fall was a reprise of their second match ... falls count anywhere in the building. The second was a stretcher match and the third was a cage match. I went back and forth with the two of them and the deal we reached was ... they would get paid for three matches. That was Cactus and Eddie's biggest payday ever. Again, my figures could be off, but I'm pretty sure I paid them $350 per match, which means they got $1,050 each. Independent guys don't make $350 today, and they sure don't make $1,050. And the thing is, Eddie and Cactus earned every cent that night. They gave me — and the fans — our money's worth.

It's funny ... if you talk to Cactus today, he'll tell you that the matches he had with Eddie were a big benefit to him because that propelled him to the big-time. I'm not saying it was anything *I* did or my shows. It was what he did with his program with Eddie. Their pictures were in all the magazines and the matches were discussed in the dirt sheets. They helped propel him to superstardom.

The first problem I faced was the presentation of the matches. You can't have a stretcher match, have the bell ring, and go right into a cage match. First of all, if you're being carried out on a stretcher, how do you get right back up? Plus, we had to put up the cage! It was my idea to spread the matches out on the card. The *falls count anywhere* match was the second match of the night. Luna and Madusa wrestled next, followed by the stretcher match. The longest period fell between the second and third matches, which would — logically— give the loser of the stretcher match time to recover. The four matches that filled that time went somewhere around an hour, and when you add the cage setup and intermission, it may have been as much as two hours.

Eddie Gilbert vs. Cactus Jack

One problem I always had with a steel cage match was that it required about a 30-minute break, so it's always the last match on the card. Well, our shows were never designed to run for two hours, so when we started bringing the cage out, a lot of people said, "*Well, it's time for me to go.*" By the time the bell rang for the cage match, we probably only had 400 to 500 people in the building.

You had a cage match one night where you had the cage up from the opening bell. Was that because it took so long to set up?

No. That was the night we had the last blood battle royal. It was the first match on the card, so when the people came in, we already had the cage set up.

During the stretcher match, Eddie broke what was said to be a non-gimmicked bottle over Cactus' head.

Yep. It wasn't gimmicked. Eddie did that on his own. In fact, Eddie talks about it on a YouTube interview. He emptied a trash can in the middle of the ring, right on top of Cactus. He found the bottle and, for a split second, he thought, "*Should I or shouldn't I?*" After the fact, Eddie told me that his concern was that he could seriously cut Cactus ... or even himself. It was one of those ah-ha moment for the fans. Nobody expected him to do that, and when he did, nobody doubted that it wasn't a real bottle. One thing about Eddie and Cactus ... they had this eerie communication between them. They could talk to each other through their eyes. When Cactus saw Eddie pick up the bottle, he knew what Eddie was thinking, and he mouthed the words, "*Do it.*" And Eddie did. He nailed him.

My biggest fear was that — with the glass being real — that the shards would fly out into the crowd and cut somebody. All I could think about was getting sued because a piece of the glass hit them or a piece went into somebody's eye. Luckily, nothing happened that I'm aware of. But, no. That bottle was *not* gimmicked and the spot was not scripted. It was totally ad lib.

It's hard to believe that a bottle could actually break without fracturing the skull of the person who took the shot.

Watch it on video. It's scary ... but the place popped. The place actually popped. Watch the videos of Cactus and Eddie doing their thing. When you see the things they did in the crowd, it's a wonder that I didn't get sued by somebody. And the seats on the floor were moveable seats. By the end of the night, you were not sitting in the same seat. Abby and Sheik did the same stuff when they went onto the stage. Everybody — the whole crowd — ran towards the stage, then they had to go back to their seats. It was unbelievable!

What you said about the fans leaving before the cage match is true. Many of them left, not so much because it was late, but because they were burned out.

No question. It was overkill. People were leaving while we were setting up the cage. I'll tell you, when people came to my shows, they always got their money's worth. My goal wasn't to have eight matches. It was to have eight main events. My philosophy to the wresting fans was, get to the matches on time because the first match will be a main event.

That's amazing because that's the total opposite of how promotions were run in the old days.

Total opposite. My goal was to have the first match be a great match, and if people showed up late, they'd be really pissed. I'm one of those guys who, if somebody tells me to meet them at five-fifteen, I'm ready at five. That's just who I am. My father drilled it into me. "*If you're on time, you're late.*" I wanted people to get there early ... not because I wanted them to buy food because I didn't share in the food proceeds. My first match was a part of the show. I wanted eight main events.

Shifting to a completely different subject for a minute, did you ever get a cut of the concessions at McGonigle or Penn Hall?

I didn't get a cut in any of the venues. They got a cut of my concessions, though. In my contract, if I sold shirts, or whatever, in Penn Hall, they got 40 percent, so if I sold a $10 shirt, I wound up with six bucks. So, when I ran Pennsylvania Hall, the price of that $10 shirt jumped to $12 to help me recover some of the cost. If I remember correctly, I kept my concessions at McGonigle and they kept theirs.

Okay, back to Cactus and Eddie.

Now, on the night that Eddie and Cactus wrestled three times, it was absolutely exhausting to just watch them. At no point did I give them time limits. At no point did I tell them I need ten, 15, 20, or whatever. "*Just go do your thing.*" And nobody had to tell me that the fans were tired and burned out. I remember driving home that night. *I* was exhausted from watching them. Yep, those two guys gave us three main events during the course of the show.

The finish to the cage match saw Cactus taking a bump backwards from the top of the cage to the floor on his back. He was doing that insane stuff even then.

Cactus had matches with Eddie where Eddie would be on the floor and Cactus would jump off the ring and land on Eddie with an elbow. There were times when he just dove. He did a move one day — and Cactus told me afterwards that he had called the spot outside the ring — but he and Eddie were looking at part of the fence that surrounded the ring. You can see on the video ... Cactus tells Eddie, "*Toss me.*" Eddie throws him against it and Cactus flips over the fence and lands on his back on the concrete floor. I never had mats around my rings. There was none of that shit that Vince does where everybody is falling on carpet and padding.

Eddie and Cactus went outside the ring one night and got up on top of a table ... and one of them dropped the other with a piledriver, not knowing if the table would hold them or what would happen if the table fell.

A bloody Cactus Jack traps Eddie Gilbert against the cage.

I remember one time when Terry Funk was beating the shit out of Kevin Sullivan. [Philadelphia, Sept. 21, 1991] Kevin picks up Terry and drops him balls-first on the railing that surrounded the ring. I don't care how good a worker you are. At times like that, you can't protect yourself. You just can't. I think the hardcore things the guys did at my shows were, in part, their way of showing their appreciation for me overpaying them. It was amazing.

The cage match ended in a double disqualification when Eddie's brother, Doug, and Bam Bam Bigelow did run-ins.

Doug Gilbert wouldn't have sold a single ticket for me. On the night he was there, he came up with Eddie. He was just a throw-in. Now, whatever Eddie asked me for, I gave him. I never had an issue with Eddie, God bless him. He called me up one day and asked, "*Do you mind if I bring Doug and we'll work him into the show?*"

I said, "*Fine.*" So Doug was there, but I don't recall paying him. I may have, but I don't think I did. Eddie was simply trying to get his brother some notoriety for the magazines. We needed a fuck-finish for the cage match, so I let Cactus and Eddie figure it out. How many promoters do you know that tell their main event boys, "*Call it on your own*"? But that's how I ran things. I let the artists be artists. Go do your thing. At times I would tell them I needed 15 minutes, 20 minutes, whatever, but I never personally told them what I wanted or how I wanted it, except for the local guys. Larry came up with some ideas. That's the job of the booker. I was always of the belief that a promoter promotes, a booker books, and the wrestlers wrestle. Too many promoters try to get their hands into too much shit ... and that includes Vince.

If I remember correctly, Eddie Gilbert takes the microphone in the steel cage before the match starts and says if he loses he retires. Again, I didn't call for that, but when he said that, it scared me because I thought it meant that Eddie wasn't going to lose ... and in my mind, that meant *Cactus* was going to lose. I didn't know they had a fuck-finish planned with Eddie's brother and Bigelow in the mix. I knew Doug was there, but I didn't know how he was going to get involved. After all, how do you get involved in a cage match? But Eddie and Cactus themselves called that finish.

In hindsight, that three-fall match was a match that people still talk about today, and yet, if you look at the numbers from that night, it was my worst-drawing card.

As much as I thought they were main event, these guys really weren't main eventers. I don't think a two-out-of-three fall match has ever been done again ... at least not in the way I presented it, with the stipulations spread over a card.

You're correct about the attendance figures. For the record, of the four times that Cactus and Eddie met in singles, in 1990, the Sept. 15 card drew 1,500, March 2, 1991 jumped to 1,735, attendance dropped to 1,253 on May 18, and the two-out-of-three match drew just 562.

There you go. Of all the shows I promoted, this was the most disappointing. I really thought we'd sell out the building. I had smaller crowds, but those were later when I ran shows in the Original Sports Bar, and that was only because we couldn't get more than a hundred people in the building.

Why do you think attendance dropped so much?

First of all, my records show that we had 837, not 562. I guess we can probably get some official record because it was at the Civic Center, but the place has been refurbished, so I don't know if they still have the records. However, my personal records show 837. I've seen that number published.

The reason it dropped so much was, in Philadelphia, it was a summertime show, which was always tough. It was so blasted hot that nobody wanted to come out. My guess is that the heat was the culprit. The show was Summer Sizzler and it was hot as hell. The temperature that day was in the mid-90s. It was the worst drawing card that I ever had. Then, in the fall, when it came to Autumn Armageddon [Sept. 21, 1991], attendance went back up to 1500. However, looking at the bottom line, the two-out-of-three-fall match was a great idea, but it just didn't sell tickets.

I wonder why that was. It seems like it would have been a big deal.

It *was* a big deal, but quite frankly, what that meant was that Eddie Gilbert and Cactus Jack were almost half my matches. People just didn't think it would be that interesting, and in hindsight, I understand that. They missed out, though, because it was an incredible night of wrestling.

Even more interesting is the fact that attendance at your next show jumped to 1,524. Your shows normally drew anywhere from 1,200 to 1,700, something like that.

Yup. Those numbers ... again, my records show my numbers being more than 2,000, but that also included the freebies I gave out, so you may have the actual paid numbers, the gate numbers. It's interesting ... Penn Hall held 3,000, and if you see some of my shows on video, you know there's more than 1500, so I'm not sure those numbers are accurate.

That being said, the building was phenomenal. Like I said, the two-out-of-three-falls was the best show I ever saw. I will tell you, in hindsight, there was so much violence on that card. I'll also admit that, by the end of the show, there may have been no more than 400 in the building. The show went too long ... too late.

You can watch it on YouTube. Doug Gilbert did a run-in with Bam Bam Bigelow. Nobody in the building knew who Doug Gilbert was. I mean *nobody*. We never announced that Doug was going to be there. The smart marks figured it out, though. They knew what was going on, but nobody else knew who the hell he was.

My original game plan was to have Eddie and Doug Gilbert go up against Cactus and Bigelow. That's why I had Doug come out. When it came time to book it, though, for whatever reason, I couldn't get Doug.

That whole scenario is so interesting. The deal I had with Cactus and Eddie was that I paid them for three matches. Cactus talks in his book about it being one of his biggest paydays ever. What independent promoter ever paid $350 a match, and that was back in the early '90s! I told them both, *"I'll pay you for three matches as long as you give me three matches."* We used to have three-way telephone conversations, okay? There were no Zooms back then, so we had a phone conversation.

It was my idea to have two out of three different falls, but it was Eddie and Cactus' idea as to what the three falls should be. Falls counting anywhere in the building always worked with my group. Then they had the stretcher match and the cage match. Okay? They came up with the whole idea. They booked it all.

One thing I want people to understand is that — and I've already said this, but I want people to understand — by using the professionals that I used, I gave them the freedom to book all their own matches. Ask Lawler, Idol, or Cactus ... I didn't care what the finish was. I didn't care who went over. They worked it out between themselves. As an example, when Idol got pinned by Lawler, that was Idol's finish. Idol called that.

I read a report that you had an old-timers battle royal planned for Aug. 3rd, and two of the names mentioned were Bulldog Brower and Killer Kowalski. Was that really in the works?

That was something I wanted to do, but it never got off the ground.

Why not?

It was a matter of trying to get them all to come down on the same date. They all wanted top dollar, you know, and again, I get that, but if you have a ten-man battle royal and each guy is charging you $500, that's a really expensive match. Financially, it just wasn't feasible. The other thing I had to contend with was, who was going over? They all wanted to know who was going over and why. My plan was to put Brower over because he was working with me. Kowalski wasn't. And to bring Kowalski down and have him get in the ring to put Brower over ... that just didn't seem to be right. Kowalski was an old man by that time, too. You know, the devil is always in the details. Something sounds like a great idea until you try to figure it out ... and then it just doesn't work. Even if I had worked out all the logistics, I don't know if it would have sold any tickets.

I doubt it. You had a ton of talent already. You had the Fantastics there that night, too.

I talk to Bobby Fulton now and then when he does appearances. I was sorry to hear that Tommy [Rogers] passed away. I know I keep using the words *true professionals*, but that's what they were. They worked for me three times and they had great ring presence. Tommy was like Ricky Morton, although to a lesser extent. He was the guy the girls wanted to get to know. It was really strange when the Fantastics came in to work with the Midnight Express. It was in Philadelphia, and in my crowd, the Midnight Express were the babyfaces. What happened was, the people cheered for Tommy and Bobby when they came to the ring, but all of a sudden, when Midnight and Cornette came out, the people switched. Suddenly, they were for Cornette and Midnight. (laughs) Bobby and Tommy weren't sure what the hell to do.

And that was because Philadelphia was a heel town.

Exactly ... all the time. I had Lawler and Funk. They wrestled in Memphis and Lawler was the babyface. Lawler comes up here and everybody is cheering for Funk. When Cactus wrestled Eddie Gilbert, they were cheering Cactus. Okay? As a rule, whenever I had a heel and a babyface, the heel would get cheered. There's no arguing that. It happened all the time. And as much as wrestling fans *hated* Jim Cornette and the Midnight Express in the NWA, they cheered them in Philly.

It seems like it would be tough for the heels to do what they were supposed to do.
 Yeah, yeah, it was. It was tough. Cornette and Midnight were trying to be heels. Jimmy would do his thing on the microphone ... and everybody cheered. When Cornette stood on the second rope and waved that tennis racquet, everybody in the world booed him ... except in Philadelphia. In Philadelphia they gave them a standing ovation. So, yes. It was tough. That's why Lawler, Dave Brown and Lance Russell told our guys in Memphis that they couldn't cheer the heels. They were expected to boo them.

Jumping ahead to Aug. 3, 1991, when you were promoting your own shows, Jim Cornette teamed up with Stan Lane against The Fantastics ... Bobby Fulton and Tommy Rogers. The Fantastics were booed the entire night, and while the people were still booing, Bobby picked up the house mic and said something like, *"Okay, for all you kayfabe sheet readers, the Fantastics are the greatest tag team ever and you're too stupid to realize it!"* The booing continued and Bobby said, *"Thank you very much! We love you, too!"* Do you remember that?
 I don't remember that, but it would not surprise me. It's weird because I remember that match itself. They had such a difficult time because it went against everything they did down south. It just didn't work. Jimmy was running the match, and it was a classic match, and in theory, it should have been a *great* match, but it was difficult. The crowd didn't cooperate at all. It's funny that I'd remember something like that. There's a video of that show somewhere. If there is, I'd like to see it.

That's what was reported, but you never know. I can see Bobby getting frustrated because that must have been as hard for them as it was for the heels to be cheered while they were trying to be hated.
 I'd like to see a video of that.

At the August show, you announced that Eddie would return in September with his brother, Doug, against Bigelow and Cactus Jack. It ended up being a mixed match with Eddie and Madusa against Cactus and Luna, and it was reported that Doug was supposed to work against Bam Bam Bigelow in a "first blood" match. Why did it all change?
 A couple of things. Bigelow had signed with WCW. Then Cactus signed with Crockett. His contract stipulated that he couldn't work in the ring, so I kept him and Eddie outside the ring as seconds to Madusa and Luna. I couldn't have a standard tag match.

You made several other announcements that night, one of which was reported in the *Observer* as a strong hint that Flair vs. Terry Funk would headline his 9/21 show. Flair's name was never mentioned directly, but the implication was that Funk would wrestle against a champion whose name can't be mentioned for legal reasons until Sept. 21. Flair wasn't on that card. Did you really have plans for a Funk-Flair main event, or was that all just hype?
 No, there were plans. I had conversations with Flair. If I remember correctly, he had left Crockett.

Yes. He signed with Vince on Monday, Sept. 16, five nights before your Penn Hall show.
 I had spoken to Flair several times before that. It was not a signed deal, so I jumped the gun a little bit. When Flair left Crockett, *nobody* believed that he would go to Vince. And everybody knew that I was dumb enough to pay Flair his number to get him on my show. My recollection was that Flair wanted five grand. Back then, that was ridiculous, stupid money ... but I would have paid it. So, we

were having conversations. Can you picture Flair/Funk on a local independent show?

A few years earlier, Flair and Funk had the "I Quit" match on TBS. [*Clash of the Champions IX*, Nov. 15, 1989] I never would have put two main-eventers like them in an "I Quit" match because someone actually loses, but when Flair and Funk did that, you talk about a work of art! It was unbelievable! Funk did the job for Flair, and afterwards, Funk comes off looking great. That was when Gary Hart turned on Terry.

Anyway, when I was talking with Flair, he kept asking me, *"Who am I working with?"* So, my immediate thought was ... Flair against Funk. I never gave thought to him wrestling anyone else. The contracts, however, were never drawn up or signed. Funk was in, Flair was in, but we didn't get it done.

After you mentioned this to me the other day, I went back and looked at the video of the [Aug. 3] match. I never promised Flair/Funk, but I'm sure the fans chanting *"We want Flair!"* may have led to the confusion.

Well, in the Aug. 5 *Observer*, Meltzer wrote that Flair had agreed to at least one date that I know of with Joel Goodhart in September, so that put fuel to the fire. Meltzer corrected his statement in the next issue when he admitted that Flair's name was never mentioned directly, but was only implied. One other thing that may have led to fans thinking that it was a done deal is that, after making the implication about Flair, you said your trademark *"Goodhart always delivers!"* statement. You also announced that Keiji Muto and Jushin Liger would be working for TWA by the end of the year. Were there actual plans for that?
I started working with New Japan when I had Owen Hart against Takayuki Iizuka. I told them, *"You have two wrestlers — one match — that I want to have on my cards, and we'll bill it as a New Japan Pro-Wrestling match."* They saw me as a foothold into the U.S. market. Think about that! Who the hell was I? And yet, they were working with me to have a New Japan match. At the time, Jushin Liger was just over. Nobody knew Iizuka, but I was booking him against Owen Hart, so it didn't matter. At some point, if New Japan came in with their other talent, they'd get to call their matches, but as far as Takashi Iizuka went, they understood that Owen had to be put over. There was no issue there.

Just as a side note, if you ever watch that match on YouTube, the rope broke during the match, but when it was over, everybody in the building gave them both standing ovations. It was clear to me that smart marks knew what was going on, but the whole building got into it. I ran out at the very end of that match and I called Owen's name two or three times to a standing ovation. It was very cool. Nobody knew who the heel was, although everybody knew Owen. It was classic, working with a broken rope. But getting back to New Japan, I said, *"Give me Jushin Liger."* We had conversations at that point and it seemed to be a given that he would be working on one of my shows.

While they were trying to fix the broken rope, the fans were chanting "boring." Do you remember that? Did that worry or bother you?
No, because if you ever watch a scientific match, it's boring. The kicker was that there was no storyline to that match, and it wasn't the smart marks who were yelling "boring." It was all the other fans. As the rope was being fixed, the guys actually had to change their match around a bit to do the mat work. And the fans weren't chanting "boring" that long. I had a small number of guys at every show who yelled "boring" at everything. To those guys, it was just the thing to do. I remember the fans booing the shit out of Sheik and Abdullah because the match

Owen Hart flies off the top rope onto Takayuki Iizuka
Photo by Craig Prendergast

ended in a double count-out. [March 2, 1991] They weren't booing because the match sucked. They were booing because the match was over. But the booing stopped just as quickly as it started because Sheik and Abby fought outside the ring for another 20 minutes. If you watch the Owen-Iizuka match now, you'll see that it was a scientific match with a lot of moves, and some people find that to be boring. Even so, I'll bet you there wasn't more than 50 people booing. It wasn't that big of a deal.

As a whole, the match did get rave reviews. I think WCW had a business relationship with New Japan. If your association with New Japan had continued, do you think WCW might have balked at them working with you?

I don't know. If there was concern on their part, it never got back to me. My relationship (pause) ... and I forget the gentleman's name ...

Tokyo Joe.

Tokyo Joe. [Joe Daigo] I had breakfast or lunch with him on the day of the show. As we sat there and talked, I was thinking to myself, *"This is pretty cool. I'm sitting here with Tokyo Joe and we're talking about tonight's match. I wish somebody was here to videotape this."* It was weird because, on the one hand, I was smart enough to recognize that I'm just one guy in Philadelphia doing shows. On the other hand, I started to get the idea that I was really a player ... and I don't use that term loosely. I do believe that in 1990, 1991, I was a player in the wrestling business. I knew I would never have the stature of a Crockett or a Vince. That was never going to happen, but I do believe that in the independent world, I may have been the top independent promoter in the country. That being said, I think my promotion got more press than the Florida or Pacific Northwest territories, which were bigger companies by far. Word had spread about me and I had no problem getting talent. The guys wanted to work for me. Of course, they wanted to work for me because they would get a great payday. I knew that. I'm not stupid. But here I was having breakfast with Tokyo Joe, who flew 24 hours to be there!

This goes off-topic, but Dan Geringer, who wrote an article about me in the *Philadelphia Daily News* ... I think I told you the story about talking to Bruno Sammartino and Ric Flair. I was in my [insurance] office and Flair called to ask me for Bruno's phone number and to help put together something with Bruno. I didn't give him Bruno's phone number. Instead, I told him, "*I don't give out phone numbers to anybody."* When guys gave me their phone numbers, I protected them. They knew their numbers wouldn't be given out unless they gave me permission to do that, and they respected me for that. I called Bruno and helped negotiate a deal to get the *Halloween Havoc* thing together.

When I brokered that deal, I was doing things I never dreamed I'd be doing. I called Bruno and said, *"Ric wants to talk to you about something. Do you mind if I hook the two of you up?"* He gave me permission. Now, I had three-way calling capability in my office, so I called Ric. Ric answers and I said, *"Ric, I'm gonna put you on hold and call Bruno."* What? Who puts Ric Flair on hold? (laughs) Then I get Bruno on the line. I put *him* on hold. I hit a button and now they're both talking to each other. (laughs) There I was, sitting in my office in Philadelphia, Bruno is in Pittsburgh, Flair ... probably in Charlotte. They're talking to each other about the *Halloween Havoc* show that was coming up in Philly. Flair tells Bruno that they wanted him to be the special guest referee.

On Oct. 28, 1989, in Philadelphia, Ric Flair and Sting wrestled Great Muta and Terry Funk in a Thunderdome Cage Match with Bruno as the special referee.

They negotiate and (pause) ... I wish I could remember the number, but I think Bruno wanted $5,000. Flair agreed to it. I was such a fan-boy that I never even thought, *"What's my cut for brokering this deal?"* I was just glad to be a part of it. Bruno says, *"Okay, that sounds good. What do you need me to do."*

I'm sitting back saying to myself, *"I'm a player!"* At least I was in my own head. After *Halloween Havoc* was over, Bruno came to the back and thanked me for putting the deal together. I wasn't acting as Bruno's agent, though. I was just doing what I could to help make it happen. I helped make it happen behind the scenes. Flair never said thank you, but it was cool.

I didn't tell that story to anybody until I told Dan Geringer. It goes back to that line of kayfabe, but at some point, I just had to tell somebody. Today, if a promoter called John Cena, or whoever, the details of that phone call would be on the Internet 30 seconds after they hung up the phone.

Anyway, Dan wrote the whole story for the *Philadelphia Daily News* and titled it *The Gods Are Good to Goodhart*. To this day, when fans ask me what my number one moment was, it wasn't something that took place at a TWA show, or even a TWA show itself. It was that moment when I connected Bruno and Flair on the phone.

There's so many others things to talk about regarding that August show. What was the reason for Jim Cornette working?

If I remember correctly, Bobby Eaton was hurt. I haven't talked to Jim in a while, but he would probably remember. We talked about this earlier, but it was messed up. Everywhere Bobby Fulton and Tommy Rogers worked, they were *over* as babyfaces. They came out for my match and they got booed to shit. Stan and Jim Cornette were really over as heels, but with my crowd, they got cheered. Bobby and Tommy were walking around the ring trying to shake everybody's hands, but they were getting booed. That match was the complete opposite of what they normally worked.

Bam Bam Bigelow was a special referee on that card for the six-man tag. Was that because he had signed with WCW?

Yep. His contract prohibited him from wrestling, so we made him a referee.

Crybaby Waldo
Photo by Craig Prendergast

You had a guy on that card named Crybaby Waldo. He won a handicap match against Rick Perez and the Spoiler. Who was Waldo?

Crybaby Waldo ... God bless him. He's dead now. His name was Walt McDonald. He was a big, heavy guy, who later wrestled as Big Slam. Larry Winters came up with the idea to call him Crybaby Waldo. Here's this big 300-pound guy wearing a pink body suit and carrying a big baby bottle. Every time someone hit him, he'd go to his corner of the ring and cry. We thought we could make him into something. He was big enough. The crowd loved him. When he walked out, everybody started rubbing their eyes, like they were crying. He was trained at Ringmasters. He was still promoting wrestling shows a few years ago. He had a lot of health problems ... diabetes, heart issues. He was a very nice guy. But Crybaby Waldo was Larry's idea and Waldo ran with it. It was hilarious. It was promotion.

Every time we talk, when we finish, I look up my shows on YouTube. I watched one yesterday from beginning to end. Holy shit. That show drew 2,000 people, but as I watched, I found myself thinking, "*That show only drew two thousand people.*" Well, when I was on the radio, I had 22,000 listeners per quarter hour according to the Q ratings. How could I have that many listeners and only draw 2,000 people — less than ten percent — to one of my big shows! It pisses me off to think that, if I had drawn even 4,000 people — not even 20 percent — I'd still be in the business. Everybody was getting a free ride on my radio shows and not coming to my live shows!

You should be in the book business. It's no different. Most wrestling fans talk about how much they love wrestling, but they won't open their wallets and support people like you.

Well, I already told you that I know I'm not getting rich off this book. If we make something, fine. If not, at least my story is out there and maybe somebody can learn from my mistakes. I can't tell you how many wrestling fans have said to me, "*You did all this stuff! You worked with all those superstars! You have got to write a book!*" That's where I came up with the idea to do this. That's when I hooked up with Dan Murphy.

I'm thankful for that because his encouragement really set the stage for what we're doing now.

Yeah! How many guys will be able to say they have a book co-written with Scott Teal?!

We talked about Al Perez. Who was Rick Perez?

Joel & Dan Murphy

Rick was trained at Ringmasters. We gave him the name because he looked similar to Al, but he was much smaller. I think his real name was Rick Petine.

What about your parents? Did they ever go to any of your shows, and what did they think about what you were doing?

They never went to a single show. My father and mother thought I was nuts. I had let my hair grow, my beard grow. I had turned into an individual they never expected. Even though he never went to a show, my father was supportive. He got up every Saturday morning to listen to the radio show. He had no idea what I was talking about, but that was his kid on the radio. My mother, on the other hand, thought I was crazy. My cousin got married on a Saturday night and I couldn't go because there was a Crockett show at the Civic Center ... not a TWA show, a Crockett show. There was a line my mother didn't think family should cross, and missing a wedding for a wrestling show was that line. You know, in hindsight, she was right. The Crockett show wasn't that important. The show would have gone on without me. They could have found another ring announcer.

Now, when my promotion started getting bigger, my mother kind of bought into it. However, she never let up with the *"I can't believe you threw away your career and your family."* She was more upset that I was getting separated than what was going on with my career, but I think my mother saw through everything. I think she realized that I would never be able to make a career out of wrestling, so she figured she'd just let me play and I'd eventually come to my senses.

My father, on the other hand, would sit down and talk with me about it. I'd tell him my dream of opening up a wrestling franchise. I used big brushstrokes to paint him a picture of my plans. He believed in me. My father was a podiatrist, and whenever he'd talk with patients, he'd tell them about his kid being on the radio. "You need to listen to Joel on Saturday morning." I doubt any of them did because they weren't wrestling fans, but every once in a while, one of his patients would ask him, *"Does Joel know Hulk Hogan?"* or something like that. I'm sure there were a lot more wrestling fans than I knew about. There were people who woke up every Saturday morning to watch wrestling on TV, who were wrestling fans from afar, who never bought a ticket to a house show. Again, that was part of my downfall. *Rasslin' Radio* had thousands of fans, but they didn't buy tickets.

You've mentioned both Penn Hall and the Civic Center. They were the same venue, right?

Penn Hall is actually Pennsylvania Hall. The Philadelphia Civic Center included Pennsylvania Hall, so we were literally in the same complex where the NWA wrestled. Penn Hall was just a smaller venue. The Civic Center held ten to 12,000 people, while Penn Hall held 3,500 to 4,000.

Did you ever promote a show in the Civic Center proper? Or were they all in Penn Hall?

No, they were all in Penn Hall. The only thing I did at the Civic Center was co-promote the NWA shows, but the answer is, no, I never did shows in that part of the venue.

Why did you move there from McGonigle Hall?

I had to run on Saturday afternoons at Temple University because people just wouldn't go into that part of town at night, but it was tough because I was flying guys in. Having our shows in Penn Hall, which was in the same complex as Crockett, and on Saturday nights, both made us look more legit. We shared the same parking lot, the same complex as Crockett, as well. Penn Hall wasn't used too often. Big events took place either in the Civic Center or at The Spectrum, like Vince. Penn Hall was more suited to guys like me.

You also promoted at a place called the Original Sports Bar, which you mentioned earlier.
Sports Bar was a local restaurant. It only held around a hundred people. We ran the Sports Bar shows *in addition to* the other shows. The actual name of the bar was Philadelphia Original Sports Bar. It was located at 8th and Market Street. If it held 150 people, I'm saying that's a lot. It was an actual bar. The guy who managed the place was a wrestling fan, but I forget his name. Mike Schmidt, a Hall of Fame third-baseman from the Philadelphia Phillies, was part owner. He eventually got out of it.

Where did you get the idea to promote there?
I don't remember the guy's name, but he was a cop. They were advertisers on the radio show. The guy that ran the place asked me if there was any way I could have wrestling shows there on a week night. Sports bars were usually dead on week nights, so he thought it might bring traffic into his place.

The shows there were awesome. First of all, I couldn't use a regulation-size ring, so the guy who worked as the Bounty Hunter had a smaller ring. The ring just fit between two poles in the bar and the fans were sitting ... well, the people in the front row could literally put their foot into the ring. They were that close, which was scary because those people were really too close for some of the shit we did. On one side of the ring, the seats were literally rope high, so if somebody got thrown against the ropes, we had to make sure there was enough room between the ropes and the audience. The poles were monster poles that held the building up. There was no give to them at all, so, of course, we used them, too. (laughs)

You didn't use that ring at Penn Hall, did you?
No, no. Cheetah Kid, Ted Petty, it was his ring. Teddy's ring didn't fit in the Sports Bar, but Bounty's did.

Did Ted's mats look bad from all the blood that soaked into it each week?
He had them cleaned every week. I remember the mats being clean *every* week before the show started. Let me tell you about a ring that looked nasty. If you watch the videos from the Mid-South Coliseum in Memphis, that mat *always* had blood on it. I don't think they ever cleaned the damn thing.

Was your fan-base the same fans who went to your shows at Penn Hall and Temple?
They were your typical smart marks. It was a Tuesday or a Wednesday night, never a Saturday night, because the bar didn't need us there on a Saturday night. It was also the future home of what I had plans to create, which was a legitimate, physical wrestling hall of fame. It never really got off the ground, but the first person who was inducted into the Philadelphia Wrestling Hall of Fame was Superstar Billy Graham. I actually flew Billy in for the induction. Our original game plan was to have a wall of fame with pictures of the hall of famers. Our plan was to, once a year ... well, we never got to a second year. But when Superstar came in, it was phenomenal. Because it was a sports bar, it had big TV sets ... big screens. We showed the video of when Superstar beat Bruno in Baltimore for the belt. The place popped when he won the belt. Well, everybody knew what the result was going to be, but he was the original Hulk Hogan.

But getting back to the Sports Bar, when we did the matches there, they were crisp, stiff matches because, quite frankly, when people are sitting that close, you can't fake it. You just can't. The bottom line was, it was more exposure for the local guys. They would tell their friends and families that they were going to wrestle at the Sports Bar and they'd have six or seven guys show up. Larry booked all the matches. And you know what? Those guys got better and better because they were put into situations where they had to grow up really fast.

It grew to a point where we decided to have a Sports Bar champion, so we held a two-night tournament on shows we called "Bar Wars." On the first night, I had sixteen wrestlers and eight matches. We put the names of the wrestlers in a bag and the people in the front row put their hands into the bag and picked out a name. The first two names drawn out wrestled first, the second two wrestled second, and so on. It could have been face vs. face, heel vs. heel, partner vs. partner. When all sixteen names had been drawn, Larry and I ran downstairs and booked the card in such a way that Tony Stetson would be the champion. Of course, that meant that Cactus Jack would be putting one of my guys over. That was my one exception to us having a name wrestle one of my local guys. I don't think it took ten minutes to book the tournament.

The Dog Pound
Don E. Allen &
Johnny Hotbody

Aug. 3, 1991
The Original Sports Bar

Photo by Craig Prendergast

A masked Jimmy Jannetty gives Glen Osbourne a chairshot.

Aug. 19, 1991
The Original Sports Bar

Photo by Craig Prendergast

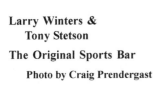

Larry Winters &
Tony Stetson

The Original Sports Bar

Photo by Craig Prendergast

12 Five-Foot Seven ... in Both Directions

Philadelphia, Pennsylvania: August 19, 1991
Original Sports Bar
1st round
• Tri-State Bar Wars Title Tournament
  Glen Osbourne beat Jimmy Jannetty
  Mr. Sandman beat Michael Bruno
  Johnny Hotbody beat Rick Perez
    Tony Stetson beat Rockin' Rebel (count-out)
  D.C. Drake beat CN Redd
    The Bounty Hunter beat Ghetto Blaster
  J.T. Smith beat Crybaby Waldo
    Cactus Jack beat Johnny O

Before the opening bell rang, my local guys were downstairs changing and Larry was telling them, "You guys get ready. The first match is in five minutes. Figure out your match. Here's what I need to happen." Larry always told the guys who was going over. The biggest concern was the length of the show. When you have an eight-match tournament, you can't have 30-minute matches, so the matches had to be eight to ten minutes, give or take. A couple of them only went three to four minutes, or whatever. Here's Cactus sitting in the dressing room with all these green guys. (laughs)

By the end of the night, we had whittled the field down to eight wrestlers. Of the eight men remaining, one of them was Cactus Jack, who knew he wasn't going to be the Sports Bar champion. There I was, spending $500, or whatever it was, to bring a name like Cactus Jack in ... and he was going to do a job. I was spending stupid money. I didn't need Mick there, but I had made a commitment to him and everyone else. If you can be at my shows, you're working.

Those guys worked harder than they ever had before. Every one of them tried to impress me. That was tough for some of them because they came directly to the bar from work, or they had to work the midnight shift after the show. Since the shows were on Tuesday, Wednesday, or Thursday nights, there were a few guys who couldn't make the bar shows because of their jobs. Cactus would drive down from New York. Buddy Landel was willing to come up. Of all the matches I promoted, they were probably the best because they were crisp and stiff. They were believable ... and the fans loved it!

The only dog match out of the eight first-round matches was Bounty Hunter against Ghetto Blaster. Ghetto was a true, green rookie who trained at Ringmasters. He couldn't wrestle for shit, but Phil did his best to make it a decent match. Phil — Bounty Hunter — knew what he was doing. After the match, Phil looked at me and said, "Thank God you're paying me." (laughs) He actually worked for free. I was paying him for his ring. I rented it for the two nights, so he got a nice payday.

We brought Ghetto in because we needed to get more black athletes in the mix. He was one of those guys who looked like he was a wrestler ... 5-foot-9 or ten. I never gave him a shot in a match, but I used him in battle royals and underneath matches.

He wrestled in a taped-fist match at the Sports Bar against someone named Titan.

Okay, so there you go. The Sports Bar was more of a tryout kind of thing. Titan has since died. He was 5-foot-7, but he was 5-foot-7 both directions. (laughs) The guy was solid, though. He was really put together. I don't remember that match, but neither one of them could wrestle. I probably put them together in a taped-fist match because they could just beat the hell out of each other.

Did Titan work for anybody else after you quit?

Not that I'm aware of. If he did, it was small indies. Let's put it this way. He might have been in the ring for somebody else, but he didn't wrestle for them. (laughs) Seriously, though, he was a nice guy and he lived near me. Louis something.

There was another guy named Johnny O.

Johnny O. His first name actually was John, but I don't remember his last name. Our original intent was to promote him as Glen Osbourne's brother, Johnny. At some point, he dropped the Osbourne gimmick and just went with Johnny O. He had freaky hair and was another small guy who started at the school. I don't know what he did after I got out.

I don't know why I haven't asked you about Glen Osbourne yet.

Nightbreed | Glen Osbourne-Bounty Hunter

Glen is still around. To this day, Glen gives professional wrestling the credit for paying his college bills. He was small when he trained at Ringmasters and I emphasized, over and over, that he needed to gain some weight. He tells the story of being on my Max Myers Playground show and seeing Iron Mike Sharpe, who was built like a tank. That was when he realized that he had to pack on some size. The deal I had with our gym students was that they could use the gym whenever they wanted. Glen would show up an hour or two early every night to work out. Today — and he's probably 50 years old — he's still built like a brick.

What can you tell me about CN Redd? I love the name.

Good old Chet [Czescik]. The one thing Larry Winters once told me was that redheads never make it in wrestling. (laughs)

Yeah. Bob Backlund didn't do well at all. (laughs)

(laughs) Larry said it was because, when they get hot, their faces get red. (laughs) Well, CN Redd was a redhead, but he was a great worker. I think it was Larry who came up with the name, likely because he just didn't like redheads. Chet walked away from wrestling a long time ago, but he was a classic ... a great worker.

Philadelphia, Pennsylvania: Aug. 20, 1991
Original Sports Bar
• Tri-State Bar Wars title tournament
2nd round
Glen Osbourne beat Mr. Sandman | Tony Stetson beat Johnny Hotbody
D.C. Drake beat The Bounty Hunter | J.T. Smith beat Cactus Jack (count-out)
3rd round
Tony Stetson beat Glen Osbourne | D.C. Drake beat J.T. Smith
Final
Tony Stetson beat D.C. Drake

Note: Tony became the first, and only, Bar Wars champion. He held the title until the promotion closed.

What jumps out at me from the Aug. 20 show is Cactus. I'm sure the fans thought he would make it to the second round of the night, and possibly lose in the final match, but Larry did the unexpected by taking him out in the first round of the night.
 (laughs) Well, I'm not sure we actually planned it that way. (laughs) If I remember correctly, Cactus wanted to get home early. I think he actually asked me something along the lines of, "If I'm not winning this thing, let me get out of here in the first round." (laughs) You can give us credit for it, but I can't honestly say it was what we had planned.
 If you think about it — if it was Cactus against Stetson in the final — there would have been no way that Stetson could have legitimately beaten Cactus. Stetson would have had to do a clean pin on him. You can't do a fuck-finish on a show like that, or in such an important match. No, Cactus got beaten by J.T. Smith. J.T. was phenomenal, and Cactus had no problem doing the job for him.
 Some part of what you said is true, though. Everybody came out the second night assuming Cactus was going to win the tournament. When he lost in the first round, they were completely in the dark as to what was going to happen.

That was smart booking. I'm impressed. The other thing that stood out is that Rockin' Rebel was one of your top guys and he did a job on the first night. Was there a reason for that, too?
 Nope. The one thing Rebel didn't have was ring savvy ... psychology. Larry never really liked him, either, and it was Larry who booked it. I'm sure there was a reason why Larry had him go out in the first round. I'm sure part of the booking was because the fans, at that point, kind of knew who my top guys were ... D.C., Rebel, Stetson, Sandman ... I couldn't have the second night being all my top guys. So who did Rebel wrestle?

Tony Stetson, and he lost on a count-out.
 There you go. I mean, it was somewhat of a fuck-finish if you will, and he lost to the guy who would ultimately be the champion. Yeah. In hindsight, when we booked those cards, there was logic to what we did. Larry knew the business. It's funny, but if you ever get into booking matches and you use local guys, you always worry about losing a local guy. Again, Rebel sold tickets. He was the one guy who sold the most tickets. To his credit, Rebel did everything we asked him to do. We rewarded him by making him the first TWA champion, and he loved that, even though he knew he would be wearing that belt for about 32 seconds.

Tony Stetson and Johnny Hotbody worked together a lot. Rockin' Rebel said that Stetson worked with Johnny because nobody else wanted to.

I don't that that was the case. I think it was more the way we booked the matches. I booked the feuds and Stetson/Hotbody had a certain chemistry, similar to Drake/Winters. Hotbody was a guy who put his body on the line every night. I've only seen Johnny a few times since I got out of the business. He had neck problems, he had back problems. He put it all out there. He was smart enough to know that Stetson had history, so he just rode the back of Stetson. But I don't recall anybody ever saying "I don't want to work with Johnny." If Rebel said that, I'm surprised.

Rebel said Johnny wanted to look better than the guys he worked with, but his matches would get sloppy, so the guys complained to you.

The thing about Johnny was, Johnny was small. One of the things you learn about independent wrestlers is that the main reason those guys didn't make it big is because they weren't 6-foot-4 and they didn't have the physique. I'll bet you Johnny was five-ten. One of the problems I had when I was a ring announcer at my shows was that I was taller than some of the wrestlers, but I certainly didn't have a physique. But if you saw Johnny on the street back in those days, you'd never know he was a wrestler. When he was in his ring gear, though ... well, he was put together. I think he was a roofer by trade at one time. No, when I booked the feuds, there was no reason to mix those guys up. Hotbody had more of a following than Rebel, so that may have been some jealousy on Rebel's part.

Did you have an actual title belt?

No, I never got a belt.

And you never changed the title. I think it stayed on Tony until you folded the business.

Yeah. He was the only guy to hold the title. Tony used to kid me all the time. "The only belt I ever held was the one I won in front of a bunch of drunks at a bar." (laughs)

Which brings me to the next question I was going to ask. Did it concern you at all about mixing alcohol with wrestling? Fans were wild enough without having the alcohol in them.

Well, the answer to your question is, I never worried about it. The bar owners may have had some concern initially, but we never had any problem. As a rule, wrestling fans weren't rich, so they didn't have a lot of money for drinks, but we didn't charge for the matches. We just asked them to eat and buy a drink.

For the most part, you made money at the Sports Bar?

Yeah! They were sold shows. The owner paid us for the shows. We had a lot of wrestling fans who drank, so they made it up in liquor sales. The fans wouldn't order food, though. Some of the fans might order a soda or something. I'd walk around and ask them, "Do me a favor. At least buy something from the bar." They didn't have to pay anything to get in, so the least they could do was show a little monetary support for the bar.

13  The City of Brotherly Hate

1991_09_21 Program lineup
Philadelphia, Pennsylvania: Sept. 21, 1991
Autumn Armageddon II, Penn Hall, att. 1,524, $27,000
• Last blood battle royal
  Winner: Sandman
Other entrants: Mr. Anthony, Ernesto Benefica, Michael Bruno, Cry Baby Waldo, Ghetto Blaster, Jimmy Jannetty, Johnny O, Glen Osbourne, Rick Perez, Rockin' Rebel, Sabu, and Tony Stetson
• TWA title match
  J.T. Smith pinned D.C. Drake w/Woman (12:48)
• Tony Stetson pinned Sandman (7:04)
• TWA tag team title match*
  The Blackhearts beat
    Johnny Hotbody & D.C. Drake (sub for Larry Winters) (16:03)
• Owen Hart pinned Takayuki Iizuka (21:40)
• Terry Funk DDQ Kevin Sullivan w/Fallen Angel (11:02)
• Eddie Gilbert & Madusa Micelli beat Cactus Jack & Luna Vachon (12:22)
• Steel cage match
  Abdullah the Butcher beat The Sheik (5:17)

Let's move on to your Sept. 21 show in Pennsylvania Hall, you had the Gilbert-Madusa vs. Cactus-Luna match. That was a hair vs. hair match, wasn't it?
 Yes. Before that match, though, Eddie Gilbert — and this is actually on video on YouTube — Eddie actually confronted Cactus, and I don't think this was planned. Maybe Cactus would tell you differently. I haven't talk to him in a while, but Eddie took the microphone and ...

Eddie Gilbert, before the match on Sept. 21, 1991.
> "You just wait a second, Joel. I want everyone here to know, of all the Philadelphia wrestling matches that we've had, the barbed-wire matches ... the last time we were here, we had a stretcher match, falls count anywhere in the building, a cage match ... and what did you do? You ran off to Atlanta, Georgia, and you sell your soul! You sell your soul! You sold me out, you sold every one of your fans out. I had the same chance you did, but you know what? I said, 'No-oooo!' You want to be on Channel 17, you want to be on CNN Center, you want to be a part of Jim Herd and his crew. Well, I've got one message ... one message for you to take back to Jim Herd and World Championship Wrestling. You can tell him to KISS MY ASS!"

That's when the fans started their "*Jim Herd sucks!*" chant.

Eddie Gilbert, after the match.
> "I want to thank you for one thing, and that's for being the toughest guy I've ever met in the ring in my life."

The Tri-State Wrestling Alliance
AUTUMN ARMAGEDDON II:
GORY, GORY, HALLELUJAH

Saturday, Sept. 21, 7:30 PM
Philadelphia Civic Center -- Pennsylvania Hall

!!! BARBED WIRE STEEL CAGE !!!
Abdullah the Butcher
vs.
The Original Sheik

FIRST BLOOD
Bam Bam Bigelow
vs
"Dirty" Doug Gilbert

BEAUTIES VS THE BEASTS
Mixed Tag Hair Match!
Eddie Gilbert & Madusa Miceli
vs
Cactus Jack & Luna Vachon
The person who gets pinned loses his or her hair

THE DEVIL MADE THEM DO IT
Terry Funk
vs
Kevin Sullivan
(with Fallen Angel)

NEW JAPAN
PRO WRESTLING

Owen Hart
vs
Takayuki Iizuka

TWA HEAVYWEIGHT TITLE MATCH
(Champion)
J. T. Smith
vs
(Challenger)
"Mad Dog" D.C. Drake
with WOMAN and
Devious Don E. Allen

TWA TAG TEAM TITLE MATCH
(Champions)
The DogPound
Larry Winters & Johnny Hotbody
vs
(Challengers)
The Black Hearts

THE BATTLE ROYAL OF ALL BATTLE ROYALS
ARMAGEDDON -- LAST BLOOD
Once a wrestler bleeds -- he is eliminated. The only man left <u>NOT</u> bleeding is the winner!
Featuring the stars of the TWA

Tickets $25, $15 & $12. Available at the Philadelphia CIVIC CENTER Box Office,
all TicketMaster outlets and the Squared Circle at 215-745-8315
For more information listen to Rasslin' Radio every Saturday morning from 8 to 9 am on 610 WIP AM

Cactus Jack, after the match.

"Hey! Hey! You want to stand there and call me a traitor for going to Atlanta. Well, just go ahead, but remember one thing. It's your own fault, because if it wasn't for you, I wouldn't be there! You tell all these people that it's your fault that I won't be back!"

I don't think Eddie and Cactus planned that at all. Cactus was great on the mic. I don't remember the storyline, but I remember one line he said. He says, *"All right, time for a Cactus Jack story. I'm a mental, social, and sexual loser."* Those aren't the exact words. I'll have to look it up, but it was absolutely hilarious. Again, that was part of Memphis. Memphis did a lot of mic work. Lawler used to do it all the time and all his lines were great. There was a guy at Temple University, a fan. He was at every match and yelled at all the heels. Lawler took the mic and, in front of 700 people, pointed at the fan and says, "*This is what happens when cousins marry.*" In any normal situation, people would get pissed off about something like that, but everybody popped. They popped! It was hilarious. Austin Idol got on the mic one night and said to the same guy, "*Before you were born, your mother wanted a girl and your father wanted a boy, and when you were born they were both happy.*" It was the best line.

Great stuff. Back to the Madusa/Luna hair vs. hair match. So the deal was that Cactus could be involved in a match, or the schmozz at the end of a match, but he just couldn't get into the ring.

He could get *into* the ring, but he couldn't wrestle, and since Cactus couldn't wrestle, I had him and Eddie stand on the ring apron and second the girls. Of course, as I said, Eddie called Cactus out before the match began. Keep in mind, in *my* building, as far as *my* people were concerned, Cactus was the babyface, even though Gilbert was calling *him* out. In the day, that was a big deal. Eddie knew that whatever was said in my ring would be in the press in no time, so he made a point of calling Cactus out. I don't know how many people realized it, but there was a whole lot going on that night other than just a match.

At some point during the match, Cactus reached through the ropes and tripped Madusa. Eddie ran over to Cactus and they started fighting ... *outside* the ring. If you watch the video, you'll notice that nobody was watching the girls. Madusa and Luna were putting on a solid wrestling match and Cactus and Eddie were beating the shit out of each other ... and the crowd was watching *them* instead of the women. In fact, the referee was outside the ring trying to get those two guys to break it up while the match was going on in the ring. Cactus and Eddie weren't even in the match! I remember, afterwards, having a meeting with the ref. I told him, "*If you're the ref, you have to stay in the ring.*"

I don't know the exact wording in Cactus' contract, but the rules were real specific. I had to deal with it twice ... once with Nikita and once with Cactus. I told them both, "*Hey, guys, I announced you. You have to be there. Let's do what we have to do. We'll make it work within the parameters of your contracts.*" In both cases, they got involved outside the ring. Look, I didn't want to get in their way of making money. As long as Crockett respected me — and he never gave me any problems — I respected their situation.

Those two girls were amazing. I could put Madusa on any show and she could sell. And the neat thing about Madusa is, she was a beautiful woman, and she was *sexy*. The kicker was, Madusa never wore the sexy outfits like the so-called divas that came along later. The one thing with wrestling fans, when you had women on your show, they were usually on the first match and the fans weren't looking for wrestling. They were looking for an ass shot. They wanted to get a tit shot. Guys are guys. Madusa, however, was respected as a wrestler. On the flip side, Luna was respected as being a nut, but in her own way, she was as sexy as hell. They were as different as night and day, but it was pretty cool how things worked out. Luna recognized that she had to let Madusa call the match.

Madusa was a true, true professional. She was great. Her work was phenomenal. You could put her in a scientific match and it would be phenomenal, and Luna was somebody who would go along. Luna was phenomenal. I remember her telling me, "*I don't pull anything. I'm gonna beat the shit out of Madusa and Madusa is going to beat the shit out of me.*" And they did.

How did the hair vs. hair stipulation come about?

That was Luna's idea. Luna called me up and told me that she wanted to go back to the *veins in the head* gimmick. Her suggestion was that I bill the match as a *loser loses her hair* match. It was all her idea. She said, "*I don't want to go totally bald. Just promote it and we'll come up with a fuck-finish.*" She wasn't totally shaved, but Madusa cut the hair on one side of her head and held up a handful of hair. She dropped the hair and cut another handful. That's when the Blackhearts came out to kind of finish it up.

Luna gave you the idea. Did you have to pay her extra for the haircut?

(laughs) Yes! How dumb was I? She sold me on the angle and then said, "*What's it worth to you?*" And like a mark, I paid her an extra hundred bucks. It was all about the payday. (laughs)

Something else that was interesting about that show. We had Woman come out as "Woman" and manage D.C. Drake. She came out later in the show as Fallen Angel. I believe that was the only time that Woman and Fallen Angel appeared on the same card. I asked Kevin if we could do that and he said, "*Sure.*" You should have seen her in the back between her matches. If you remember, Fallen Angel had frizzy hair, so she had to spend the whole time fluffing up her hair before she came back out as Fallen Angel. That was kind of neat.

You used the girls quite often. How did Luna Vachon come into the picture?

I loved Luna. I absolutely loved her. I'm trying to remember the exact storylines here, but I got Luna through Madusa and I had them work against each other. [Philadelphia, Aug. 3, 1991] Luna and Madusa really put it on the line for me. I loved both of them. Madusa, to me, was an Owen Hart. She was a professional wrestler. Luna was showbiz. Luna was a nut, and I say that in a very positive way. Luna and I became very, very close. In fact, I still have a letter in the closet somewhere that Luna wrote to me when she was having marriage problems. The Blackhearts [Tom Nash & David Heath] was Luna's idea.

The Blackhearts & Luna Vachon   Photo by Dr. Mike Lano

The Blackhearts won the tag team title at your September show. How did that come about?

When Luna came to me about the Blackhearts, she said, *"Let's bring these guys in from Florida. I think it will work."* Well, not only did it work ... God bless Larry Winters. Larry never told me the finish. I did not know the Blackhearts were going to win the straps that night.

So they came in with Luna?

Yes. Luna was in Florida. She called me and said, *"We've put together a masked tag team here called the Blackhearts. We'd love to work your shows."* She was really upfront with me because she admitted why they wanted to come in. *"I'll be honest with you. We know the New York magazines are at your shows, so by us working your show, we'll get notoriety."* That was one of the things I loved about Luna. She didn't blow smoke and she was always truthful.

I was a little bit torn because I had to fly three people up from Florida. You know, it's funny, but here it is, 30-plus years later, and people are still talking about TWA, but a good reason for that is because I spent more money on transportation than I did on talent. Anyway, we put it all together and they came in ... and they were an immediate hit. For one thing, the Blackhearts looked like wrestlers. The local guys had a tendency to be smaller.

So, Larry Winter put the Blackhearts with Johnny Hotbody and D.C. Drake. At the time, Larry and D.C. were the TWA champions, but Larry broke his leg, so D.C. took his place. Everybody thought Larry's broken leg was a work, but it really was legit. Well, when the Blackhearts won the match and the title, it was as much a surprise to me as it was to the people in the audience. That was all Larry Winters' idea. It totally knocked me for a loop.

One of the Blackhearts slams Johnny Hotbody on the arena floor.
Photo by Craig Prendergast

That was one of those matches ... if you ever watch the video, that match was so wild, so out of hand, so out of control. All four guys were wrestling all over the place, and outside the ring you had Woman, you had "Devious" Don E. Allen, you had Luna Vachon. It was so wild. They were beating the hell out of each other. They were *stiff!* There was a point where I almost stopped it because it was so out of hand, and I had no idea how the match was going to end. I had no clue of the time or anything. They beat the hell out of D.C. Drake and took the belts. Even after the match was over, they went on for another five to ten minutes of stuff. Yes, that was Larry's from beginning to end. I had no clue. The story there was, there was no story. I didn't know a thing.

Did you prefer to have the guys work a more stiff-style match?

Absolutely! I used to tell the guys, when you're outside the ring, you better freaking hit each other. If you pull the punches, the word *will* get out because the smart marks will see it. And that match was more outside the ring then inside. It was ridiculous. I'm watching the match ... and all of a sudden, the Blackhearts beat them. Larry Winter, my booker, called for a title change that the promoter didn't want! It wasn't that I didn't *want* the Blackhearts on my cards, but by giving them the title, I *had to* put them on every card ... or, at least, on every major card.

Again, it was entirely Larry's call about the Blackhearts getting the straps from our guys. You know, I was trying to keep our belts local, mainly because, if we put the strap on a big name and we wanted a title defense, we'd have to fly them in.

Tell me about David Heath. He's a guy that I don't know much about. I mean, he's had quite a career, but I just don't follow the business anymore.

He came in with Luna. I didn't know anything about him other than what Luna told me, but he had been wrestling in Florida with Tom Nash as the Blackhearts. Later on, when he wrestled with the WWF, they named him Gangrel. I didn't know anything about their work ethic, but David and Tom put it all on the line when they came up here. I flew all three of them up from Florida. Fortunately, airfare was reasonable at the time. From the first night they appeared for me, it was clear to me that they had the potential of being major stars. Luna was great as their manager. She had the look and clearly knew the business.

Tom was married to Luna at the time, right?

Yes, but I didn't know that at the time. I was one of those guys who didn't get involved in the personal lives and I'm glad I didn't. The less I knew, the better. When I booked them, I didn't realize they were a couple. I didn't realize the politics of that whole scenario. Later on, Luna called and told me that Tom was out and she was bringing in someone else.

Dave Johnson.

That's right. I was kind of disappointed because I liked the team as it was, but again, I didn't like to get involved in the personal lives of the guys and gals. I see David Heath every once in a while at conventions and we talk about the old times.

The Blackhearts only worked three shows for you.

Yes, because shortly after they won the straps, the worst happened. The Blackhearts broke up. Luna got divorced from Tom and later took up with David Heath. It's really amazing to think about how much time has gone by. I just can't believe I'm 71 years old. I talk to David — Gangrel — all the time, and he's had hip surgery. Robert Gibson told me that he's 66 years old and he's had hip surgery. I don't know about you, but I picture Robert Gibson as a 34-year-old.

The positive thing about the Blackhearts winning the title was that it boosted TWA into a different league. The guys holding the belts weren't just local guys. Now we had national champions ... guys who had worked Calgary, Florida, and other territories. I got national notoriety by having Luna and the Blackhearts on my shows. Watch the crowd on the videos. They had great music to come out to, and the photographers were taking pictures like crazy. We only had cameras back then. We didn't have cell phones, but I wish we had because we would have thousands of pictures.

You were one of the leading bookers of lady wrestlers in regards to using them in featured spots.
There was something about women wrestling that I thought would draw in the fans ... and I'm not talking about the sex angle because Vince already had that wrapped up. The girls I booked — Misty Blue [Simmes], Kat LeRoux, Linda Dallas, the local girls — they were wrestlers first, females second. I took it to the next level when I booked Woman and Baby Doll to come in and act as seconds to the guys.

Luna died much too young.
Absolutely. When Luna passed away, one of the things I wanted to do was keep her name around. That's why I changed my name to Joel Blackhart for my management bookings with local wrestling promotions ... mainly a small promotion called ECWA. They've been around for a long time. It's just my small way of saying thank you to Luna.

You had a "last blood" match on the same night as the Luna-Madusa hair match.
Matches like that were what got me my real reputation. I kept coming up with matches (pause) ... I'll call them gimmick matches. For instance, there were fans who absolutely loved blood, so I came up with the idea of the "last blood battle royal" match [Sept. 21, 1991], which was the opposite of a "first blood" match and a twist on the old over-the-top-rope battle royal. A wrestler was eliminated when they bled, so I had 19

Cactus Jack & Luna Vachon
Photo by Dr. Mike Lano

guys guaranteed to bleed! I had a reverse steel cage battle royal. [Sept. 15, 1990] The wrestlers, all locals, all started *outside* the ring on the floor and the winner was the first one to climb *into* the cage. You had guys fighting on the floor outside the ring, climbing up the cage, and getting knocked down to the arena floor. It was different and it was incredible. I think it was the first match on the card.

Yes, it was.
It takes a long time to set up the cage, so the cage match better be a big draw. If you have Abby and Sheik in a barbed wire steel cage, people will stick around for that. If you have Eddie Gilbert against Cactus Jack in a cage, they'll stick around for that. But a "last blood battle royal" with 20 nobodies has to go on first.

One of the funny things about the last blood match was, Kevin Sullivan liked Glen Osbourne. Kevin was doing the devil worshiper gimmick, so he came to me before the matches and asked if he could have Glen as his disciple. Kevin came to the ring during the battle royal and commanded Osbourne to get blood and eliminate himself. That was sort of weird, but it showed the people that Kevin had supernatural powers and could make people do things they didn't want to do.

It was one of those deals where, if I had really known what in the hell I was doing, we could have promoted it the right way and really built on it. The problem with doing it with a local guy, though, is that, if you're going to do a devil-worshiper gimmick, you'd better be a devil worshiper. Kevin plays the part all the time, but I'm not sure the local guys would want to do that.

That was the first time Kevin worked for you. What was your impression of him that night.

Kevin Sullivan was fantastic. He was a true professional. I know I keep using that term — true professional — but it's the best way to describe a lot of those guys. Kevin worked many of my shows and he was always a pleasure to work with. The very first night we met, he came to me and asked, "*How much time do you need?*" He made no demands and did everything I asked.

Terry Funk vs. Kevin Sullivan
Photo by Dr. Mike Lano

Where did you get the idea for the "last blood battle royal"?

It just popped up in my head. Back in my day, wrestling fans loved color. They loved to see red, but you can't have blood in every match because it's overkill, so the local guys didn't have the opportunity to get juice too often. They were willing to do anything, so I came up with the idea and gave them all the opportunity.

From everything I've read, your matches had a *lot* of blood in them. In the old days, if a guy on the undercard got juice, or did something outside the ring, the guys in the main event would go ballistic because big stuff like that was supposed to take place in the main event. Did the big-name talent ever come to you and say, "*Why are you letting these guys do all this? We've got to follow that.*"

Yeah, they asked me that a lot. Cactus tells a story in his book about how he and Eddie Gilbert were planning this big to-do and they're sittin' on the stage watching my first match, which was that "last blood battle royal." While he's talking with Eddie about what they could do in their match, he's watching the last blood battle royal and sees 12 guys getting busted open. There was blood all over the place. How were they going to follow that? They were trying to figure out how to compete with that.

So, yeah, that came up a lot. My answer was, "*Then do something to beat it. That's why I'm paying you as much as I am. You guys know what to do to make the house pop, so just do it!*" I never had anybody come to me and say, "*I'm not working for you because it doesn't work for me.*" They would, however, ask me questions like, "*Why do you have so much talent on the same card?*" The reality is, that was a great question, and it's one I asked myself many times. However, here we are 30 years later and people are still talking about those shows.

Every independent show had six undercard matches and one main event, and the main event was typically a name against some local guy. I was running shows where four matches were big names and four matches were my guys. I was spending all this money and these guys were questioning why I was doing it, but here we are writing a book 30 years later about what happened with me. I mean, how many independent promoters back in those days could write the stories that I write? In hindsight, it was stupid business. It was dumb. But, on the other hand, 30 years later, I can say that I gave the fans their money's worth, and then some. I would bet that people talk about Eddie Gilbert and Cactus more than they talk about *Starrcade* or *WrestleMania*.

November 9, 1990. Jim Cornette and Dennis Coralluzzo booked a benefit show in Philly for a critically ill wrestling fan named Tom Robinson. Since

it was a Catholic high school, they banned the use of the blade, but it was reported that the guys you sent didn't follow their guidelines.

I heard about that, but here's a couple of things. Number one, when they booked the show, Dennis had me do some ring announcing for the show. Tom Robinson was a fan of my promotion, as well as Coralluzzo's. Here they were using guys I used regularly on my shows ... Cactus Jack, Eddie Gilbert, D.C. Drake, Jerry Lawler, Midnight Express. They tried to replicate what I was doing, but they held it in a high school gym. They didn't do it in a legitimate building. I was so naïve. I was thinking we were all helping raise money for Tom Robinson. I didn't see it as competition. If anything, they were actually validating what I was doing. But that was Dennis' way. I don't know if Larry [Sharpe] was pulling strings in the background or not, but that was their way of coming into Philly and doing a show. The tape is out there. And we all cooperated.

In terms of my guys, what I had told them was, my guys would be doing *my* matches. You're not booking my matches. We're doing *our* matches. If you want to use my guys on the card — just like when I used their guys — I'm booking my matches. We had two or three undercard matches and I told my guys, *"We're giving them TWA matches. We're not doing Monster Factory. So go out there, do your thing, get out of the ring, get into the crowd, and make sure people talk about our match before their match."* That's what I said to them. At no point did I say anything about blood. I didn't say anything about it. To this day, I never told any wrestler that I needed color ... not a one. Now, the guys who were in my last blood battle royal got it. They knew what they had to do. But I never said to any main name, any main-eventer, "You need to do this." Never. Never, ever! When you saw guys in my show get color, it was their choice. It was never my choice.

Or Larry Winters, or whoever was calling the shots.

Nobody on my team ever told anybody to color up ... not even Larry. Here's the thing. When we had a match at Temple University between Stetson and Hotbody, we called it "The City of Brotherly Hate" match. The guys knew what they had to do. When we had matches — and I'll use the main-eventers as an example — they would do it because they knew the photos would show up in the magazines. When it came to photos with no blood and photos *with* blood, the blood photos always showed up in the magazines. I guarantee you, Apter and Napolitano did more for red than any promoter because they featured those shots in the mags. When I booked Abby and Sheik, I didn't have to tell 'em. I mean, just a glance at their foreheads will tell you that they've done that for years. Nobody had to tell 'em. I don't believe that Larry ever told anyone that they needed color, because quite frankly, the way our cards ran, if you didn't bleed, it stood out. When you have a show called "Gory, Gory Hallelujah!" — I came up with that all by myself — I thought that was great. The main event was Abby and Sheik. Gory, Gory Hallelujah! Do you think we had to tell them [to bleed]?

Your Sept. 21 show drew 1,524 fans and a $27,900 gate. WCW was in Philly just three weeks before that and only had 650 paid.

That was another show where I outdrew them. Clearly, that was huge for an independent show. There's no question. However, I have to go back to the money again. I had some tremendous numbers during my run. If I remember correctly, my largest gate was about $33,000. What people don't realize, though, is that I didn't make a whole lot of money. When I moved to Pennsylvania Hall, I was working with Ticketmaster. Back then, you could call the state of Pennsylvania on Monday and find out the gate. They used to report gate size. I enjoyed the fact that I had a $27,000 gate. The problem was, the city of Philadelphia took six percent. Ten percent — or whatever it was — went to the building. By the time I paid the talent, the ring, and whatever other expenses I had, there wasn't much left.

As far as me beating Crockett, he was bringing in shows that were shit. They were absolutely horrible. He deserved to not beat me. Crockett had television and he had name talent, and there I was with local radio. We had some decent gates, no question.

When I was in the business, the promoters made a boatload of money by skimming off the box office before the final count was made so they didn't have to report it to the commission. Of course, ticket sales then were all cash. Were independent promoters in the '90s able to do that — and *did* they do that — or was it so tightly controlled that you *couldn't* do that? We'll figure out a way of saying this without implicating you.

(laughs) I wasn't able to do it. When I hooked up with Ticketmaster, it became more of a legitimate business. The smaller school shows were sold-shows, so there was no play there, either. The one thing I had in my contract for the sold-shows was that I got 20 comp tickets. Other than that, there was no way to skim, no way to hide money.

Abdullah and the Sheik worked in a cage match that night. It was reported that Mitsuharu Misawa, Richard Slinger, and Masa Fuchi were there to scout for new foreign talent. Do you remember that?

I didn't, but now that you mention it, yes, I remember them being there, but I had no interaction with them whatsoever. I remember somebody — and it escapes me who it was — call to ask me if they could get tickets, so I gave them tickets. It was weird because, at that time, I didn't understand the politics of All Japan versus New Japan. New Japan actually started working with me ... Tokyo Joe and that whole crew. I think Meltzer did a lot for me internationally because those guys read about my shows. Where in the hell else would they hear about my shows? The magazines were always three to six months behind, so it was definitely Meltzer's sheet that did that, or one of the others that was out there. They scouted us for talent, though, no question about it.

One of the complaints sent to the *Observer* about the Sept. 21 show had to do with security at your shows. One of the readers wrote: "When the wrestlers are brawling all over the building, people are running all over the place to see the action. The security does nothing to control the fans. I saw people pushing chairs over and throwing them around [...] some people told security that they weren't controlling the rowdy people around them, and then the security people hassled them because they said something." Any thoughts on that?

Yeah, that was one of the bigger issues we had. In hindsight, 30 years later ... with Vince, everything was so orchestrated, so the security people were always in the right place at the right time. Well, that wasn't the case with us. I didn't know when they were going to go outside the ring, and my fans followed the action. Nobody sat in their chair. If you watch some of the videos, you'll see a swarm of a thousand people rushing towards the stage to see them. When they try to go back and find their seats, they can't find them, because the seats are all kicked around. Our seats weren't bolted to the floor. Again, somebody could have gotten hurt. *Did* anybody ever get hurt? Not that I'm aware of.

So, yeah, security was an issue because we never had enough security and the security we had basically worked the aisle when the guys walked from the dressing room to the ring. Tell me, if Sheik and Abby wanted to battle outside the ring, would you want to be a security guard? What are you gonna do when five hundred people rush in that direction? I mean, seriously! So, the good news was that the fans got to see the action up close. The bad news was that they were in the line of fire. But again, during all the time we ran, we didn't have one claim of anybody getting injured. We didn't have a single lawsuit, either.

I think the complaint from most people was that they bought a ticket for a specific seat and then couldn't see because the match wasn't in the ring.

That was a valid complaint! If you were sitting on one side of the ring and they were battling outside the ring on the other side, they couldn't see. The flip side of that is, if every match stayed in the ring all the time, people would have said we were doing the same thing Vince did. We wanted to give the people something different from what Vince gave them. One of the first lessons I learned as a promoter was, if you try to make everybody happy, you're in trouble. So, you don't go that route. You go with your style, and if somebody doesn't like it, they may not come back, but I could never please everybody.

On the subject of chairs, the wrestlers hit each other with chairs, but the fans also threw chairs when the action got a little heated. Did you pay for a lot of broken chairs?

Yes, I did. (laughs) I already told you about having to pay for the chairs at the Sheraton when I had Brody and Abdullah. Now, the chairs at Pennsylvania Hall were padded. I remember being told that they cost $300 apiece. Those chairs were as heavy as hell, so we didn't get too many broken chairs there, and it would be tough to hit somebody with one of those chairs because they must have weighed 20 pounds. I did get a couple of broken tables. You can see that happen in some of the videos.

One of the things we used to tell the guys was, if you're going to use the mic, give it back to the ring announcer when you're through. I can't tell you how many times guys with Crockett would use the mic and then throw it down. One of the mics I had to pay for cost me more than $300. You can see Lawler, Cactus, Eddie, all use the mic in the videos, and they handed it off to someone when they finished. They were pros. I don't remember who it was, but one of local guys threw a mic down and I told everybody in the dressing room afterwards, "*If you break my mic, it's coming out of your pay.*" I know the guys thought it looked good to do that, but it was on them if the mic got broken.

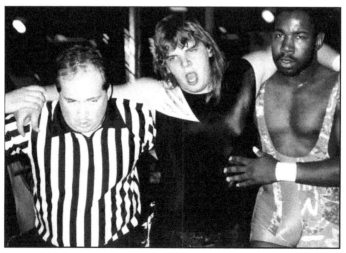

Ref Jim Molineaux & J.T. Smith assist Jimmy Jannetty

Photo by Craig Prendergast

14  The Bones That Talked

This seems as good a place as any to talk a little about other promoters. Tell me what you know about these promoters and whether you had any problems or dealings with them. Dennis Coralluzzo.

Dennis and I had a lot of history. I'm not sure where or how I met him, but it probably was at the Monster Factory because he had worked with Larry Sharpe. I never had any issues with Dennis. Dennis ran his shows in Jersey, I ran in Philly. Obviously, when I created the TWA ... I mean, even if I did run in New Jersey, my shows were so different from any other shows that I didn't see it as competing against Dennis, just as Vince, obviously, never saw *me* as competition. I *never* looked at Dennis and Larry as competition, but at one point, we did have a handshake agreement that we wouldn't run against each other.

Now, I had a wrestling school — Ringmasters — while Larry had The Monster Factory, but we never looked at each other as competitors. Monster Factory was already established. I was the new kid on the block. If there was any heat there, I never heard about it. In fact, there's videos of Dennis sitting at ringside at my shows. I will say this. If I needed a money mark, Dennis was a mark. I mean, he just loved being around the guys. But, again, no heat. The unwritten agreement was that we didn't compete against each other. I even had Dennis on my radio show. Dennis ran an angle with himself as Jerry Lawler's attorney, so we were both in with Jerry, but there was no heat.

I should have done my homework before asking this question, but was Dennis an attorney?

No, no. Dennis was actually in the insurance business. A different side than mine, but he was an attorney for Memphis wrestling.

I see. You said you didn't compete, but didn't Dennis promote a few shows in Philly?

Dennis may have run a few benefit shows, charitable shows, in Philly, but when I was promoting, no. Dennis and Larry had a better philosophy than me. Their goal was to make money at every show. If they drew 75 to a hundred people, they made a profit. I will actually argue that they knew what the hell they were doing. Larry was a local in the area, but he was a name. Larry's philosophy was that you didn't need a name on the card. He once told me, "*We'll run our local shows, we'll get our seventy five or eighty people, and we'll make money.*" You know, he was right.

Did either of them ever call you and ask why you were doing things the way you were?

No. In fact, I think they realized that I was my own worst enemy and that I couldn't last. The radio show was heard in New Jersey, so I'm sure they felt like they had to work with me. They may have figured that if they got heat with me, I could have buried them on the radio. I mean, I didn't pull punches on that shit. We never had that problem, though.

Do you remember any specific interaction with Larry?

No. I did go to Larry's funeral. It's funny, but I always saw Larry as a guy who had wrestled. He was never a main-eventer in the Northeast, but he had worked the Garden. He worked the big shows. He knew all the people I knew, but I didn't know all the people *he* knew. On the flip side, I came into the wrestling as a businessman. And yet, in many ways, he was much more of a businessman than I was. He was light years ahead of me in business. I think about it at times and I wonder if he could have helped me, but he never even came to one of my shows.

Gordon Scozzari?
The name doesn't ring a bell.

He ran the American Wrestling Federation in New Jersey.
No, I don't remember his name.

Okay. John Arezzi. He didn't promote, did he?
I don't remember John promoting, but John had a radio show up in New York and he booked bus trips down to my shows. I'd give him a block of tickets and preferred seating. On YouTube, he did voiceovers on my Cactus Jack/Eddie Gilbert matches that are phenomenal. John and I were pretty good friends. In fact, we were both on the ECWA Super 8 Chickfight show in [Woodbury Heights] New Jersey in 2017 [Oct. 21]. I was a manager, John was the ring announcer, and my friend Dan Murphy was the co-emcee of the show with Honky Tonk Man. The last time I saw John was just a few years ago in Vegas.

When you say you gave John a block of tickets, do you mean you *sold* him a block of tickets?
Oh, yeah. I'm not that charitable. If he was bringing 35 or 40 people down, I'd give him a block of seats. They weren't front row, but they were good seats. I'm assuming I gave him a discount. I can't say I did for sure, but if somebody bought 40 tickets, I gave them a discount.

You said earlier that, at one time, you flirted with the idea of being a manager.
I never managed at any of my shows, but I did several years ago at ECWA shows. There was a wrestler by the name of Napalm Bomb [Derrick Green, Jr.]. He was a good guy and he wrestled out of Baltimore. Anyway, I managed him one night and I'm standing in the corner of the ring giving him instructions. His opponent whips him into the corner and into me. I was going to hold onto the ropes and act like I was hurt. Well, he comes in so hard that he knocks me off the damn ring apron. I tumbled to the floor, my glasses flew off ... there were no mats out there. That was about ten years ago, so I would have been 61 years old. I'm lying on the floor dead and thinking, "*What the hell am I doing?*" Of course, he loses the match because of that and they dragged me to the back. Bomb comes over and says, "*You okay?*"

I said, "*I'm fine, I'm fine.*" I'm 50 miles from home. I get in the car at the end of the night and, as I'm driving home, every bone in my body was talking to me. "*You're never doing this shit again!*" (laughs)

Did you ever have any dealings with Joe Pedicino?
No, none at all. If I remember correctly, the only time I ever spoke to Joe was when we did a tour of Atlanta and I met him, but I never had any real interaction with Joe or Bonnie [Blackstone].

Rob Russen?
Another good guy. In fact, he's on Facebook. He ran shows under the IWA banner, and when he had a few TV tapings, he asked me to ring announce. He used some of my guys ... Larry Winters, Johnny Hotbody. All I asked was for him to respect my territory and not bury my guys. He basically kept to that. He was ahead of me because he had TV. He ran shows in the middle of Pennsylvania

Joel with ECWA-TWA tag team champions
Chris Rockwell & Sam Shields, the Midnight Sensations

that I had never been to. In fact, he ran a TV taping in Nanticoke, Pennsylvania, which is in the middle of nowhere and a good solid three hours from here. Wouldn't you know it, of all times, the engine in my car blows on the way home and I was in nowhere land. AAA took forever to find me. Back then, they'd ask you for a mile marker. Well, there was no mile marker. There weren't any lights on the road. They eventually found me. Rob paid me $100 to ring announce, but I must've spent $2,000 on an engine. You always hear stories about the guys in the business who run old cars into the ground. Well, I had a piece of shit car and it died that night. Regardless, Rob Russen was a good guy. I had no negative interactions with him.

Did you do ring announcing for other promotions?
Yeah. I ring announced for Larry Sharpe and Dennis Coralluzzo one time. I'm sure the reason they had me ring announce was because they knew that if I was going to ring announce, I would promote their card on my radio show. I think I did a decent job. I wasn't Gary Michael Cappetta, but I had my little shtick. It put me over some because I wore the tuxedo and most of the guys in this business couldn't afford a tux. I had a little credibility because I had announced for Crockett when they had 7,000 people at the Philadelphia Arena. [Jan. 16, 1988] Now, to be honest with you, if Rob Russen had been able to get Gary Michael Cappetta to do it, that would have given him a lot *more* credibility. Who in the hell was Joel Goodhart? I don't know if Gary couldn't or *didn't* want to do it, but I was kind of like the next ring announcer on the list.

Are there other promoters you had dealings with, or do you have memories of other promoters?
The only one I can think of is Gary Juster. Gary was one of Crockett's promoters. If Gary was running the show, I could get ahold of Gary through Elliott Murnick. I never had any real interaction with Gary, but we worked together for Crockett. There was Gino Moore in Allentown. Gino ran a couple of shows, but nothing major. We were 45 miles apart, but nobody knew what the hell was going on in the other territories. Gino was one of those big, heavy, 350-pound guys who was fat ... not solid like some of the guys. He's since passed away. I don't have

anything negative — or positive, for that matter — to say about Gino. I just worked with him.

Your referees ... John Finegan, Joe Zanolle, and Jim Molineaux. Which one of them came first?

John Finegan. He was already a referee and he was my main guy. He was never a part of our booking committee, but he was at every show. In fact, he trained both Zanolle and Molineaux. John went on to referee for ECW and referees now for ECWA [East Coast Wrestling Association].

Zanolle was a ring photographer before he became a referee. One of the first matches he refereed was Terry Funk against (pause) ... who was it? Terry threw him right out of the ring. Today, Joe is about 250, 300 pounds, but back then, he was a young kid, and he was skinny. Zanolle was on a lot of my big cards at Pennsylvania Hall.

Molineaux was my third referee. I heard Molineaux on a podcast a few years ago, but I haven't talked to him in a long, long time. Jim got his start working for Larry Sharpe at the Monster Factory.

There was a fourth referee by the name of Rich Ingling. Rich refereed some of my shows in McGonigle. And the fifth referee was Sal Corrente. Sal refereed some of the Jerry Lawler/Austin Idol matches. God bless Sal. He wanted to get involved in every friggin' match. Sal never worked a match at Pennsylvania Hall. He just worked at McGonigle. I haven't talked to Sal in a long time, but I keep seeing his Facebook stuff.

Eddie Gilbert & Woman
Photo by Dr. Mike Lano

Bam Bam Bigelow & Luna Vachon
Photo by Dr. Mike Lano

Owen Hart & Cactus Jack
Photo by Dr. Mike Lano

15   Hot Oil Wrestling

Philadelphia, Pennsylvania: Oct. 1, 1991
Original Sports Bar
- Crybaby Waldo & Michael Bruno beat John Rock & Bounty Hunter
- Glen Osbourne beat Johnny O
- D.C. Drake beat Glen Osbourne.
- Jimmy Jannetty beat Rick Perez
- Mr. Anthony drew Rockin' Rebel
- TWA title match
  J.T. Smith beat Johnny Hotbody
- Tony Stetson beat Mr. Sandman

Joel Goodhart was the special guest ring announcer at Wizzard's Lounge for Hot Oil Wrestling on Wednesday, Oct. 9, 1991.

Okay. This is probably the most important topic I'm going to cover. Tell me about Wizzard's Hot Oil Wrestling. The ad reads, *12 Battling Beauties*.
(laughs)
 (laughs) You'll love this one. When things were going south towards the end, and I was trying to generate money, I created a women's group that wrestled at a place on Chestnut St. called Wizzard's. Wizzard's was one of our advertisers. I ran shows in a couple of places in Philadelphia ... the seediest places you'd ever want to wrestle in.

The ad said you were the special ring announcer. I didn't realize it was your company.
 Yes, it was. In fact, I used the TWA initials. TWA stood for Tri-State Wrestling Alliance, so I simply changed the words to *Tits With Ass*. We would feature three matches, sometimes four. When I was promoting Tri-State, we also trained women at the Ringmasters school. We weren't just getting strippers to throw each other around in hot oil. Women actually came to the school and we taught them moves.

 Each match was two out of three falls and I paid the girls $50 each. They wrestled in bikinis. In the state of Pennsylvania, you couldn't do topless or bottomless, so they wore in bikinis. The girls would wrestle and then we'd have an auction, with the guys bidding to be their seconds between the matches and help them wipe off the hot oil or spaghetti. Of course, the guys would get to cop a feel. That's all they were getting. There was nothing else. Some guy would bid a hundred bucks to be a second and the money was the girls to keep. We had a one-minute break after a girl wrestled for a minute or two and then he would dry her off. I remember one guy paying $300. Now, this was in the late '90s when $300 was real money. That girl was a knockout. She was gorgeous. He started taking liberties with her. (laughs) We stopped the guy at some point. There was just so much we could let them do before we were pushing the line.

I made more money on those sold-shows than I was on the wrestling cards, and I didn't have to worry about getting guys into the building. They were already there. If I remember correctly, I sold the show for $1,000. The girls cost me 300 to $400 and the hot oil, mud, or spaghetti cost me another hundred or two. I would make $500 in a night. It was tough making a $500 profit when I was promoting a wrestling show.

At some point, TWA started having ring girls, and they were girls from Wizzard's. They'd accompany the wrestlers to the ring. Those girls knew what they were doing. They knew how to strut their stuff. It was a good little relationship and it worked for me.

You said spaghetti. You had spaghetti in the ring?
We had spaghetti wrestling, hot oil wrestling, mud wrestling. The girls came up with the ideas. You can't just have hot oil matches. You had to have some variety, and we used spaghetti because they could throw it. It was as messy as all hell.

One of the topics I used to avoid was the subject of the arena rats ... the wrestling groupies. In a strange way, though, they played an important part in the wrestling business. Were they still a thing in your day?
Yes, we had the arena rats. We called them ring rats. I remember one girl who wanted to screw Buddy Landel. She bugged the hell out of me. I remember saying to her ... her name was Janelle. I just remembered that. Wow! (laughs) I said to her, "*If you want Buddy, you've gotta have me first.*" (laughs) She agreed! (laughs) We went upstairs, did our business, and the next week, I hooked her up with Buddy. I mean, I figured, what the hell! I might as well benefit from it. (laughs)

This is interesting because a lot of the best stories aren't about the wrestling, it was the party afterwards. When Crockett was in Philly, the parties at the Marriott were unbelievable. Unbelievable! And the rats were all there. They knew what their role was and the wrestlers knew who they were. The wrestlers kayfabed a bit. The heels stayed on one side and the babies on the other. But the ring rats were still around and at our shows, no question. Those girls would just line up to go to bed with a wrestler ... *any wrestler*!

And the one thing you learned was that the guys all had rats in the different cities. Bruno was faithful to his wife, but he told me stories about the guy working the cities. If they had a tour that went from Philadelphia to Washington D.C., to North Attleboro, to Scranton, to Baltimore, to Boston ... if they had to stay at a hotel, that took a chunk out of their pay, so if they had a ring rat in town, they'd stay with her. She'd make them a home-cooked meal so they didn't have to spend more of their payoff at a local restaurant. They got to spend a few hours with the girl and get laid, they'd take a shower, and then take off for the next town. They had ring rats in every city to keep their expenses at a minimum. The women didn't care. They understood that they were getting sex in exchange for what they gave. When the wrestler left their house, though, most of them thought they were connected. Well, the truth is, the guys were using them for no reason other than they wanted to save the 50 bucks they would have spent for a hotel room.

In a lot of cases, the guys did that in order to survive because paydays — especially in the smaller territories — were so small, and by the time they took out the cost of gas, food, hotels, and whatever else, they weren't left with a whole lot. Of course, the wrestlers also rode together and shared hotel rooms so they could split the costs. And to be fair, a lot of the guys may have saved money by riding and rooming together, but many of them spent the money they saved on drugs or partying.

I'll never forget the story Bruno told me about his early days in the business, when he had to drive 500 miles or more a day. Later, when he became the WWWF champion, he was driven everywhere, so he sat in the back seat instead of the front.

Pine Hill, New Jersey: Oct. 26, 1991
Overbrook High School
Pine Hill Punishment
- Loser eats dog food match
  Pitbull Rex pinned Johnny Hotbody (or D.C. Drake?)
- Tony Stetson pinned Rick Pérez
- Handicap match
  Crybaby Waldo beat Michael Bruno & Johnny O
- D.C. Drake pinned Glen Osbourne.
- The Blackhearts, Apocalypse & Destruction* beat Rockin' Rebel & Jimmy Jannetty
- Special referee Buddy Rogers
  Steve Williams beat Bam Bam Bigelow (dq)
- Eddie Gilbert DDQ Kevin Sullivan.
- TWA title match
  Buddy Landel beat J.T. Smith (title change)

Which brings us to your show in Pine Hill, New Jersey ... the night when Buddy Rogers appeared in the ring for the first time in many, many years. I'd like to talk about a few things regarding that show, but I don't want to tackle the story about Rogers just yet. Tell me about the "loser eats dog food" match between Pitbull Rex and Johnny Hotbody.
We took a can of dog food and cleaned it out, then put beef stew in the can.
Your promotion being what it was, I'm surprised that you didn't use real dog food.
My only problem was ... how was I going to get someone to agree to eat the dog food? So, we gimmicked it up.
You mentioned earlier that you didn't match up local guys with the big names. An exception to that was J.T. Smith beating Cactus in the "Bar Wars" tournament. There was one other. You actually put Buddy Landel over J.T. Smith for the TWA title.
I got some heat for that. To me, taking the strap away from the local guy and putting it on somebody like Buddy Landel was a step forward. For the first time, the strap would be recognized nationally with a name that people recognized. J.T. did the job. Afterwards, I heard some of the guys saying, *"What's left for us?"* That led me to play around with the idea that we could have another champion that we could push to whatever degree we wanted.

Buddy Landel

Was Buddy willing to return on a regular basis to defend the title?

I talked to him about that when we talked about him winning the strap. I told him that I needed him up here whenever I ran a show. Buddy gave me the commitment of time similar to what I had with Cactus. I took preference over any other promoter when I needed him. As long as I had that deal with the guys, I was fine with it ... even when Larry Winters decided to give the straps to the Blackhearts. Now, the Blackhearts certainly weren't a major name at that point, and they were out of Florida, so they weren't local. When they beat Drake and Hotbody, everybody in the arena was stunned. You see, I was torn between having a local champion and wanting to get some national attention. I was moving up in the world, so Buddy Landel was a natural extension for me.

You said Larry Winters made the decision to change the tag belts. Did he normally have to get your approval for an important decision like that?

I usually came up with important things like that. I'd float the idea to Larry and he'd do the booking. In the case of the tag team title change, though ... I had no idea that he was going to do that. It was a total shock to me. Now, the breaking up of the Dog Pound, that was all planned by Larry, as well.

Larry and I would meet a week before a show and I'd tell him, *"Here's the order I want the matches in, here's who I want to go over, and here's the time element."* Larry took it from there. I left the finishes completely up to him. Larry was the artist. In fact, once a show started, I seldom, if *ever*, went into the dressing room. Larry took care of everything.

I wish I could have talked to Larry Winters because I'm sure he could have shared a lot of the backstage stories that you probably weren't privy to.

It pissed me off when I went to Larry's funeral. There was a couple of local guys there, but I was looking for Tony Stetson, Johnny Hotbody, Glen Osbourne ... for those local guys to come en masse. Larry was *the man* when they were just rookies, and yet they couldn't find the time to come to his funeral and pay their respects. That really bothered me.

I went to Larry Sharpe's funeral, even though I wasn't all that close to him ... and everybody thought we had heat! Davey O'Hannon was there. There might have been ten to fifteen local guys there, but he trained a *lot* of guys. Davey O'Hannnon, one of the WWF stalwarts was there to show his respect, but it's a shame that more of the WWF guys didn't take the time to pay their respects to Larry. Larry Sharpe and Larry Winters both deserved better than that.

If you could talk to any wrestler from the past — and it doesn't have to be somebody who worked for you — who would that be?

I'm torn. I have two answers. One would be Spiros Arion. I never met him, but when Spiros was with the WWWF, he was *the man*. I would really love the opportunity to talk to Bruno Sammartino again. For 30 years, I had an opportunity to talk to Bruno, and I never went out of my way to do it. I'm actually going to amend that. The one person I would love to talk to is Dominic DeNucci because he was at the store when we first opened. He was my first booker, my first promoter. Dominic is another guy I didn't stay in touch with, and now he's gone, as well. I said I wouldn't drive five hours to St. Marys. If he was still alive, I'd get in my car right now and drive five hours to go see Dominic.

Is there anybody you would have liked to book, but never had the opportunity?

Harley Race.

Oh, really? Okay, now that leads to another question. Let me see if I can find it here. The July 8, 1991, *Observer* mentioned your upcoming show on Aug. 3 that featured the two-out-of-three-fall match with Cactus and Gilbert. Meltzer said you had Dory Funk Jr. vs. Harley Race scheduled as the semifinal that night. Was there anything to that?

I don't know where that came from at all. I never booked Harley and I never spoke to him ... ever! I would have *loved* to have Harley on one of my shows. But if I had planned to book Harley, I wouldn't have put him against Dory. I would have put him with *Terry*! That would have been a dream match, but again, I never spoke to Harley. I had to book a lot of guys many months in advance. If you called them up a month, two months before a show, they were already booked. That's another reason why I went to four big, quarterly shows. They allowed me to book way ahead of time and I'd get a guy set for four dates in a row.

It makes me wonder if you might have said something to someone about wishing you could book Harley against Terry and they, in turn, called Meltzer and told him that you already had it booked. Then again, people fed Meltzer bogus information all the time, so who knows where that came from.

That's very possible. There again, Dave would never call me to confirm a story. It may have been a smart mark who called him. It could have been one of the boys. It wasn't me. If Dave heard a story about me booking Harley and Dory, would logic dictate that he call me for confirmation? That's why I almost never read the sheets. To be honest, unless someone told me about something going on in the wrestling world, I never knew what the hell was going on. I didn't care what Meltzer thought, you know. To me, Meltzer was one person's opinion. I never used him as a drop, either, although I probably should have fed him information on what I was doing because a lot of people were reading his newsletter. Meltzer could get the word out about anything. Now, I don't recall speaking to Dave *ever!* It's possible that Dave will tell you that he spoke to me somewhere along the line, and we may have. It's possible we interacted, but if we did, I don't remember it.

While we're on the subject, did you ever take the guys aside and tell them not to be calling Meltzer and giving him background, inside information?

I never had to say that because I think it was understood. Let me explain it this way. I have a designation as an accredited investment fiduciary, and as a fiduciary, I'm held to the same boundaries as an attorney. If you tell me something, I can't repeat it, end of story. That's just the way it is ... client privilege. Well, in the wrestling business, the boys understood that what we talked about in meetings was privileged information. Of course, Dave Meltzer and Wade Keller were exposing the business in their sheets. It used to piss me off when someone would tell me about something they read about TWA, especially when they printed things that were just assumptions, or downright lies. That told me that they were *not* journalists, despite what they claimed. Journalists went to the source and confirmed stories before they went to press. None of those guys did that. They never called me to find out the truth.

The sheets weren't all bad. They did get information out that was helpful, both for the business and to the fans. For instance, people from California were flying in for my shows. Well, they sure didn't hear about them on my radio show. They must have read about them in the newsletters. So, on the one hand, they [the newsletters] were helping sell tickets, but in the long run, they were killing the business and spreading disinformation.

Back to the show at Pine Hine High School … somebody said a teacher there said the school board would never allow another wrestling card to take place at the school because of the violence.

I never heard that. Now, that being said, we never went back, but I don't know if it was because of that teacher making that comment. The common denominator is that our wrestling was a step beyond the quote-unquote norm. In the old days, the majority of a match took place in the ring. In fact, on an eight-match card, all but one of the matches took place in the ring. However, I always contended that, if you really have a feud going, why would the participants keep it within the confines of the ring.

That being said, there's no doubt that our product was much more violent than anything people saw on television. There's no question about that. That's the first I ever heard of a teacher making that comment, though, but again, it wouldn't surprise me. I mean, the match that night between Kevin Sullivan and Eddie Gilbert went all over the gym. But that's what we did. That was one teacher's opinion, but he or she must have had some clout to take it to the board and have them keep us out indefinitely. I was out of the business not too long after that, so I never pursued returning, anyway. The other thing is, a lot of times, when one person complains, it becomes a story. There may have been 20 teachers who thoroughly enjoyed that match, but it's like the *New York Times*. They only print what they want to print. If more than that one teacher thought my show was too violent for the school, then I'd wear that as a badge of honor.

Did you ever have parents come up to you and say they'd never bring their kids back because of how violent it was?

If I was going to rate what we did, I would give our shows an R rating. I mean, there were parents who brought their kids to every show and there were other parents who quite properly thought it was too violent. Well, when a parent told me that, I smiled because that told me that I was achieving my goal. When professional wrestling is done right, it isn't for the seven-year-old. It just isn't. It's a violent sport and they may not understand the storylines. So, I took that as a badge of honor.

16   The Dream Match

Let's jump into your dream match between the two Nature Boys — Buddy Landel and the legendary Buddy Rogers. You booked Landel several times during your run with TWA.
  Buddy Landel first worked for me in Newark, Delaware. [May 4, 1991] I had him scheduled to wrestle Buddy Rogers at Penn Hall on Jan. 25, 1992, three months after he won the TWA title.

How did you get in touch with Rogers?
  Buddy Rogers was living in Lauderdale-by-the-Sea, Florida, and had talked to John Arezzi about an appearance at a wrestling convention in New York.

John had Rogers at a wrestling fan convention he promoted in New York in Aug. 1991. That was *big* news at the time.
  Absolutely. I got in touch with Rogers and he agreed to appear as a special referee at one of my shows in Pine Hill, New Jersey. [Oct. 26, 1991] However, my connection to Buddy was really through Carmela. Buddy and Carmella had been friends for many, many years before that. In fact, when Carmella and Paul were married, they bought a Lincoln from Rogers. They were very close to each other.

  Now that I think about it, I'm not sure if Carmella called Buddy or if he called me, but at some point, he said he wanted to get involved. He didn't say he wanted to wrestle. He just wanted some involvement. He was 70 years old at that point, but he was solid. He was physical. Carmella probably remembers exactly how it all went down. The one thing you learn about Carmella is that she always tells the truth.

  Now, there was no reason to have Buddy as the special guest referee, other than the fact that Buddy's hometown of Camden, New Jersey, was about 10 miles from Pine Hill.

  I came up with an angle to involve him in a match in Pine Hill, New Jersey. It was the night Buddy Landel won the TWA title from J.T. Smith. Buddy Rogers was the special referee for the Steve Williams-Bam Bam Bigelow match. After the match, Landel challenged him. Buddy said something about Rogers being the *old* Nature Boy — putting an emphasis on the word *old* — while he — Landel — was the *new* Nature Boy.

  Rogers told Buddy and the fans that he didn't want to wrestle and he turned around to leave, at which time Landel nailed him with the title belt. That set the stage for the match between the Nature Boys.

I understand that Rogers hit Landel a few times and looked pretty good, even though he was 70 years old.
  Rogers looked great. After they separated him and Landel, Rogers told the crowd that he had one more good match left in him.

Step back a bit and tell me what led you to book Rogers as a referee for that title match.
  I was trying to establish what I would call *The Super Supercard*. One of the big problems I had back then was, with every show, I had to build off the previous show in some shape or form. I booked the big supercards quarterly. I was trying

to make every quarterly show my *WrestleMania*. Rogers was originally from Camden, New Jersey, which was only five miles or so from Philly, so he was familiar with the area. I wanted to feature him against Landel because I could bill it as the *Battle of the Nature Boys*. The show in Pine Hill was supposed to set up the angle between Rogers and Landel.

Now, Rogers hadn't been in the ring in years. He wanted to get involved, but he didn't want to wrestle, so Larry Winters came up with the idea of making him a special referee. Pine Hill was no more than 20 minutes from where he lived, so getting him to come to the show was a breeze. I remember asking him to buy a referee shirt. He told me he already had one, but when he tried it on, it didn't fit, so he had to buy another one.

Landel ripped off Rogers' shirt when he attacked him. Did Rogers or somebody else gimmick the shirt so it would tear away easily?

I'll give you an honest answer. I don't have a clue. When I looked at the video, it certainly didn't look that way. I would have preferred it not to be because, if we gimmicked the shirt and it looked like we did, we were dead meat. That would work with most promotions, but in our world, we couldn't get away with it, so if the shirt was gimmicked, nobody told me.

My original plan for the *Supercard* was to have Flair against Landel, but shortly after I started making plans, Flair signed with WWE, so I couldn't get him. That was all Buddy Landel's idea. Again, I was the best booker in the world because I didn't book anything. Landel said, "*Here's what I wanna do. I want me against Flair. If you can get Flair, it's me against Flair.*" Again, Nature Boy against Nature Boy. They would have had a great match and it would have drawn a lot of people, not to mention publicity.

Buddy knew that we wouldn't have been able to get Flair a second time, so his plan was to beat Flair — some kind of a screwjob finish — and then have Buddy Rogers come out to challenge Landel.

Flair worked for me one time for that dinner. After that, we stayed in touch, so when it came time to book that card, I called him and he was like, "*Yeah!*" There was no hesitation. We agreed on money. When the word got out that it was going to happen, everybody at the Civic Center was yelling, "*We want Flair! We want Flair!*" But when Flair signed with WWE, there was no way I could get him. Things just didn't fall into place.

Did the show at Pine Hill draw well?

The show in Pine Hill drew about 600 people if I remember the number correctly. There's a video out there — although it's a handheld — of that match.

Philadelphia, Pennsylvania: Nov. 7, 1991
Brawl in the Hall #2, FOP Lodge #5 | Match results unavailable.

Boothwyn, Pennsylvania: Nov. 16, 1991
Chichester High School
- Johnny Hotbody pinned Rick Perez.
- TWA tag team title match
    The Blackhearts beat Tony Stetson & Michael Bruno
- Crybaby Waldo beat Bam Bam Bigelow (forfeit)
- Chichester Crusader pinned Mr. Sandman
- Jimmy Jannetty beat Glen Osbourne (dq)
- Pacific Northwest title match
    Demolition Crush* beat Billy Jack Haynes

There was a card on Nov. 16, 1991, in Boothwyn Pennsylvania. Demolition Crush defended the Pacific Northwest title against Billy Jack Haynes in the main event. Was that your show?
Yes. That was my show, and that was the match that sold me not one ticket. Well, I can't really say that. The smart marks probably bought tickets for it, but neither Billy Jack nor Adams had any following out here. Billy Jack was great. I really liked him, but Adams was no big deal. The problem you have with guys that come out one time is that they don't care. They figure they're there to put in some time and they don't give the fans much. Their job is done when they show up. It's funny. I don't remember the show, but I do remember that match, and it wasn't good.

On that same card, Crybaby Waldo beat Bam Bam Bigelow by forfeit.
That was Larry Winters idea. As I said earlier, Crybaby Waldo would cry every time he got hit. Well, Larry put him in against Bigelow. He cried so much that Bam Bam just quit. He just walked out. That was Larry's way of getting Waldo over without beating Bam Bam. It was a great gimmick.

Was Bigelow quitting a shoot, or a part of the storyline?
It was planned. We wanted to promote the fact that Waldo beat Bam Bam Bigelow, even though he really didn't. I just told Bigelow, "*We have to get him over.*" Originally, the idea was to put them together as a tag team, but Bigelow told me that he couldn't promise to be on every show. So, Larry came with that idea. It's amazing that you asked that. Now Bigelow's dead, Waldo's dead. I wish those guys were alive so I could tell them how much I appreciate them.

Philadelphia, Pennsylvania: Nov. 19, 1991
Bar Wars #9, Original Sports Bar
- Johnny Hotbody beat Michael Bruno
- Glen Osbourne beat Rick Perez
- Crybaby Waldo D.C.O Mr. Anthony
- Max Thrasher beat Harley Watkins
- Rockin' Rebel pinned Jimmy Jannetty
- TWA Bar Wars title match
  Tony Stetson* beat Mr. Sandman
- New England title match
  Johnny Rodz* beat Skull Von Cross
- TWA title match
  Buddy Landel* beat J.T. Smith

On Nov. 24, one month after the show in Pine Hill, you held a press conference.
It was at the Philadelphia Original Sports Bar where we did the Bar Wars and we played it legitimate for the wrestling press. We didn't bother to ask the *Philadelphia Inquirer* to come because we knew they wouldn't have come. *Pro Wrestling Illustrated* was there, Bill Apter was there, George Napolitano was there, wrestling fans were there. That was probably the closest I ever came to being able to say I had TV. We could only do so much on the radio, so we announced the press conference and invited people to show up.

The press conference, of course, was all part of the angle. Buddy Landel came in a suit, which is a picture in itself because Landel seldom wore a suit. Rogers

Buddy Landel gives the press an idea of what he'll do when he wrestles Buddy Rogers, while Buddy, ref John Finegan, and Joel look on.

wore a sports jacket. I called Landel up to the podium and he gave a little speech. I called Rogers up. Of course, they jawed back and forth at each other.

Maybe too much time had gone by since Rogers was a thing, but it seems like you would have gotten at least *some* attention from the mainstream press.

Well, we held the press conference on a Sunday morning. The bar didn't want to do it when they were open. I did ask Dan Geringer because he always supported me, but even he didn't bite. And part of that was probably my fault because I don't think I went out of my way to contact the TV stations or the local newspapers. They were aware of it because we sent out a press release, but nobody seemed to be interested.

At that same press conference, you said you would also have Owen Hart versus Shiro Koshinaka on the card. Owen had signed a contract with the WWF just a few days before that. Was your announcement just hype? People were criticizing you for announcing that because his WWF contract certainly had language that would have precluded any wrestling appearances for other promotions.

I don't remember that at all. I'll say this ... if I announced it, it was going to happen. If Owen had signed with Vince before that, I think Owen would have insisted that he keep his commitment to me. I could be wrong. As I said, I don't even remember announcing that, but if I did, it's possible that Owen hadn't called and told me about it. There was a bond that developed between Owen and me the first time he worked for me. God bless him. He died much too young, but I think if you were actually able to ask Owen, he would tell you that the press he got from the match he had for me was, at least in part, what got him that contract with Vince ... or it started the ball rolling towards him getting that contract.

After the press conference, everybody left except for me, Larry Winters, the two Buddys, and maybe a couple other wrestlers. Landel and Rogers were talking to each other. Landel asked Rogers, "*How do you want to do this?*" Now, Landel knew we were going to put Rogers over, and he knew that Rogers was going to take the belt.

This is what Landel said. "*We'll bullshit with the fans for ten minutes, then I'll hit Rogers, and he'll flatten me like a pancake, pin me, and walk away with the title.*" That's why Rogers was so keen to do the angle. He wanted to match Lou Thesz' record of having wrestled professionally in seven different decades. Of course, after Rogers got the title, he would retire it, and we'd run a small TWA show to determine a new champion.

Was Rogers' health such that he could have actually wrestled, if even for a short time?
The Rogers-Landel match was going to last all of 15 seconds. However, Rogers had no problem going longer and doing his thing. In fact, he was itching to get into the ring ... there's no question about that, but we weren't going to take any chances. We scripted it out. Landel was going to slap Buddy and then Rogers would knock him down and pin him, and that would be the end of it ... and Landel was going to lay down and do it!

We'll get into why the match never came off in a bit, but if it had actually happened, that might have been the biggest story in the wrestling world that year.
I have no doubt of that. I think it would have been a monumental, incredible show.

With all the hype surrounding the match, I wonder how the fans at the show would have reacted to a 15-second match?
Oh, I can picture Philadelphia fans booing the shit out of the match. I thought that even then. I was really concerned about that. I'm sure everybody would have expected more out of a Buddy Rogers match. The smart marks would have understood what was going on, but the fans would have booed and I would have been pissed if that had happened.

That would have been a shame for Rogers, too. You or someone else wrote an article in one of the TWA arena programs that I thought was really cool. You tied Lou Thesz, former NWA world heavyweight champion, into the storyline by saying you had asked Rogers to wrestle, but Thesz talked him out of it, so you brought Rogers in by offering him the opportunity to be a special referee for the Williams-Bigelow match.
I remember the article, but I don't know if Larry Gallone wrote the article or if we collaborated on it. In wrestling circles, Rogers making a comeback was a big story. I could picture Buddy calling Thesz and saying, *"You know, I'm thinking about wrestling. What do you think?"* The idea of Rogers calling Thesz for his opinion was pretty cool. Also, you have no idea how excited I was that Buddy Rogers was willing to run an angle with me.

How much did you pay Rogers for the referee gig and did you come to terms on what his payoff would be for his match with Landel?
I don't remember how much I paid him to referee. I'm sure I underpaid him for what he was bringing to the table. You have no idea.

The one thing that impressed me was Landel's attitude. Buddy was going to do a ten-second squash for Buddy Rogers. The one thing you learn about true professionals is, they don't have to win to be over. Again, we go back to Flair telling me, *"Hey, look at the record of the Four Horsemen. We have the worst win-loss record of anybody."* But they were over! Manny Fernandez was another one. He didn't care about who won or who lost. That didn't matter.

Manny and I recently talked about three shows I promoted on a Friday, Saturday and Sunday. The main event on all three was Manny Fernandez against Wahoo McDaniel. Now, you know those guys enough to know that it wouldn't be a wrestling match. It would be a chop fest. During their match on Friday night — and I swear, without exaggeration, I still feel it — those two guys killed each other. On Saturday night, they did it again, and Wahoo's chops all but took Manny's head off. The next day, I remember telling Manny, "*I don't know how you got out of bed this morning.*" On Sunday afternoon, they did it once again.

Manny laughs about that. When Carmella interviewed him on her podcast, she said, "*You beat the hell out of each other.*" She wasn't there, but she said I had told her about it. Manny said, "*We did that match for two years.*"

Scott, if somebody watched a match between those two, there's no way they could tell me that wrestling is fake. It was unbelievable. Manny wrestled for me six times ... once against Nikita Koloff, once against Abdullah the Butcher, once against Ivan, and three times against Wahoo McDaniel. For a promoter, that's heaven. Anyway, I got off on a tangent again.

Let's table the Rogers-Landel scenario for a bit. We'll come back to it. In Nov. 1991, Sandman and J.T. Smith showed up in Memphis for Jerry Jarrett and Lawler. Did you send them down there, or did Lawler set that up when he was working in Philly?

No, I didn't send them down. I was never an agent per se. Johnny Hotbody had wrestled down there the year before. [July 1990] Hotbody didn't stay long, though, because he had a regular job and was making good money. At some point, we became a feeder. Even Dennis Coralluzzo was in an angle down in Memphis where he was an attorney for Jerry, or against Jerry. I don't remember which. Of course, the Philly fans didn't know what happened in Memphis. If J.T. and Sandman went down there, that was something they worked out on their own.

Sandman didn't stay long. He said he couldn't afford to.

(laughs) From what I've heard, Jarrett and Lawler didn't pay their guys anything. Lawler, who owned a piece of Memphis, stood in my dressing room and told my local guys, "*Look, you don't get paid to go to college. You pay them.*" So he paid his guys a hundred bucks a week and they had to live on that.

Did any of the TWA guys let their success go to their heads?

Rockin' Rebel. I hate to be negative about the guy because I really liked him, but he always thought he was a superstar. Now, to his credit, he would sell tickets, but he was the only one I can think of who really let the shit go to his head. It's funny, but the local guys who *should* have let their success go to their heads didn't! J.T., Sandman, Hotbody ... those guys never got too big for their shoes. And the reality was, back then, they all had full-time jobs. Wrestling was a sideline gig. They understood that they probably wouldn't be going full-time. They weren't going to be on WWF TV. There were exceptions, but they looked at the wrestling business realistically. There weren't that many places to go. If you weren't in the big leagues, you couldn't find work on Monday through Friday nights. Independents were pretty much weekend gigs. We did some weeknight shows, but it wasn't enough to where they could quit their full-time jobs. They had families they had to take care of. (pause) ... I don't even remember the question you asked ... (laughs)

(laughs) Success going to somebody's head.

Oh, yeah. Rebel was the only one. When he walked into Ringmasters, you wanted to ask him where his entourage was because he always had that air about him. Now, there was one other guy who let success go to his head that I haven't mentioned.

Who's that?

Me. The answer to your question is ... me! I let it get to my head. That's the reality. I'm the guy who quit his full-time job. I'm the guy who sunk all his savings into the business. I'm the guy who brought in more talent than he should have because he was the ultimate fan-boy. So, the best answer to your questions is ... me!

I didn't quite see this going in that direction, but that's a good answer. That's the answer.

Philadelphia, Pennsylvania: Dec. 5, 1991
Brawl in the Hall #3, FOP Lodge #5
Match results unavailable
Philadelphia, Pennsylvania: Dec. 7, 1991
Terror at Tabor, Tabor Rams Youth Association Building
• Crybaby Waldo beat Dynamo
• Rick Perez beat Jimmy Jannetty (reversed decision)
• Tony Stetson beat Glen Osbourne
• Mr. Sandman beat J.T. Smith
• Max Thrasher beat Rockin' Rebel
• The Pitbulls, Spike and Rex, beat Johnny Hotbody & Don E. Allen
• TWA title match
  Paul Orndorff beat Buddy Landel* (dq)

I don't remember what this is in reference to, but in my notes after the Dec. 7 card, I have a note to ask you about J.T. Smith having a falling-out with you and Tod Gordon at some point. Was there heat there?
Not that I'm aware of. I don't recall that. It might have happened during the ECW days, but it didn't happen with me. You keep bringing up shit I don't remember. I ignored a lot of that personal shit. I came from a business where everybody was an independent contractor. We all worked together, but everybody was competing with each other. Wrestling is very much the same. If there was heat in the dressing room, most of those guys made sure I wasn't aware of it because I was a hothead. If I found out some guy was giving heat to somebody else, I'd fire them. They never wanted me to be put in that position. I've always believed in the public hanging. If you're going to let somebody go, you don't just do it privately three days after a show. You do it right in the friggin' dressing room. You have to prove a point and set a standard. If that happened, that may be why the boys made sure I didn't hear about it. You'd probably have to ask J.T. about that one.

Ambler, Pennsylvania: Dec. 14, 1991
Ambler Ambush, Wissahickon Middle School
Match results unavailable

Note: Joel ran three shows this week headlined by Paul Orndorff defeating Buddy Landel by disqualification.

New Castle, Delaware: Jan. 24, 1992
Canceled

Philadelphia, Pennsylvania: Jan. 25, 1992
Pennsylvania Hall, canceled, scheduled matches
• Buddy Rogers vs. Buddy Landel
• Steve Williams & Terry Gordy vs. Dan Kroffat & Doug Furnas
• Falls count anywhere
  Eddie Gilbert vs. Kevin Sullivan
• Chris Benoit vs. Shiro Koshinaka

Okay, now let's get back to the card in Philadelphia with Rogers against Landel. You also had Steve Williams and Terry Gordy booked to wrestle Dan Kroffat and Doug Furnas that night.

Steve Williams helped me set that up. Steve and Terry had worked for me in the past. With the Rogers-Landel match going so short, I had to get some matches that were going to fill some time. My shows were normally three-hour shows. Well, Gordy and Williams were a big-name team and I knew they'd give the fans something they'd love.

This may be a good time to get into why the Rogers match never took place.

Okay. I think Gordy and Williams were in Germany, so getting them to the States was going to cost me more money than all the other talent combined. I had to purchase their airline tickets ... and that's when I realized I didn't have the money to do that. That's when I realized that the show just wasn't going to happen. I remember trying to figure out how in the hell I was going to pay the guys. The problem with the Philadelphia Civic Center was that they didn't settle up with me until two to three days after a show. My credit cards were all tapped out and I didn't have any cash. What little cash I received from my season ticket sales went to paying my rent. You know, this is fascinating. This is the first time that I ever sat down and gave serious thought to what went down.

I had to make a decision. Now, I don't know how that show would have drawn, or what the final numbers would have been. The show was getting a lot of mention in the magazines and the dirt sheets. I had fans flying in from Japan, Texas, Tennessee, Florida ... all over the place.

And attendance could have turned out like the Cactus Jack-Eddie Gilbert card.

That's where I was going with this. I don't know if the Rogers-Landel match would have drawn with the general public ... the Philly locals. I don't think Rogers really meant that much to them. I mean, if the show had come off, I suspect that it might have drawn a thousand people, and that being the case, I would have lost at least twenty grand ... and I didn't have the twenty grand to lose. I wasn't about to lose my reputation, either. Everybody *always* got paid. That was always my number one priority. Nobody ever got stiffed on a check and nobody's check ever bounced. There were a few guys who demanded cash, but the guys who knew me were good with a check. I just didn't have the cash to cover the checks.

Part of my issue was that I always thought — and I was mistaken — that everybody else wanted to see what I wanted to see. If I wanted to see Adrian Street above the Mason-Dixon Line, everybody must want to see Adrian Street above the Mason-Dixon Line. Clearly, I was wrong. The one thing you have to learn from your experiences is to realize where you made your mistakes. There's an old quote: *"Don't learn from your own mistakes. Learn from somebody else's mistakes."* I never subscribed to that, so I made a lot of mistakes. The mistakes I made were me not recognizing that what I liked wasn't necessarily going to draw 3,000 people every quarter ... every three months. Some of my bucket list matches didn't draw flies. I know I keep going back to this, but the Kevin Von Erich-Chris Adams vs. Austin Idol-Al Perez match was an *expensive* match! It didn't mean shit to anybody. I thought it would draw because nobody had seen it anywhere else, but I obviously was wrong. I wish the hell I had known what the hell I was doing back then. Tod Gordon was smart enough to bring in Paul E. and Eddie Gilbert. Yeah, he lost a fortune, too, but they were able to go national because they knew what they were doing.

17 Taking a Financial Bath

When you made the decision to leave the wrestling business, you just walked away and never looked back. Tell me the sequence of events.

I did the radio show on Jan. 4th and Jan. 11th. I made a decision to get out of the business on the Tuesday [Jan. 14, 1992] before the Jan. 18 radio show. I still (pause) ... I don't know what the word is — stupid, naïve, whatever — I just thought I could disappear. When I went on the radio, nobody in my inner circle, including Larry Winters, knew that I was getting out. I opened the show with the announcement that it would be the last episode of *Rasslin' Radio* and that the Jan. 25th show was not going to happen. The calls flooded in, with everybody basically saying the same thing. *"I'm sorry to hear that you're going out of business."* People called in to wish me luck, to thank me. I kept thinking to myself, *"All these people who are calling, did they buy tickets?"*

I closed the show with an apology. The last thing I said on the radio — I have the tape somewhere in my garage — the last thing I said was a variation of my catch-phrase ... *"We wrestled, we brawled, we tried it all ... and failed,"* and I went off the air. It all ended with that statement.

Marla was with me that morning. We walked out to the car and ... there was so much weight lifted off my shoulders. We left the radio station and went right back to the apartment and just sat together. I was a beaten man ... as devastated as anyone could have been.

It was nice that you were able to be your own man and could promote the matches that *you* wanted to promote, regardless of what it cost. At what point, though, did you begin to think, *"Man, I'm just not enjoying this as much as I used to?"* In other words, when did it become tedious and more like a job.

It's interesting that you put that last spin on it. I *always* enjoyed it, so it never became tedious. However, what *did* become tiresome was having to build the quarterly big shows ... *Autumn Armageddon*, *Spring Spectacular*, *Winter Challenge*, *Summer Sizzler*. The pressure to try to build up those shows was tough. WWE has hundreds of employees, but I don't know how they handle it all. They seem to have a pay-per-view every three days and they're working months, maybe years, in advance. Again, I was a one-man operation, and to book talent for the big shows every three months was tough. I kept my ear to the ground in case somebody left Crockett, or Vince, and tried to get them while they were hot. The problem was, with their newfound fame, even the newer guys wanted to charge an arm and a leg for an appearance.

When you quit, you already had super shows booked for Jan. 25th, April 25th, July 18th, and Oct. 10th.

Well, maybe I should back up a little and explain how it all started — or maybe I should say *ended*. Nine months before everything came to a screeching halt, Marla got pregnant. Marla getting pregnant was a reality check for me. I knew it was time to get back to work ... and when I say work, I mean a real job where I made real money. It was time for the long hair and stupid glasses to go, and for me to pick up where I left off. My wrestling business was a success. Let me rephrase that. My wrestling business was a success in the respect that it was working ... but I wasn't making a living. It was quite the opposite, and as a provider for my family, I was a failure.

At some point, with a baby on the way, Marla and I had a conversation about getting married. So, yeah. Nine months before the end was when Joel Goodhart the family man began to have long talks with Joel Goodhart the wrestling promoter. I'm not an idiot, you know. Nine months before it ended, I saw the finish line and I knew it was all but over. If I could have made a living in wrestling, I would have continued to do it, but it was clear that it wasn't going to happen. I had two sons, I was going to have a baby in a couple of weeks, and it was clear that it was time for me to go back and make a living again.

Marla, bless her heart, always stood by me, even though she was watching money fly out the window every week. Over those nine weeks, though, she'd ask over and over — and I can't blame her one bit — *"How are we going to pay for this?" "Our electric bill is due. Where is the money going to come from?"* She was due to give birth in February, so by January, I knew it was time to cut my hair and get back into the insurance and investments business, and more importantly, become a daddy again.

Within a week, week-and-a-half, after the final radio show, Danielle was born, and it's amazing how life events take on a life of their own. I moved forward and never looked back. I faced the challenge of rebuilding my life all over again.

What was Marla's reaction to your decision?
Marla missed the spotlight ... not on her, but on me. I did, too, so it was tough for both of us. That being said, she was more than ready for me to move on. She never lectured me about it, but we both knew it was time.

You said you didn't talk to anyone about wrestling after you walked away, but I found an article by Dan Geringer in the May 4, 1992, *Philadelphia Daily News* in which you were quoted. You talked about your losses and why you left the business.
I guess I did. I had forgotten about that, but other than that, from the day I quit until 2009, during those 17 years, I didn't watch wrestling, I didn't follow ECW, I didn't make a phone call to any of the wrestlers who had worked for me. I disappeared. I went off the radar. It wasn't until 2009, when I got a call from Michael Tartaglia, that I talked to anyone from the wrestling business. I'll get into that later on.

In the article, you told Geringer that you lost $130,000 in 26 months, but in our talks, you keep saying it was $168,000. What's the discrepancy?
It was 168.

So what you told Dan was incorrect?
Yes, that was incorrect. The true number was 168,000 because I had taken money out of my pocket. I told Dan Geringer that it was 130,000, but that didn't include that personal money. When I did all the accounting, it was $168,000, to the penny.

Before we move on to what you did *after* you quit, let's talk a bit about a few things that took place a week or two *before* you quit. Shortly before you walked away, the *Observer* reported that your connection with New Japan Pro Wrestling, which was through Tokyo Joe, had fallen apart, so the Chris Benoit vs. Shiro Koshinaka match was in jeopardy. When Owen Hart went to the WWF, do you remember booking Chris Benoit in his place?
I don't remember that. I don't remember the New Japan deal falling apart, either. Who was New Japan in bed with at that point ... Crockett?

I think so.
I do remember thinking, *"I'm just too small-time for these guys."* But they came to me and we worked together. I think their talent sold some tickets, but they'd come in for one match ... they'd fly for 24 hours here and 24 hours back for one match. I couldn't afford to book them for that. Those matches were for the smart marks, no question about it. Again, if I had had TV at the time, there's no telling what I could have done.

While we're on the subject of New Japan, after you mentioned to me that some people were booing the Owen Hart-Takayuki Iizuka match, I watched that tape again. It's really clear ... maybe a dozen people booed. I watched that whole friggin' match trying to figure out when they booed and I heard maybe a dozen people ... if that! That was it. At the end of the match, they got a standing ovation. There again, though, the fans enjoyed the match, but I don't know how many people bought tickets to see that particular match. Again, I put on all those super shows, and the shows, in their entirety, weren't drawing as well as they should have given the talent on the cards.

When people go to NASCAR, they go because they want to see Dale Earnhardt, or they want to see Jeff Gordon or Kyle Busch. Very few people go to see a race. Very few people go to a WWE show to see wrestling. They didn't in the '80s, either. They went to see Hogan. They went to see Roddy Piper. Well, there were 600 people in the building the night Owen wrestled Iizuka, so nobody came to see him. They didn't buy tickets for Cactus-Gilbert, either. I made mistakes. I made a lot of mistakes.

Back to Tokyo Joe ... it was reported that the New Japan deal fell apart because you weren't returning his phone calls.
That could be. I remember the time difference always being a real problem for me. That being said, he called quite often because he wanted to put a guy on every one of my quarterly shows. That put financial stress on me because his guys were costing me a fortune. That was a good example of me biting off more than I could chew. Then he'd call and ask where on the card his guy were ... are they third on the card, are they main event, who they would work best with, that kind of thing. He'd call and tell me, *"I want this guy to work with so-and-so and this guy to work with whoever."* And not only was it costing me a fortune to bring the guys over from Japan, the guys he wanted them to work with were costing me a fortune. Owen Hart is a classic example. Owen was a phenomenal wrestler, but in Philly, he wasn't someone who could sell enough tickets to justify the expense. Sure, the smart marks wanted to see him, but how many smart marks came to my shows? But Joe's guys wanted to work with Owen. I understood that, but that didn't mean that Owen was available. He'd mention names, like Jushin Liger, and countless others.

So it wasn't so much me not returning his calls because I didn't want to talk to him. I loved talking to Joe because we had some great phone conversations. I was thinking, *"I've finally made the big-time! This establishes me!"* Well, yeah. On the one hand, it established me, but on the other, it cost me a gazillion dollars. As finances were going south, I ran into things like that a lot. I was making financial decisions based on emotion, and emotion leads to mistakes. I really bit off more than I could chew.

In the *Observer*, it was reported that Buddy Rogers said you weren't returning his phone calls, and that was before you made the decision to quit.
That's one that there's no truth to at all. I'm curious as to where Meltzer got all that information. I know his name comes up a lot, but a lot of what he wrote was bullshit. I've heard guys say he'd hear one person tell a story and he'd print it, and

people would think "*If it's in the Observer, it must be true.*" He never checked other sources for confirmation. If there was a phone call to Rogers that I didn't return, it was probably during the week before the radio show on Saturday [Jan. 18, 1992] when I announced my decision to hang it all up. I remember sitting down with Marla early that week. I was devastated. My dream was blowing up. On that Tuesday, or at least early that week, I had my phone disconnected. It's possible that Buddy called me after that, so if he didn't get an answer, that's the reason why.

That makes sense.

You see, I woke up that Tuesday morning and thought, "*It's over!*" The signs had been there. I knew the end was coming, so when I made the decision to close up, that was it. If I hadn't changed my phone number, I'm pretty sure it would have been ringing non-stop. Then again, for all I know, maybe not one person called me. If anybody did, all they got was a message telling them, "*This number is not in service.*"

So you never called Rogers after that?

No. Doug Furnas, Dr. Death, Terry Gordy ... no, I never called any of them. I'll give you one better. I didn't call anybody. I assumed everybody listened to the show.

Did you get any feedback from any of them over the fact that you didn't let them know?

I never heard from them because I shut my phone off. That was interesting. Tod Gordon says that we spoke after I went off the air. To this day, I don't recall that at all, but Tod doesn't lie. Maybe he called me, maybe he didn't, but I don't remember talking to him. I do remember talking to Johnny Hotbody, but I didn't call any of the main-eventers. I didn't even call Larry Winters, my booker. He heard about it on the radio.

In hindsight, I would not have done it the same way. I would have let everybody know. But I was going to lose $30,000 on that show. I had a thousand ticket advance, but I needed 2,000 seats to break even, or I was going to take a financial bath. Man, that card would have been phenomenal, but it is what it is.

The very week you walked away, it was reported that you were in discussions with people about promoting shows in Daytona Beach and Pompano Beach. What was that all about?

Well, it wasn't so much about promoting shows. I don't remember the guy's name now, but somebody from Florida contacted me. I was the kind of guy who — good or bad — if somebody called me from Daytona Beach and said, "*I'd like to bring one of your shows down here,*" I'd announce it. I felt like that gave me credibility. There were a lot of things like that which never came to fruition. At one time, we contacted MTV to see if they would use one of our videos. That never happened. But, no. I never went to Florida to check out venues or anything like that. It was simply a conversation that never got serious enough.

I *did* talk to Sullivan, Landel and Austin Idol about it. If I would have promoted Florida, those were the guys I would have booked on my cards. The one thing I did hear was that Florida was a very difficult place to get established in. The main problem with Florida was, your competition was the weather. If it was a nice day, your walk-up was the shits. That's an interesting subject because we never ran TWA in Atlantic City, which is only 60 miles from here. The only guy who did well in Atlantic City was Vince. Vince had a couple of *WrestleManias* there. Nobody ran there because they were competing against the ocean in the summer and there's nobody there in the winter. Nobody goes to Atlantic City because they want to spend a night at the wrestling matches. Florida was very similar, and fortunately, I had a lot of people who told me it wasn't a good idea.

Back to your mention of the videos you wanted MTV to air. What were the videos?

I knew a guy who worked at Camden County Community College. He was an IT guy. His first name was Oleh ... O-L-E-H. I can't pronounce his last name. He says to me one day — again, his idea — he said, *"Do you mind if I put together a video?"*

I didn't know what he had in mind, but I said, *"No, put together a video."*

He edited music into highlights of the matches. I asked the people at MTV, *"If I send you a video, would you consider putting it on?"* Well, they were tight with Vince, so that wasn't going to happen, but I was of the "nothing ventured, nothing gained" mindset. But that video was put together by Oleh because he loved to do that kind of thing, and it took him forever to put it together. We never sold it, but we could have. We wouldn't have had to get permission from the wrestlers because we owned all rights to everything. It was no big deal. Still, to this day, that video is excellent. I watch it now and then and I just can't believe it's something that came from something I created. But I didn't create the video. That was Oleh's idea. He did it all. Oleh created two or three videos in all.

What was the reason for creating videos if you weren't going to sell them?

We had plans to do that, but we were waiting to see if MTV was interested in airing them on their network. We just never moved ahead with them.

You also had a television taping scheduled for Jan. 27 in Philly. You were said to have had plans to tape TV every third week. What was that all about?

Let's just say that wishes sometimes do come true. I made a contact at a TV station. I always go back to the fact that I was a one-man operation, but I had no clue what the hell I was doing. At least when Tod took over and opened up ECW, he was smart enough to bring in people to help. It helped that he had money behind him and he was able to get television. I kept hoping for TV, hoping for TV. I'm trying to remember the details. I do know I had the guys scheduled for a TV taping on the 27th, which was a Monday. Obviously, if I did the TV taping on a Monday, it was going to cost me a fortune to keep the guys in town after the show on the 25th, so that wasn't going to happen. I wouldn't have Gordy, Williams, or any of those guys there. I would have relied on my local talent, which was one of the conversations I had with Larry Winters leading up to the show. It would have been much too expensive to bring somebody in for a Saturday show and keep them until Tuesday after doing TV on Monday.

Did you have a contract with the TV station?

I never signed the contract. The conversations I had were ... let's call them pie in the sky. They were going happen on the 27th, though ... *if* I had stayed around. There's no question about that. My plan was to shoot three weeks of TV because I couldn't afford to bring in guys for one shot. It was going to be the old "have three weeks' worth of angles in the can". What I didn't consider ahead of time, though, was that I couldn't afford to keep the guys around that long.

You announced Eddie Gilbert, Buddy Landel, Kevin Sullivan, and The Blackhearts for the debut taping.

Yep. Cactus lived in New York, so that wasn't an issue. Eddie would have hung around. Eddie and Cactus would have done anything I asked them to do. Buddy Landel would have, too. I'm not sure about Kevin Sullivan, but that wouldn't have surprised me.

When you got out of the business, did Larry continue to train people at Ringmasters?
I don't know. I never asked him. I assume that it closed up because I had the rental agreement with CFI Gym. I'm assuming that I went off the air on Saturday and the guys closed the school on Monday, but quite frankly, I don't know what happened. I just walked away. Then again, on second thought, they had the school when Tod took over and started Eastern Championship Wrestling, so they probably never missed a lick. The only contact I had with anybody after I got out of the business was the state athletic commission. They had my $10,000 cash bond, of which I never got one penny back. I assumed the $10,000 was sent out to the ticket holders. I couldn't tell you how the fans got their refunds other than filing with the state to get them. I don't know if the state got ahold of everybody, but every once in a while, I run into somebody who tells me that they never got their money back. The people who bought tickets through Ticketmaster didn't have a problem because they had a record of everybody who bought the tickets.

Okay, so here come the tough questions. My understanding is that anyone who purchased a ticket had to go to the Philadelphia Civic Center box office to claim their refund. In lieu of that, they had to request a refund from the Pennsylvania Boxing Commission.
That may be. I didn't get involved, so I don't have any idea of how they got their refunds. In fact, the state never contacted me about anything ... no correspondence whatsoever. For all I know, the state athletic commission kept my $10,000 and didn't pay anybody back.

It was said that $30,000 in ticket stubs were returned to the commission, so the people who purchased advance tickets received 30 cents on the dollar.
Well, if there was $30,000 worth of advance tickets sold, I would have ran that show. Those numbers are absolutely false, and the only tickets that would have been returned to the athletic commission were the season tickets that we sold at the Squared Circle. Ticketmaster would have made good on the others. Now I can't confirm the 30 cents on the dollar because I never heard from the state. The bottom line is, if I had $30,000 from advance ticket sales, I would have run the show. That's the first time I've heard that.

Did you declare bankruptcy?
No, I didn't. I just moved on with my life. The problem with filing bankruptcy was, I wanted to get back into the insurance and investment business, and if you have a bankruptcy on your record, you can't keep your securities license.

In the Jan. 27, 1992, *Observer*, Meltzer wrote "Goodhart's bankruptcy announcement came just one week before a scheduled big show in Philadelphia, which insiders had known was falling apart." Which insiders would have known it was falling apart?
The bankruptcy claim is blatantly incorrect. The only person who may have said something about the show falling apart was Larry, but Larry didn't know that until I was gone. I talked to Larry about that years later and he told me he didn't have a clue. The only person who knew was my fiancée. She's the only one who knew. I didn't call anybody. I didn't call Cactus. I didn't call Eddie. I didn't call anybody. After Jan. 18, 1992, at 9:00 a.m., I didn't think about wrestling and I didn't watch wrestling on TV.

After you walked out, how much time went by before you talked to Larry again?
Seventeen years. It was 2009. It's funny how Meltzer seemed to know everything about me and TWA, but he never once called me for a quote. He never asked me one question.

So you don't remember having any personal interaction with Meltzer?
I don't recall ever meeting or talking with him, but if we had talked, it would have been over the phone. Meltzer never called me to get results or to find out what was happening behind the scenes in the dressing room. All the shit that was on his sheet was coming from fans. I know that good and bad things were written about TWA. My philosophy was, as long as they were talking about you, it was good. It would have been nice, though, if he had gone to the source rather than taking the word of readers who really didn't know the story of what went on behind the scenes. A good reporter would have called me and asked, *"Hey, I've got this story. What's going on?"* But that never happened.

In the March 16, 1992, *Observer*, he published a letter from Dennis Coralluzzo, who wrote, "the commission didn't seize Joel's bond, but seized a letter of credit for $10,000 through his bank."
No, it was cash.

And that was considered a bond.
Yeah. It's either cash or credit. I had no credit. I gave them $10,000 in a CD.

What about your promoter's license? Did they revoke it?
I'm assuming they did. Again, I didn't get anything in the mail from them. I could probably call the state athletic commission and find out. I'm sure they have a record about something like that.

I never had much respect for wrestling and boxing commissions. Their only concern was to collect revenue.
It's all about money. They get tax revenue. The state athletic commission did nothing for me, but I have to say, they didn't nothing against me, either. The face of the Pennsylvania Boxing Commission was a guy by the name of Frank Talent. Frank was a super-mark. He came to every one of my shows. Back in that day, we were going over the line all the time, but Frank didn't care. Frank was a guy who just loved to be around the wrestlers. He used to do ring announcing for Vince. He just loved to be around the guys. I have nothing but good things to say about him. He was a great "in." I never spoke to Frank after I walked away from the business, but I understand that he has since passed away.

One of the interesting state laws was that the wrestlers had to be at the venue an hour before show time. That was tough for the main event guys because, even though they weren't going on until nine-thirty or ten o'clock, they had to be there around six o'clock.

That was a state law?
That was a state law. One of the commission regulations was, if you're going to be announced, you had to be there an hour before.

I never heard that! Wow!
So what did the guys do for three or four hours ... before they went on? They played cards, they sat in the dressing room, they told stories, and they watched the matches. And here's the kicker. They couldn't eat during all that time because they had to go out and bust their ass in the ring.

When they were done with their match, they'd take a shower. They were starved, so they'd go out and eat. Some of them would go out and party. Of course, the main item of business for most of the guys was getting laid. They'd wake up the next morning, go to the gym for an hour and a half, take a shower, get in the car, and drive to the next town, where they'd start all over.

What did they do during the two to four hours they were on the road driving to the next town? They talked about what they did after the matches the night before. They talked about angles, they talked about fan reaction, they bad-mouthed the promoters, they talked about the rats they had screwed, and they threw around ideas. The guys don't do that today because they're flying everywhere, and if they do drive, there's not much to talk about because their ideas don't matter. Everything is scripted for them. They can't talk about anything personal, or knock anybody, because everything has a funny way of getting back to Vince.

It's amazing that, with all the hardcore stuff you did, you never had a problem with the commission.

Never. I should expand on that a bit. There were times when Frank asked me to cut it back a little bit, but he never threatened to shut me down. The main issue we had was that Philadelphia had a curfew, and at times, our shows would run too long. I don't recall ever having an issue with blood. One thing that Frank always told me was, "*You better make sure your insurance covers this shit.*" But that was it. And before you ask, the insurance did cover it. Frank — or nobody else from the commission — ever gave me any heat.

Did you have heat with anyone regarding your walking away and leaving people with worthless tickets?

Oh, yeah, but it wasn't until 2009, when I started going to some of the matches. I was out of sight from 1992 to 2009. Every once in a while, somebody would come up to me and say, "*You still have a hundred dollars of my money.*"

I said, "*All you had to do was contact the state athletic commission. The money was there, so that's not my fault.*" But, yeah, people would occasionally say that to me. I had one person come up to me — I'm trying to remember who it was — he came up to me at one of the ECWA shows and told me, "*I'm still pissed that you walked away with my money.*"

I said, "*Look, I'll tell you what. When my book is published, I'll give you a free book.*"

We might be giving out a lot of books!

(laughs) The problem is, anybody could say they didn't get a refund. I don't have a list of who paid and I don't have a list of who got reimbursed by Ticketmaster or the state. I realize that some people lost money. There's no question about it. Of course, in my mind, I justify it by saying I lost $168,000. I didn't want to hear about someone losing a hundred bucks. That doesn't make it right, but that's how I justified it in my head. To be honest with you — and I've thought about this many times — if the state of Pennsylvania had given me a list of all the people who didn't get their money back, I probably would have paid them back over the years. To this day, I don't know who did and who didn't, and of those who tell me they didn't, I have no way or knowing whether or not they're telling me the truth.

Maybe we should put an announcement on the website. (pregnant pause) **I'm kidding.**

I'll tell you what would happen if we did that. I'd get 1300 people ask for a refund, when in fact, I sold less than 200 tickets. Wrestling fans are wrestling fans. Even if somebody came up to me today, I'd ask them to prove it. Again, I don't know who or how much the state paid out. Maybe they paid out *more* than $10,000. I don't know if they paid anybody. I had zero communication from the state.

Do you remember what the advance for the show was?

No, I don't remember. I do remember that it was more than $10,000, but I don't remember what it was. I do know that I wasn't going to make my money back on that show. That's the main reason I walked. I wouldn't have been able to pay the guys. In my own weird cockamamie way, I sometimes blame the fans that it all fell through. I mentioned to you before … I had 22,000 listeners per quarter hour on the radio and I was drawing 1,000, 1500, 2,000 people to the Civic Center. If I could have drawn just 3,000 people — around 15 percent of my listeners — I would have had no problems! All the freeloaders who listened to my radio show and didn't support me were the problem. Now, that's certainly not the case, but that's how I justified it in my mind.

Did you ever get any complaints from the Better Business Bureau or the Consumer Division of the Attorney General's office?

None. None that I'm aware of.

Another mention in the *Observer* said, "Joel Goodhart sent a form letter out to all his former wrestling customers advertising his new insurance and investments business."

Yeah. It's funny that you mention that. I was starting up in the [insurance and investment] business again. I went out on Jan. 18 and I think I hooked up in May. I thought, "*I'll just send out a letter to all my mailing lists.*" The insurance business is all about getting the word out to as many people as you can, so I figured I'd send out an announcement. Yeah, I was an idiot. I didn't think people hated me, but by sending that out, everybody had my address and phone number. They could have come to my office and caused me all kinds of trouble. Nobody did, though.

So, you lost some $168,000 during the course of your promotional career. Was that in addition to lost wages from not being employed, or was that not even counting what you lost in compensation?

The 168 grand was real money, money I paid out. That didn't include what I could have made on the outside because God knows what that number would have been ... but that $168,000 was a real number.

That's unreal. Where did you get the money?

It's embarrassing to admit this, but I cashed out my retirement plan. Theoretically, if I had kept that $168,000 in my portfolio, it would be worth a million dollars today. So, yeah. I can honestly say that I lost a million dollars in today's dollars, and I probably lost another million in money that I could have made. Now, keep in mind, when I was promoting, I wasn't paying myself a salary, so I was taking my rent out of the $168,000. I lived on a portion of that 168,000, but the majority of it went into the wrestling business.

That's unbelievable.

That's one of the reasons why I was a one-man operation. I couldn't afford to hire anybody. I did have one employee who I hired to answer the telephones and what have you, but I did everything else. Booking, promotion, marketing ... you name it!

In a shoot interview with Tod Gordon, when asked if he was aware that you had money problems, he said he told you not to take the ticket money for that next show because there was no way you could afford to put it on. He said you split with all the money.

That's a bunch of shit. Tod Gordon wasn't aware of the financial crunch I was in. Now, he knew I needed some working capital because he lent me $15,000. I don't know if he thought he would ever get it back. Tod certainly had enough family money that he was able to do it. Bob Artese also lent me $10,000. They were there for me, and I can't ever thank them enough for that.

Did Bob Artese ever do any ring announcing for TWA?

No. Bob was a ring announcer for Tod when Tod opened Eastern Championship Wrestling. Bob was a fan of wrestling, and specifically, TWA. He and his wife,

Lex, used to sit on the front row. I see him once in a while. He's a great guy and his wife is a great girl.

Did he ever ask for the money ...

No, not one time.

He never even mentioned it?

Well, one time we had a conversation. He said he knew that he took a chance when he gave me the money because he had a feeling that the business was going under. He did the ring announcing for Tod for many years, as well as a lot of TV. Bob now manages a skating rink out here. He's done that for a long time.

Tod was my ring announcer and he sat at ringside. Watch the videos sometime. He was my contact at Variety Club and got me on the board, so we always put each other over. He was my contact for the insurance, as well.

What insurance was that?

I contributed $5,000 in exchange for using the Variety Club's insurance. Their insurance covered.all of their fundraisers. Tod and I worked well together, but he didn't have anything to do with the actual business ... the booking or the promoting. I guess the best way to say it is, Tod was always around, but he never told me to not collect ticket money. That's a bunch of crap.

There were a few times when Tod came to me with ideas. I was always willing to listen, but I don't remember doing anything based on what he suggested. It is possible, though, because Tod was a smart guy and he would have had good ideas. I don't remember him giving me tips on better ways to run my business, either, but if he had, I should have listened because he knows how to run a business.

Were you having any problems with Tod towards the end? Did he ever complain about not getting any return on the money he loaned you?

No, there was never any heat or anything like that. The thing is, the money was a loan. He wasn't a partner or anything like that. Bob Artese wasn't, either. When the thing fell through, I got one phone call from Tod and he asked me what I thought he should do [regarding an opportunity to promoting wrestling]. I told him to keep it going. He had family money from a hundred years before. I don't know how wealthy he was, but I knew he had some kind of money that *I* didn't have. But I gave him my blessing. I told him, "*Go do what you want to do,*" and history shows that he did it well.

Other than the few people who said they never got their refund, I don't think you have heat with anyone.

From the business side of things, I was even with everybody. Obviously, the boys lost a payday, but there was nothing tangible lost because they didn't make the trip. Of the fans who might have been there who bought tickets at the store — I'd say there were around a hundred — yeah, they probably have a right to be pissed. Ticketmaster would have refunded everybody else.

As far as the industry is concerned, I was top-notch. Yes, I'm sure some of the fans who didn't get refunds were upset with me, and understandably so, but I justified it in my mind that I used my personal money to give them the matches they dreamed about. If they lost a hundred dollars, or $30 if the commission refunded just 30 percent, they got their money's worth with all the stuff I gave them. Now, that's how I justified it, and I understand how someone could be upset over losing that money, but it's not like I lived a frivolous lifestyle and used their money to buy a Cadillac or go on luxury vacations. In fact, I could have had all those things if I hadn't promoted wrestling, but I chose to give them as much — possibly more — entertainment than any other promoter of that era.

For all the accolades people throw at ECW and Paul E., when they went out of business, many of their regular guys were owed six figures. I don't know how much you know about it, but at least you didn't owe the boys money when you folded.

Well, the only thing I've heard — and I don't know if it's true or not — is that, when WWE bought them, it was just to pay off the debts they owed. I don't think anybody got paid a lump sum of money. And if I lost $168,000, I know Tod lost a lot more than that. I never talked to Tod about this, but my guess is, if you're going out, you just have to disappear. Well, ECW was a much higher-profile company than TWA ever was. I mean, they couldn't just fold up their tents and disappear. Again, think about this ... if the fans of Philadelphia lost *anything*, it was miniscule compared to the great wrestling Tod gave them with ECW over the years.

TRI-STATE WRESTLING ALLIANCE 1992 SEASON TICKET PLAN

WE WRESTLE!
WE BRAWL!
WE DO IT ALL!

WINTER CHALLENGE III
—·—·—·—
SPRING SPECTACULAR III
—·—·—·—
SUMMER SIZZLER III
—·—·—·—
AUTUMN ARMAGEDDON III

Season Ticket Plans

The TRI-STATE WRESTLING ALLIANCE Season Tickets are offered in a variety of affordable plans. Each plan guarantees you the same great seat for each of the four cards. Most season ticket holders also receive a discount on all TWA cards held at locations other than the Philadelphia Civic Center.

V.I.P. PLAN $140
A limited number of front row seats are available. This is the premiere plan for TWA fans. In addition to being on top of the action, the plan includes a 10% discount on outside cards.

PLATINUM PLAN $100
Enjoy the TWA from some of the best seats in the building. The Platinum Plan includes a 10% discount on outside cards.

GOLD PLAN $60
An economic way to acquire very good seats to the TWA. The Gold Plan includes a 5% discount on outside cards.

SILVER PLAN $48 *
Be part of all the exciting TWA action in 1992.

(*24 for kids under 12)

Season Ticket Orders

Be at the Philadelphia Civic Center for all four of the TRI-STATE WRESTLING ALLIANCE Supercards. Choose one of four plans and guarantee your seats for all the action!

PLAN	Price	#Tix	Total
V.I.P.	$140		
PLATINUM	$100		
GOLD	$ 60		
SILVER	$ 48		
SILVER-Kids	$ 24		
GRAND TOTAL ENCLOSED			$

Season Ticket Deadline: January 25, 1992

Individual event order form
Individual orders will be processed when received

Event	$35	$25	$15	$12	$6	Tot.
Winter Chal.						
Spring Spec.						
Summer Siz.						
Autumn Arm.						
Grand Total Enclosed						$

Please make check or money order payable to:
SQUARED CIRCLE
Total remittance must accompany all orders.

Please Print
Name _____
Address _____
City _____ St ____ Zip _____
Phone (d) _____ (n) _____
VISA and MASTERCARD Accepted
Type of card _____
CARD # _____ EXP. DATE _____
SIGNATURE _____
Mail to: SQUARED CIRCLE, PO BOX 57068
Phila., PA 19111
Tickets can also be purchased at all TICKETMASTER locations and the Philadelphia Civic Center Box Office

Flyer promoting Tri-State Wrestling Alliance season tickets

18 Sleeping Well at Night

Okay, take me back to the day after the last episode of *Rasslin' Radio*.
 The next morning — Sunday morning — when I woke up, my first thoughts were, "*I've gotta get my life together. My daughter's gonna be born. I've gotta get back to work. I've gotta pick up where I left off. The experiment failed. I have to move on.*" Then it hit me. I had nothing to do that day. Part of me felt like I was just a total failure ... and I was absolutely broke. I had spent every penny I had. In fact, shortly before the end, I actually had to borrow money from my father-in-law to pay the rent. It was a humbling and embarrassing moment.

 I can't say enough good things about Marla. As bad as things were, she stuck by me the whole time. After I made the announcement, I think we both realized that it was just the two of us. We were going to have a baby and start a new life. It was time. It was time.

How tough was it emotionally to just walk away from the business?
 It bothered me for about 20 seconds. During the nine-month period I mentioned earlier, I prepared for it mentally. I'm not one who accepts defeat, so the biggest issue I had was what I call my personal public hanging. I had to go on the radio and make the announcement that I was going to close up. I didn't tell *anybody* until after I made that announcement because I knew that if I told anybody, it would be in the dirt sheets before I could announce it publicly. And when I say I didn't tell *anybody*, I mean *anybody!* I didn't tell Larry Winters, D.C., nobody. Nobody knew I was folding up.

 I guess I should revise my answer to your question. Wrestling is like a drug. You get addicted. And quite frankly, I knew that the only way I would ever get out was to go out cold turkey. I don't think most wrestlers look back when they get out, although with so many autograph shows taking place now, they get to live their personas again, but the rest of the time, they live normal lives. If you're a fan and you tell one of the old-timers that you watch *Monday Night Raw* or one of the other programs, they look at you funny. That's me. I promoted wrestling for a career ... if you can call it that. I'm not gonna watch it now. It's funny, but I'll bet 99 percent of Lawler's fan don't realize that Jerry was wrestling in the early '70s. They think he got his start with Vince.

When did you and Marla get married?
 We weren't married when I left the business. My daughter was born on Feb. 5th and we got married that next December. We wanted to be married in the same year that my daughter was born, although she obviously was born out of wedlock. The reason we got married was because Marla was working for a company down in Center City and they gave her health insurance benefits. In January 1993, her father was giving her his business, but she wouldn't have any benefits, so by becoming my wife, she got my benefits. So I guess you could say I got married, not out of love, not out of lust, but because Marla needed benefits.

Philadelphia, Pennsylvania: Feb. 25, 1992
Market Street Mayhem, Eastern Championship Wrestling, Original Sports Bar
• Jimmy Jannetty draw Stevie Richards (20:00)
• Glen Osbourne beat Crybaby Waldo
• Super Destroyer #1 beat Michael Bruno
• Tony Stetson beat Ivan Koloff
• Jeff Royal beat Max Thrasher
• D.C. Drake & J.T. Smith vs. Johnny Hotbody & Larry Winters (double DQ)

After you walked away, Tod Gordon launched his Eastern Championship Wrestling promotion. He held his first show at the Original Sports Bar on the very night you had planned for the Rogers-Landel match. I always wondered why Tod didn't contact Rogers and use him that night.
I have a feeling that Rogers health was really on the decline at that point. It may have been that Rogers wouldn't have been able to even appear for me. I don't know that for a fact, but he passed away just a few months after that show would have taken place. I don't know. I don't know why Tod didn't do that. For all I know, he may have asked Rogers, but Rogers turned him down.

Rogers may have been unable to make the shot, but I did ask Tod about that the other day. He said he just wasn't interested in Rogers. Did you pay attention at all to what was going on when Tod Gordon was running Eastern Championship Wrestling?
None. I avoided it like the plague. I gave him my blessing. He didn't need that, but I told him to go do it. The whole concept of Eastern Championship Wrestling was his. I had nothing to do with it. To this day, I've never watched an ECW show — Eastern or Extreme — and I know DVDs are available. I didn't even watch the show where they brought out somebody who was supposed to be me! [Feb. 25, 1995] I think his name was Joel Hartgood.

How did you get back into the insurance business? Did you call on your old clients? We already talked about you sending out letters to your list of wrestling fans, which I think is hilarious.
That took balls, didn't it? (laughs)

It did.
I just chilled for about a week, and then I decided it was time, so I started to do some research. Now, here's the good news. A lot of my old clients stuck with me. It wasn't like they went out looking for more insurance and had to go find another insurance agent. I got a lot of positive responses. *"Hey! Welcome back! Sure, let's get together."* Now, I did lose a few clients, but a great majority of them stuck with me. In fact, a lot of them had been listening to the radio show. They weren't wrestling fans, but they got a kick out of the fact that someone they knew was on the radio. Then I had several clients who *were* wrestling fans, but when I went to talk to them about insurance, I couldn't have a one-hour appointment. The appointments were two to three hours long because they wanted to ask me a million questions about wrestling.

My biggest decision was finding a company I wanted to join. Back then, I wrote much more insurance than investments. Today, I'm 90 percent investments, but back then I was probably 75 percent insurance. So, I started looking at the ads and interviewed around. The problem I had was that I hadn't yet made the physical change. I still looked like Joel Goodhart the ring announcer. I still had the long hair and wore snakeskin boots. I did some interviews and I wound up going to a Prudential office in Blue Bell, which is a suburb of Philadelphia.

Now, I always had an issue with Prudential. There was just something about the company that bothered me. Anyway, I went in and sat down ... and sure enough, the guy in charge of hiring was a wrestling fan. In fact, he used to listen to the radio show. He got such a big kick out of me walking into his office. His name was Glen Pellicott. I think he's since passed away, but Glen was a basketball referee on the side. We spent three hours talking, and most of the time, we talked about wrestling. He picks up the phone and calls in this other guy ... a guy named Leon Sobolefski. We used to call him "Polish Hammer." *"Hey Leon! You've got to come in here!"* Leon comes in and guess what?

He was a wrestling fan, too.

Yes! (laughs) Before you know it, three or four other guys are in there and they're all buying into the persona. They knew that I had been in the insurance business for 13 years, from 1976 to 1989, and that I'd be coming in with an existing clientele, so it was a no-brainer. *"Yeah, we'll take you!"* There was no guarantee, no stipend, no salary. The only thing they offered was a place for me to set up shop so I could do my thing.

Now there was no finance on the insurance side. You can be financed just one time in your career. That keeps guys from jumping from company to company to get salaries. So I wasn't financed. They just had to take me.

What do you mean by being financed?

I talked about this earlier, but I don't think I used the word *financed*. When I was first hired by The Equitable — a great company, by the way — in 1976, they gave me a salary of $500 a month. You got $250 on the 15th of the month, and on the last day of the month, you got another 250. Now, during the first two years of your contract, whatever business you wrote that earned commissions, you got paid half. That was the deal. At the end of two years, if you would have made more money getting paid straight commissions, you would be paid the difference. That's what we call "being financed."

At the end of two years, you can leave and go to another company, but you work on straight commission. You don't get financed again. I was at The Equitable from 1976 to 1989. I left in 1989 and tried to make wrestling my full-time thing, and in 1992, I finally came to the realization that I wasn't going to make any money in the wrestling business, so I knew I had to do something else to take care of my family.

I was with Prudential from '92 to '01. As it turned out, it was a hell of a little career. I was so far in advance of the other Prudential guys there that I moved to another company, New England Financial, which was the worst move I ever made. I was there for two years and left in 2002 to open BIRE Financial Services, my current company. The company name was BIRE, as in fire.

Is BIRE an actual word or an acronym?

It's an acronym for the services we offer ... Business, Individual, Retirement, Estate. I used to tell people, *"If you're a buyer, I'm BIRE."* The corporate name is BIRES SWAN, so our logo is a white swan. I'm big with acronyms. SWAN stands for the phrase "Sleep Well At Night." *"BIRE clients sleep well at night."*

There's an interesting story about the origin of the name BIRE. My assistant at Prudential was a girl named Rebecca. I told her I was thinking about leaving and promoting myself. I said, *"I have to come up with a name for my own company."* Now, keep in mind, I didn't create BIRE right away. I decided to go with New England Financial, instead. Anyway, she said, *"I have an idea for a name. I thought about this a while back. You have three kids ... Ross, Mark and Danielle. Use the first two letters of each name ... ROMADA."*

I said, *"That's great!"* I called my attorney, a guy named Malcolm, and told him to put in the papers to name the company. Six days later, UPS delivers a box, about three inches high. I open it and it's a lawsuit filed against me by Ramada, the hotel company, for name infringement. I was sweating bullets, so I called my attorney. He assured me, *"You're not getting sued. What they're doing is trying to scare you. Even if they did pursue it, they'll bury you in paperwork and it would take seven years for the courts to make a decision. They know you'll beat them because you're not a hotel, you're not selling food, you're not doing anything that Ramada is doing right now. You have a legitimate reason for using the name ROMADA. I can send them a reply that should make them drop it. I need a five thousand dollar retainer."*

I told him that I didn't want to spend $5,000 on something that might open up a can of worms. He said, *"Well, then change the name."*

I went into the office the next day and told Rebecca — I called her Becky — I said, *"I'm not going to fight this. We'll come up with a different name."* Well, I used to talk about my elevator speech. She says, *"Tell me what your elevator speech is."*

I said, *"I deal with businesses, individuals, retirement plans, and estate planning."*

It rolled right off her tongue. *"B-I-R-E ... BIRE! Business, individual, retirement, estate."* I didn't come up with that. Rebecca came up with it.

The two guys who hired you at Prudential. Did they leave, too?

Glen Pellicott was a recruiter, but he also refereed basketball part-time. That took off for him and they wanted him to travel, so he left. Leon stayed with the company.

Keep in mind, Prudential actually encouraged people to go out on their own. I knew two others guys who went out on their own. Prudential was easy to work with, but I didn't want to represent just one company. They gave me a wing in their building, which was called Sentry Parkway, and our address was Suite 300. I had a separate entrance, so I went to management and told them I wanted a different address from Prudential, so they gave me Suite 301. I was on the same floor, but Prudential was in Suite 300 and BIRE Financial was in Suite 301.

At first, I called the company "BIRE Planning Group." I was a team player and I wanted to be a group, so I brought on five associates. They weren't partners because there wasn't any partnership paperwork. Now we have a group of 12 people. It's ridiculous. I didn't have a whole lot of start-up expense. I paid rent for the office space, and part of the deal was that I could use their copier and phone system. Over time, I brought a couple of associates in, but every time they brought in a significant case, they would bring it to me to work on with them, so I got busy very quickly. The bottom line is that I did what I had to do and I pulled myself up out of a very deep hole in a short period of time.

An article in the Nov. 20, 2016, *Philadelphia Inquirer* had this to say: Joel Goodhart, founder of BIRE Financial Services in Plymouth Meeting, has Slott on retainer. "I call him my 'Slott machine,'" Goodhart says, "because when IRA rule changes happen, we know about it within the hour. And we need that for our clients." What is Slott?

I don't know if you ever watch PBS, but a guy named Ed Slott had a show called "Ed Slott's Retirement Freedom!" He created a group called "Ed Slott and Company," a financial advisor group. To be a member of the group, you paid $6,000 — now it's $10,000 — and you were required to attend at least one of two conferences a year. I got hooked into Ed Slott when he hosted a training seminar in Baltimore. Now, I happen to love Baltimore. I don't eat seafood, but there's an

Italian restaurant there that I love. Baltimore is close enough to me that I didn't have to stay overnight. I could drive down and drive back. I went to Ed's one-day conference and was hooked. I signed up that day ... $6,000.

To be honest, one of the key factors of me signing up was a woman by the name of Laurin Levine, the managing partner of Ed Slott. She made the introduction that day and I had the hots for her immediately. For a while, I thought she was Mrs. Ed Slott because they were really close. They were like husband and wife. Well, as it turned out, we dated on and off for about ten years. She was just a little younger than me, so we were a great match.

I stayed with Ed Slott for 14 years and left last year because I wasn't able to travel. I can now, so I may go back with him next year. He's worth every penny. That's why I told everybody that I'm a Slott machine. I brought Ed in to speak to my firm six times at $15,000 a session. Eventually, he gave us a reduction to $12,500. We also fed everybody dinner, so it wound up being a $30,000 night. I made that money back in one month. Today, my partners and I manage close to one billion dollars in assets for business and individual clients.

My partner, Stuart Leibowitz, was an attorney for 25 years and has been with me for almost 25 years, so we have a lot of experience between us. But when we brought in Ed Slott, we were hitting homerun after homerun. Without getting into detail, people come in who have a million six in their IRA and they let us handle it. Nobody comes in that doesn't have an IRA, so Ed Slott has attracted the right people for us. Ed gave us the knowledge we needed. We were both pretty good at what we did, but Ed Slott took us to the next level.

Ed mentioned me in the last book he wrote. I'm on page 396. He listed people who contributed to his success and he had my name first. Ed and I became very close, partly because I was tight with Laurin and we'd go to dinner with him. It makes me feel good to tell people that I'm friends with Ed Slott. He would call me up onto the stage at times and endorse the living hell out of me. I'm going to bring him back at some point this year.

You seem to be very focused on whatever you choose to do. You have a strong work ethic.

If I remember correctly, my official start date was around the first of April. My baby was born in February and a couple of months later I'm starting a new business. I was driven to be successful because I wanted Marla to be a stay-at-home mom and I had to support the family.

I got my work ethic from my father, but I can get diverted real easy. That's why I'm so resistant about getting back into the wrestling business. As the managing partner, founding member, CEO, CFO, of my company, with 12 employees, I'm busier than hell. I don't want to get some stupid notion in my head about trying to promote wrestling again and throwing everything away that I've worked so hard for. I do have one wrestling event in the works, though.

We'll talk about that in a little bit. How much do you work today?

I have a great schedule. I have a 4,900 square-foot office that's an old, refurbished house. A woman named Barbara, who has been with me for 18 years, handles my calendar and everybody else's calendar. She books all my appointments. She knows that she can book me all day long, from 7:30 a.m. to five p.m., on Monday and Wednesday. Lennie, my receptionist at the front desk, was 84 years old in October, and she has more energy than all of us combined. We also have an office manager, Whitney, who has been with me from day one.

On Tuesday, Thursday, and Saturday, I have dialysis from 6:30 to noon. She can book me Zoom calls and phone calls on Tuesday and Thursday afternoons because I can do that from home. With dialysis, nine times out of ten I'm fine, but other tenth I'm tired as hell and can't do it, but I can sit there and make phone calls.

On a scale of one to 10, though, I feel like an 11. I've been through three years of hell, but I'm back doing what I want to do.

So let's talk about that for a bit. You've had some serious health challenges over the past several years.
I definitely have had challenges. My problems stemmed from the fact that I always thought I was immortal, so I never followed the advice of my doctor. On Oct. 22, 1921, I lost my right leg due to gas gangrene. Sometime during the next two years, my kidneys failed, so I'm now undergoing kidney dialysis three days a week.

What was the cause of the gas gangrene?
What they told me was ... this is the easiest way to explain it. When you shower, do you ever look at the bottom of your feet?

No.
Okay, neither did I. What I learned was, when you get gas gangrene, your skin turns black. Well, the bottom of my foot was black and I never noticed it. It was a complication of diabetes.

In October 2023, I lost my left leg. I'm learning to walk on two prosthetics and I go to physical therapy. They also discovered that I had a 95 percent LAD [left anterior descending artery], which was a clogged artery. The doctors inserted two stents in my artery.

You have really been through it.
I'm the walking six-million-dollar man! (laughs) I told the doctors at the Einstein Medical Center, *"I gave you my two legs, I gave you my two kidneys, and all you gave me back was two stents in my heart."* (laughs)

You're still as busy as ever, so it doesn't seem as if your physical limitations have slowed you down, and you still have such a good attitude.
I'm 71 years old — almost 72 — I'm still alive, I love what I do. I have no complaints. For all practical purposes, I'm in good health!

This is an amazing story. My son Ross — my oldest son — saved my life. Ross is a volunteer fireman and an EMT. He discovered an infection in my left leg after they took it off. I had to go through two more surgeries to get rid of the infection. They told me that if Ross hadn't discovered it, it would have killed me. It was because of his EMT training that he recognized the infection. He saved my life ... end of story. There would not a book if not for Ross.

In regards to your health, how has everything you've been through changed your life?
In many ways, it's been for the better. I have a better diet, I listen to my doctors ... you know, for a long time, doctors — not to mention my health — were the last thing on my mind. Now I'm going to the doctor every week. It's just ridiculous. My doctors had been telling me for years ... *"Your diet and lifestyle are going to catch up to you."*

I was like, *"No it's not!"*

They were right. I have nobody to blame but myself, and I hope everyone reading this will take that to heart. See your doctor! But more than that, *listen* to your doctor.

The office is only open four days a week, so going there on Friday is my only issue. I'm the only one there, so I worry about what might happen if I fall. If my partner has appointments there, Barbara can book me there, as well. I don't drive anymore, so my son drives me all five days. God bless him, he's really at my beck and call. First of all, he saved my life. He's an EMT and found the infection in my foot, which would have killed me if I hadn't gone in to have it treated. He's on the payroll and takes me to physical therapy. He sits in the car and listens to his music, and then takes me home. That's an easy day and he's getting paid well for that easy day. My daughter lives a half hour from me, and my other son, who lives about 20 minutes from me, doesn't drive. He's 42 years old and just refuses to drive, so Ross is the only one who can take me right now. I have another driver, Sandra, for my long-distance trips.

Like today, I'm home all day. I have you booked from six to whenever, and then I have Zoom calls that I can do from home. I don't meet with clients on Saturdays, but I do phone calls after physical therapy. So, I have two full days at the office, two half days on the phone, and I'm still the CEO and managing partner. I love Stuart Leibowitz, but if it was up to him, the office would have closed a long time ago. To his credit, when I was having my rough time, he kept the office going.

We have two full-time accountants, 12 support staff, six advisors, and we're licensed in 28 states. I have clients all over the country. When a client left Philly and moved to the Outer Banks of North Carolina, I got a license in North Carolina. When someone moved to Memphis, I got licensed in Tennessee. It's unbelievable. I have a Zoom call today from a client in Virginia. I like Zoom because I like doing business eyeball to eyeball. Even this call with you and me, I'd rather do Zoom. What I do is not physical, it's mental. You can let the issues bring you down or make you stronger. It's that simple.

You must really love what you do.

I love it! I'm not doing it for the money. Financially, I'm secure. I could retire tomorrow and never look back. I just paid my house off. I put an elevator in my house because I, obviously, couldn't get to the second floor. $39,000 for the elevator. I called my kids and said, "*Thank you for the elevator.*"

They said, "*What are you talking about?*"

I said, "*I'm spending your inheritance.*" (laughs) But I love what I do. I love a nice sit-down with a client to help clean up their mess and make them financially secure ... make them SWAN. I don't do it pro bono, but it ain't the money. I tell all my clients, "*I don't need your business.*" Well, that just makes them want to use me more! I tell them, "*If I take you on, I'm creating more work for myself.*" I meet with all my clients two to four times a year. If I take on a new client, I have four more calls to make this year. I tell my clients that all the time. There you go, I went off on a tangent again. (laughs)

That's okay. I often find that letting guys go off on tangents reveals important, interesting information. Having said that, let's continue on this tangent for a bit. Will there ever come a day when you *will* retire?

Right now, we manage a *lot* of money, and there are clients who are dependent on me, so I'm not sure I'll ever retire. Why would I? I *love* what I do! Sure, there may come a day when I slow down a little and stop taking on new clients, but I've been in the business now for more than 40 years, so two-thirds of my life has been in the business, and I've loved every minute of it! No, I don't think I can *ever* walk away from it. To me, I have a responsibility to take care of my clients.

It sounds like you'll work until you die.

Well, there's a story there, okay? My father used to tell me that the definition of retirement is working because you want to, not because you have to. Now, I could have retired a decade ago and never looked back, but again, I'm working three days a week doing something I enjoy. In the meantime, I'll be looking for someone in the company to take on some of my clients and ease my workload. So, yes! You could say that my goal is to die in the business. (laughs) I mean, I am so intertwined with a lot of my clients that they treat me like a member of their family, and I feel that. I've gone to so many funerals of clients who have passed away.

The second thing my father used to tell me is, "*There's nothing better than to make a living by helping people.*" I took that and used it as a slogan. I tell people, "*My father took care of people's health care, I take care of their wealth care.*"

So, the long and short of it is, I could never retire fully. What would I do all day? You can only play with the grandkids for a certain amount of time, and when they're in school, you can't be with them. I live in a 55-plus community, so I'd probably go to the pool and sit around talking to people. Ultimately, someone would ask what I did for a living, and I'd tell him. The next thing you know, they want me to manage their money. So, bottom line, I can't imagine ever walking away from the business. That's a long-winded answer to your very short question.

Joel doing ring announcing | 2009

19 Goodhart, Blackhart & Friendlyhart

I don't know if you know this, but I have a separate company that I call Friendlyhart Productions. I tell people I'm tri-polar. I'm Goodhart, Blackhart, and Friendlyhart. As Friendlyhart, I'm a concert promoter. We do concerts here in the Philadelphia area. We do about 20 a year.

I didn't know that.
Yeah, I bring in tribute bands. It's kind of cool because, for the first few years, I'd get to appear before the public. I'd put on my sequined clothes, sequined shoes, and kick off the shows. I didn't sing or anything. I'd just go out and do stupid stuff. I don't do that now, though.

What shows do you have lined up for the future?
I average 15 shows a year, but I have several scheduled for April [2025] ... all at the Broadway Theater in Pitman, New Jersey. I have Taylor Swift on April 10 and 12, the New York Bee Gees on April 11, and Sal Valentinetti on April 12. I book shows whenever I can, so it's another diversion for me. I've always been a multi-tasker, so when I was really booking the concerts, I had this dream of becoming the biggest concert promoter in the Philadelphia area. There are times I wish that I had given up the financial business and gone all out on promoting concerts because it's so much fun. For now, though, I'm Goodhart during the day, Friendlyhart on some nights, and Goodhart at 2300 Arena. By Sunday, I'm exhausted. It was nothing for me to be pushing myself for 80 hours a week.

That's incredible. I had no idea you were doing all that.
Oh, yeah. You should see some of the videos of me on stage when I was promoting wrestling. I'd take the microphone before a big show began and I'd say, "*Is everybody ready?*" That was my little thing to get people pumped up. I did the same thing at the concerts, but I'd do two or three minutes of silly stuff and then introduce the bands.

Let me see. I'm not sure where I was going next. You caught me off guard because I had no idea about all this concert stuff. Okay, putting the promotion of concerts into perspective with the promotion of pro wrestling, what are the differences? Which entails the most financial risk, and do you actually make a profit on the concerts?
Okay, so that's a multi-part question. First of all, it took me four-and-a-half years to make an actual profit. You have to understand that, for the first year or two, you're gonna lay out more money than you make. There's a learning curve. At one point, I took on a partner in the company who does all the P.R.

The answer to your other question is, promoting is promoting, but there are so many more avenues available today because of Facebook and many social media outlets. When I was promoting wrestling, it was a matter of putting up posters, handing out flyers, and doing a radio show. Today, it's more about making sure you get the right concert in the right venue, negotiating a deal with the venue, which I can do, negotiating a deal with the recording artist, which I also do, and then you cross your fingers. You can also pay the venue to have them send out an e-mail blast to announce an upcoming show.

Keswick Theatre 291 Keswick Ave., Glenside; 215-572-7650. www.keswicktheatre.com. ♿ The McCartney Years. $29.50-$49.50. 11/22. 8 pm. Dru Hill. $39-$89. 11/23. 8 pm. Go 90s With The Fresh Kids of Bel-Air. $29. 11/16. 8 pm. Trisha Yearwood. $39.50-$75. 11/24. 8 pm.

For example, I had a show two years ago. I'm a big Beatles fan and there's a production called "The McCartney Years" based out of Canada, and a guy named Yuri Pool does McCartney to a tee, and his wife, Jennifer, does Linda. Now, he plays his guitar right-handed, not left-handed, but he has the same vocal range and he does a whole show of Beatles to Wings. If you're a Beatles and McCartney fan, this show is freaking awesome. We did it last year at the Broadway Theatre in Pitman, New Jersey, and I lost money.

Bottom line, if illness ever got to me, or if I had to get out of the financial industry, I could promote concerts. The shows are either Friday, Saturday, or Sunday night, so I'd have the whole week off.

The guy who works with me is Robert Maffia. How's that for a name? Yeah, M-A-F-F-I-A. He knows his stuff and I pay him to do all the social media promotion. He knows the people in the industry, too. So, I could make it full-time if I wanted to. Of course, I'm not going to take the risk I took with TWA. I took a *lot* of risk back then because I thought I could do it. However, I wasn't in a position financially to sustain it, but I could do that today. I'm smarter today, though, so I won't take on that risk.

So, 2020 was the first year that Friendlyhart Productions made a profit. I showed a loss from 2017 through 2019, but it was expected. There was one surprise, but now we've turned the corner. We have it down.

What was the surprise?
It was a tribute to Earth, Wind and Fire ... Feb. 18, 2017. Those guys were out of Chicago, and if you closed your eyes while they were playing, you'd believe it was the original Earth, Wind and Fire. The concert just didn't sell, though, and I lost $13,000.

One interesting thing you'll learn about these tribute bands is that, unlike wrestling, the tribute bands are always better than the real band because (pause) ... I'll give you an example. We did one show where we brought in a tribute band for Journey. We brought in a tribute for Aerosmith. Well, the Rolling Stones today are still touring, and they're all in their 70s and 80s. God bless them for their stamina, but if you go see Earth, Wind and Fire, two out of the eleven musicians are original to the group. The others are replacements. So, essentially, you're looking at a tribute band, anyway. When you see a tribute band, you get the same flavor. And again, in most cases, if you close your eyes, you wouldn't know the difference.

There is a difference in the ticket price, though. An "original" Earth, Wind and Fire concert would set you back eight to ten times the cost of a tribute band ticket. My tickets for the McCartney show were $29.95 and $39.95. Sure, you can see the real Paul McCartney in concert, but they want $750 to a thousand dollars for a ticket, and that's if you're lucky. You just need guys to be able to mimic the music and look the part. Tribute bands are pretty damn good. We had a tribute to ELO a few years ago. It was scary how good they were. I will say, though, that some tribute bands really suck, so you have to be careful with the ones you take.

What was your most successful concert?
The Billy Joel and Elton John shows.

Do you ever have anybody today who recognizes you and says they used to go to your wrestling shows?
Yep. Every once in a while, somebody will walk up and say, *"I can't believe it! I haven't seen you in thirty years."* A friend of my sister came up just the other day and said, "*You're the guy that was on the radio. I know your sister.*" Now, back in the day, very few people knew what I did on the side, but I have clients today who will call to book an appointment, and when they walk into my office, the first thing they say to me is, "*I've gotta ask you a question.*" I immediately know where the conversation is headed. "*You're the guy who used to be on WIP radio!*" He's there to talk about money, but for the first 45 minutes, we're shootin' the shit about wrestling!

I don't necessarily mind that, but most of them have the same question ... "*Did you ever meet Andre the Giant?*" or "*Did you know Hulk Hogan?*"

"*No, but I knew Ric Flair.*" So, the wrestling connection is good for business.

Do most of them remember you when they *see* you, or do they remember your name?
(laughs) I certainly don't look like I looked 30 years ago, but Goodhart's not the most common name in the world. Once they hear the name Goodhart, "*Are you the guy ...*" It's amazing. When I went to independent shows as Blackhart, there may have been ten to fifteen people who all knew me back when. They'd walk up and, for the most part, they all looked the same. We all look a little older. It makes me feel good when they tell me things like, "*If you started another promotion, I'd be the first in line to buy a ticket.*"

They must have been the people who got their money refunded.
(laughs) That was quick! (laughs) Yes! They must have been.

Having promoted wrestling, and now promoting music, what comparisons have you seen between pro wrestlers and musicians?
I'll tell you what the crossover is ... professionals are professionals. I find that in every business. I know that sounds strange, but it's the way a professional carries themselves. One thing in music that amazes me is the way they conduct business. On the day of a concert, the venue sends out an e-mail to all the parties ... instruments show up at two o'clock, the band sets up at three o'clock, sound check at four o'clock, dinner is five o'clock, whatever else is at six o'clock. Everybody shows up exactly when they're supposed to show up. That's so similar to wrestling. You need the ring to show up at one-thirty or two o'clock. The ring has to be set up by three o'clock. Security needs to be in place at whatever time.

Now, musicians in the tribute bands look like regular people. They don't travel in limos or get treated like royalty. They're everybody, normal people who eat dinner and then go to the dressing room. However, when the show starts, they take on a whole new persona ... which is a *lot* like the wrestlers. It's a mental thing.

We have a group called the New York Bee Gees, which we've used about 20 to 30 times, and those guys really do sound like the Bee Gees. Well, when Peter Mazzeo comes in, he's just a normal guy. He gets his instruments ready, he gets dressed, he puts on his outfit, and when he comes out ... he's Barry Gibb! He's really Barry Gibb! After a while, I realized, "*These guys are just like the wrestlers.*" When Eddie Farhat was in the dressing room, we had some interesting discussions, but when he stepped over that line that separated the dressing room from the arena, Eddie Farhat vanished and the Sheik appeared.

Have you made any good friends in the music business?
It's like wrestling. Let's just call them friendlies. There's singers who are always ready to go to dinner when I ask. Of course, they probably do that because I've booked them several times. It's the same with the wrestlers. They were all friendly with me because I had the wallet. I recognize that, you know. I guess the best way to put it is, I'm not really friends with anyone, but I'm friendly with everyone.

Do you book the buildings for the concerts?
Yes, but I don't handle the negotiations with the talent. Robert does that. I'm the wallet! (laughs)

This book may reach a whole new audience for your concerts.
(laughs) That's cool. I have to keep my sanity, so that's how I do it.

That's awesome. Are any of the wrestlers clients of yours?
Not a one. Larry Winters was, but nobody else. That was more me than them. I didn't ask them and they never asked me.

What insurance and investment plans do you offer?
We don't do car, homeowners, property and casualty. We do a significant amount of life insurance, long-term care, holistic planning, and if you ever look on my company website, you'll see our mission statement.

I'm a fiduciary by designation, so when people come to me, they don't walk in with a hundred thousand and we put it in ABC. That's not what we do. We actually have a five-appointment process. I'm not gonna bore you with all this stuff, but the firm currently manages more than $900 million dollars and we have a significant amount of life insurance in force. We have an ungodly sum of disability and long-term care, and to be honest with you — I'm 71 years old — we do more life insurance on people age 65 and over than we ever did on people 65 and under.

What do you do outside of work?
At this point, I have no other diversions, other than Friendlyhart and Blackhart, and Blackhart has faded away. Blackhart, though, gave me an opportunity to kick up my ego because I was on the stage, and when the show was over, everybody walked past and told me they enjoyed the show.

20  The Legacy

Do you stay in touch with any of the wrestlers who used to work for you?
Not a one. I see the local guys occasionally, but I don't keep in touch per se. The big names ... not a single one. I spend a lot of time with Gangrel when I see him at autograph signings. I talk to Shane Douglas, Abby, Lawler. I saw Paul Heyman in Dallas, Texas. I was there for a conference and it happened to be on the same night as *Monday Night Raw* and we were staying at the same hotel. We talked for 30 minutes or so. He has his own business on Long Island, he works for Vince. Again, he didn't start with me, but I set the tone for what he ended up doing.

When I saw Jimmy Valiant — Boogie — he showed me where he mentioned me in his book. I got pissed because he called me "Joe" Goodhart. (laughs) Well, at least he mentioned me. So here comes the typical wrestling shit. We sat down and talked for a good half hour. At the end of that time, he says, *"Come on, buy a book. I'll autograph it, okay?"* So I buy a book. Now, to me, that showed exactly what those guys are all about ... the payday. Everything's about the money. Mick Foley didn't send me a book. I'm in there for 12 pages and he didn't track me down. I went and bought the book on my own.

I think the guys respect the fact that I left the business. They all get it. They all get it because most of the guys in the business *hate* the business. They love the sport, they love to wrestle, they love the atmosphere ... but they hate the *business*. It's a lot like attorneys. Most attorneys will tell you that they can't stand being attorneys.

When you look back at your career as a wrestling promoter, do you have any regrets?
No, because here we are, 30 years later, talking about what I did. I mean, in hindsight, if I would have stayed small, I could have done it forever. I recognize the fact that I was my own worst enemy. I keep going back to the match between Adrian Street and Jimmy Valiant. It cost me $1,500 for that one match, but I didn't care. That's stupid business. The only regret I have is that I couldn't keep it going. That's my only regret. Everything else! I'm satisfied because everybody got their money's worth. In fact, I overdid it. Nobody ever felt ripped off ... except for the people who lost money on the show that never happened.

Was there anybody you regretted spending the money to fly in?
Yeah ... my tag match with Austin Idol and Al Perez against Kevin Von Erich and Chris Adams. I thought the team of Idol and Perez was going to take off. They were both built like brick shithouses. It was an expensive match because it was a tag match. I flew two of the guys in from Texas and two from down south. They were on fourth or fifth from the top and the match sucked because, again, nobody wanted to be pinned. I was so frustrated that I just threw up my hands and let them call the finish. I spent all that money and the match didn't draw me one penny. There may have been one or two people who wanted to see Kevin Von Erich, but that didn't help my bottom line. In fact, the match *hurt* my bottom line.

I didn't regret bringing in Adrian Street and Jimmy Valiant, but their match sucked and didn't mean anything. I mean, I was a mark for Adrian, and when those two guys were at the height of their careers, their feud was unbelievable! TWA fans knew the storyline and they enjoyed the match, but by that time, they were two old guys who were past their prime. And again, that match didn't draw me a dime.

It's interesting that you picked those two matches because they were on the same show.
Yep. I had a lot of names on that show ... a *lot* of names. If those two matches hadn't been on the card, nobody would have missed them because I had three or four other hot matches and I would have sold the same number of tickets.

I remember promoting a show at a high school in Atco, New Jersey. Dominic DeNucci was on that card and my main event was Dick Slater against Tommy Rich. You would think that would have been a great match, but it sucked. Rich and Slater weren't a draw, either. It was the only time I ever used those two guys. Can you guess why I booked them on that card?

Because *you* wanted to see them.
(laughs) Yep! That's it! They had never wrestled up north and I wanted to see them. That may have been the first time I realized ... Tommy was a former NWA champ, but that didn't mean shit. It was a payday for *him*, but it didn't help me. I see Tommy every once in a while and he remembers the match. It's funny, but Atco High School was about five miles from where Jimmy Snuka lived, and I never used Jimmy. Not then, not ever.

You left a legacy behind because people still talk about you and TWA, whereas I don't hear anyone saying much about Larry Sharpe, Dennis Coralluzzo, or Herb Abrams.
South Jersey people still talk about Larry Sharpe. Larry was from Fallsburg. He was a good guy who did a lot for the community. I don't think many people remember Dennis, and nobody talks about Herb Abrams. His name doesn't come up much at all and he had television. He was using a lot of the same guys I used, and since he had television, he was a step above me. I don't think he used his local talent correctly, though. His focus was major talent, TV stuff. In hindsight, I think my blend of the two was better. My problem was that I would have eight matches ... four main events and four with local guys. In reality, I could have done just one main event, but hindsight is always 20/20. The fact that I lost all that money and rebounded lets me look back and laugh about it a little.

I guess the thing I'm the most proud of is the fact that there may never have been an Extreme Championship Wrestling without a TWA. I know the business may have evolved eventually, but I think TWA was the catalyst that ushered in a new era, a new style, of wrestling. I think I changed the direction of the sport. Obviously, there are a whole lot more people who made money at it than I did, but I changed the face of professional wrestling. I really do believe that.

If you could go back in time and do it over, would you rely more on your local guys and bring in fewer name wrestlers?
No, and here's the reason why. It's now 2025 and I'm on the phone with Scott Teal from Crowbar Press talking about a promotion from 30 years ago ... and it's only because I did things the way I did. Did I make profitable decisions? No! My decisions stunk. But to this day, many people consider the Cactus Jack-Eddie Gilbert two-out-of-three-fall match as the number one match of all time. I haven't picked up a PWI in years, but when they used to pick the top 50 matches, it was always in there. If I was at a convention and Cactus, Lawler, Sullivan, Abdullah

and Terry Funk were there, they'd remember me. To this day, when Shane Douglas sees me, he tells stories about the very first show I promoted ... the one at Neshaminy High School when he was wrestling as Trevor Martin. That's worth so much more to me than money. Yes, if I had stuck to just one main event, I might still be in business, but I had fun doing it the way I did and I don't regret it for a minute.

I often think that I was the best thing that ever happened to the wrestling business, but I also was the *worst* thing that ever happened to *me*! But if I was an ordinary promoter who promoted normal wrestling shows, would you be writing this book with me? I doubt it. Who the hell am I? I was just a guy on the fringe who was trying to make his way in the business.

21 Go-Go Professional Wrestling

Voorhees Township, New Jersey: Oct. 24, 2009
TWA Reunion Show, Flyers Skate Zone, att. 300
- Blue Meanie, Crybaby Waldo, & Kid America beat
   Cueball Carmichael, Jimmy Cicero, & Johnny Calzone
- Michael Bruno beat Don E. Allen
- Cujo the Hellhound beat Brian Rancid.
- Al Snow beat Steve Corino
- Larry Winters beat Jimmy Jannetty
- Tony Stetson beat Breaker Morant
- TWA title match*
   Glen Osbourne beat Buddy Landel (title change)

There was a TWA reunion show at Voorhees Township on Oct. 24, 2009. Did you go to that?
   Yep! That's the one I went to and everybody kissed my feet! (laughs)

Tell me a little about how, after 17 years, you once again found a small niche in the wrestling business.
   There was a group up here called ECWA [East Coast Wrestling Association]. They've been around since 1967.

I remember Jim Kettner, the original owner of ECWA. Was he around when you were promoting?
   He was, but I didn't know him. He ran shows in Delaware, but they were small shows, so I never saw him as competition. I don't recall ever meeting Jim. If I did, it was in passing. The local guys he had on his cards were Delaware wrestlers, and they stayed in Delaware. I don't think any of his guys ever made serious money in the business. Kettner sold the ECWA to Michael Bruno [Mike Tartaglia], who broke into the business with me in TWA. I have no idea what Mike paid for it, but I do know that he owned 100 percent of the company.

   Anyway, in 2009, I get a call at my office from Mike. *"Hey, how ya doin'!"* Yadda, yadda, yadda. He says, *"The reason I'm calling is, I want to start up a new promotion. Do you mind if I use the TWA name?"*

   Well, what was I going to say after not using it for 17 years? *"No, you can't use it."* *"I'm going to charge you."* No! I gave him permission to use it. Long story short, in the meantime, he purchases the ECWA and creates his champions ...

and then proceeds to blow up the TWA and bury it. So, since sometime in 2011, there has been no TWA.

After I gave Mike my permission — if you want to call it that — to use the TWA name, he said, "*Since you're allowing me to use the TWA stuff, why don't you come to our next show?*"

I told him, "*I haven't been to a wrestling show in eighteen years.*"

Well, I wound up going. The show was at Flyer Skate Zone in Voorhees Township, New Jersey. I'm always early, so when I pulled into the parking lot, I just sat there in the car. I was as nervous as hell. (laughs) I swear, I was sweating bullets. I'm thinking to myself, "*What the hell am I doing?*" I finally got out of the car, and as I walked towards the building, I'm thinking, "*Nobody's gonna know me.*" My biggest fear, though, was that I'd walk in and somebody was gonna ask me for ten dollars for a ticket. (laughs)

I don't remember who I saw first, but I saw Mike Tartaglia, and then I see Larry Winters. They gave me the big bro hug and all that kind of shit. Larry said to me, "*Thank god, you're here. We've missed you all these years. You are a god.*" Those were his words.

Then I see Tom Brandi, Mike Kaluha, Steve Corino. Now, I didn't know Steve very well, but he walked up and basically said, "*You know, if it wasn't for you, I wouldn't be in the business,*" and he proceeds to tell me his story. [Glen] Osbourne was there. The next thing I know, all the guys are kissing my ass. It was like I had never been gone. It suddenly hit me that those guys were still wrestling 19 years after I got out of the business. It really got to me. Those guys were still physically fit, but 19 years later, they were still getting their asses kicked in the ring. I don't think it was at the first show. I think it was at the second that Mike [Tartaglia] took me to the ring for something. I don't remember what it was, but it was cool to be in the ring and be recognized.

It was just incredible. Until that point, I had not attended a match and I hadn't watched a single show on TV. To be honest, to this day, I haven't even watched an ECW match on YouTube. They were all my guys, but I just couldn't bring myself to watch.

You actually got involved as a talent with ECWA, didn't you?

To that point, when Mike took over the TWA, I had never been involved in a wrestling match, but I thought it would be cool, after all these years, to do some heel stuff, so I created the persona of Joel Blackhart ... Goodhart by day, Blackhart by night. I got into the ring and told everybody that I was going to manage wrestlers on ECWA shows. The "Blackhart," of course, was a tribute to Luna Vachon, and I wore a black, sequined, tuxedo jacket, which was a bit like Freddie Blassie's.

My management style was different from most others. I wouldn't say I never got into the ring, but it was very seldom. I'd walk out with one of my guys and stay outside while he got in and wrestled. What I learned was that managers today really have to work the crowd because the wrestlers don't know how to do that. I didn't get involved physically, although I took a bump from the ring apron to the hardwood floor one time. I felt that for a week.

I managed a faction called the Blackharts. I didn't manage the champions, because I only managed when I had the time. I didn't work every card. I had too many other things going on to commit to every show. If I can make a show, I'll make it. If their next show was on Sept. 21st, I might not be able to be there because that happens to be the night I had to meet with an important client for my insurance business. I had the dates far enough in advance that I could usually work around them, though.

What was their average attendance?
 ECWA drew 75 to 100 people and, typically, they were the same people, but they made some money. That's what I was saying earlier. These smaller promotions are doing it right. They no longer bring in major names. They run six to eight matches and pay their guys 25 to $75. If they have a hundred people paying twenty bucks, and even if they spend a thousand on talent and three or $400 on the ring, they can actually make a few dollars.

What was the range of your payoffs?
 The guys, when they worked for me back in the day, I paid them $50 to $75. The guys working today aren't making that much. Think about this. I was paying $75 in the '80s when $75 wasn't really *great* money, but it was decent. Today, they're getting paid $75 and it costs them that much in gas and tolls just to get to the match.

Did they recognize a TWA champion?
 Yes. The title still belonged to Buddy Landel. He never lost it. Mike's first show under the TWA banner took place in Voorhees Township, and he brought Buddy up to drop the belt to Glen Osbourne. Buddy made the trip to do a job for the local guy and give the belt *back* to the local guy. If he was still with us, Buddy would have told you that he did it for the payday. He didn't give a shit about the belt. It didn't mean anything to him. He was willing to do whatever for the payday.

 After that, Mike promoted some belt unification matches and buried the TWA. Now it no longer exists. Don't think I haven't fantasized with the idea of restarting the TWA. (laughs) I've also toyed with the idea of getting in touch with Tod Gordon since the names Goodhart and Gordon both start with GO. Together we'd head up Go-Go Professional Wrestling. I'm just joking. That would never work, and even if it would, I would bet he's burned out on that shit because he kind of disappeared, too.

I didn't follow ECW and I've never studied their history, so I don't know if he got pushed out or if he just left voluntarily.
 It's funny, but part of me would like to know what happened. I'd love to sit down with Tod and discuss it. My one and only contact in wrestling, Larry Winters, who I trusted implicitly, has passed away. Larry would have been the one guy who would have told me what really happened if I ever asked him. I never did, though, and now it's too late.

I just bought a copy of Tod's book the other day, so I'll see what he has to say, although I have a stack of books to get through. From what I've read, Joe Zanolle bought the ECWA promotion from Mike Tartaglia a few years ago. I don't know if that's a work or if he actually did.
 I don't know, either. Joe Zanolle is the booker — or at least he was — and John Finegan is the chief referee, and with Mike Bruno in the mix, ECWA as it exists today, in terms of management, is really a byproduct of TWA.

A lot of the guys who worked for you were there. Did you recognize Blue Meanie as the fan who went on the bus tours with you?
 Oh, yeah. I didn't follow ECW at all, but when he came out as Blue Meanie, I said, "*Whoa!*" I recognized him right away. To this day, Blue Meanie credits me with a lot of the success he had. I mean, he made it on his own. I had nothing to do with Blue Meanie, but Brian got involved in the business through me. Brian Heffron … he was just a good kid.

I would guess you were amazed when he walked out?
 Oh, yeah. That surprised the hell out of me. I see Blue all the time. He still does his little dance in the ring.

It's funny, Bob Artese and I were inducted into the ECWA Hall of Fame the same year. [2022] Bob and I got our plaques, and after us was Steve Corino. Do you know Steve?

I know who he is, but I've never met him.

He's a good guy, and now his kid's wrestling. When he got his plaque, he thanked me because he said he got started in the business because of me. Years ago, we did a TWA show at Norristown Ford, a local car dealership. They had a big car lot and they hired me to present a wrestling card. It was a sold show. We drew a couple hundred people, plus his customers. One of the matches was Tony Stetson against Johnny Hotbody. Johnny throws Tony outside the ring and Tony lands on Steve Corino's foot. Steve was there with his mother. Steve says it was at that point that he decided to become a professional wrestler. Steve still tells me that story. He became a wrestler because Tony Stetson got thrown on his foot.

You made quite the impact on the wrestling industry given ECW — both Eastern and Extreme — and ECWA, all have ties to the groundwork you laid.

I know this will sound self-serving, but there is no question that the Philadelphia wrestling scene was a spin-off of what we did with TWA ... no question. In fact, many of the guys who wrestled for ECW came out of Ringmasters. J.T. Smith, Larry Winters, Sandman, Stevie Richards ... go down the list. Then there's Tod Gordon, who got involved in wrestling because of me. Bob Artese, who did a fantastic job as ECW's ring announcer. Bob used to sit front row. Dean Dixon, who does podcasts as HIACTalkRadio, gave me the nickname of The Godfather of Hardcore. I thought that was funny, but hardcore was here before me. D.C. Drake was doing it *long* before I promoted. I just crystalized it and gave it some notoriety. I think being in Philly is what set it off. If TWA had been based in Kansas City, it never would have taken off. It never would have happened in Pittsburgh. Philly was the right place and I was there at the right time, not to mention the fact that Apter and Napolitano were at every show.

Back to me promoting, I came real close at the Super 8 that ECWA had a few years ago. I got involved in the promoting end of it. And guess what? (silence)

I'm in suspense. What?

I lost money. (laughs) So, okay, I'm done. I'd be fine working as Joel Blackhart because I enjoy that. I've never taken a nickel from Mike Bruno. I don't get paid to do that, but it gives me the opportunity to kid him about it because, every time I work a show, I have to get my tux cleaned, so it actually costs *me* money. (laughs) But, no, it's not happening.

Are the ECWA shows as hardcore as yours were?

No, they're more family-friendly. I will say that some of Mike's guys are what I call my D.C. Drakes, my Larry Winters, my Tony Stetsons. He has some hardcore guys. Chris Wylde was one of Mike's guys. Chris was a hell of a worker and he's got a great, great build. He's really physically fit. Chris has been on Vince's shows doing jobs, but it was sad to see how they've used him. He was the guy when they did that stupid banana and hot dog run-in on WWE RAW. [Albany NY: April 20, 2015] He was the banana. Chris is a great example of the independents up here, even to this day. Some of those guys are great workers. However, they put their bodies on the line for no money. They do it for the love of the sport.

Chris happens to be a family man who has a full-time job with the Department of Corrections. He's good friends with JJ Dillon, who also worked there. You can put Chris in the ring with anybody and he would do whatever it takes to give the fans a great match. He's another of those guys who, if I was considering buying a ticket to a show, I would pay to see Chris Wylde. There is no better compliment. He can work as a heel, he can work as a babyface, he can work in a tag. He will earn every penny a promoter pays him and the promoter will reap the rewards.

Chris had a feud going with a guy by the name of Breaker Morant [Matthew Boyd]. Their matches were as good as anything I ever did. Unfortunately, the two of them had a falling-out, so Breaker doesn't work with him anymore. Mike has other guys who are really good workers, but they're only being seen by 75 people, month in and month out.

Are most of the guys who worked for you retired now?
Oh, yeah. They're done. ECWA is all homegrown talent.

How much input did you have on the show that you helped finance?
Just enough to say I had some input. We ran the show in South Philadelphia. We brought in eight boys who were sons of wrestlers ... Brian Pillman Jr., Ross and Marshall Von Erich ... I'd go down the list if I could remember them all.

The ECWA Super 8 tournament, was an annual, one-night, elimination tournament that featured eight wrestlers. The tournament Joel refers to took place on April 20, 2019, and featured second generation wrestlers:

Brian Pillman, Jr. (Brian Pillman)
 Lance Anoa'I (Samu)
  Leland Race (Harley Race)
   Marshall Von Erich (Kevin Von Erich)
    Ross Von Erich (Kevin Von Erich)
     Colby Corino (Steve Corino)
      Wes Brisco (Gerald "Jerry" Brisco)
       Tim Zbyszko (Larry Zbyszko)

They cost a fortune to fly in ... no surprise there. We flew the Von Erichs in from Texas and they had to fly back to Hawaii where they lived. Six of the eight guys had to be flown in ... even Pillman, who came from Cincinnati.

It goes to show you that nothing changes. In this case, it was me that didn't change my way of thinking. I thought, "*With this lineup, everybody's gonna come out.*" We had a great show, but we only drew 135 people. That's when I realized that the business is way beyond me. I didn't know what the hell I was doing back then, and I clearly don't know what I'm doing now. (laughs)

Mike has a funny way of promoting. Mike has his own career, a full-time job, so he hired people to create flyers, and flyers aren't going to entice people to buy a ticket. Posters don't draw people anymore, either. The one thing I learned is that promotion is 25 hours a day, eight days a week — there's a song in there somewhere — and 53 weeks a year.

I would imagine that you're at a point that you don't care if you know.
That's right! Right now, my involvement in the business is this book. It doesn't matter to me if 50 or a hundred people buy the book. I'm not doing this to make money. I'm just happy that it's being written because maybe someone who has aspirations of being a "big-time promoter" will learn something from my mistakes. Most of the wrestling world doesn't even know who Joel Goodhart is because most of the wrestling world was, and is, outside the Philadelphia area. I keep thinking to myself, "*Why would somebody in Topeka, Kansas, want to buy my book?*" Well, I don't know the answer to that. Now, I'm sure there are wrestling

fans who buy every book you publish, but I can see myself going to wrestling conventions and selling them. I can see that happening. I do think, however, that the people who will buy the book are the people who came to my matches. (laughs) I can almost guarantee you that the first day the book comes out, I'll get a phone call from somebody who says, *"Hey, I never got my money back from the ticket I bought. Can you give me a book?"* (laughs)

I just want the story to be told so people will give me some credit for triggering everything. Paul E. Dangerously — okay, Paul Heyman — to this day, he's making real money, and I'm content that he's where he's at because of what he did in ECW. But he wouldn't have been in ECW if not for TWA. There's no question as to where his roots are.

Jeannie Siciliano, Carmela Panfil Foss & Joel

Joel, Carmela Panfil Foss & Paul Panfil

22   It's Chubby Dudley's Fault

Let's get to my final questions, which have to do with what will be your final show.

Well, I've learned to never say "never," but I don't plan to *ever* promote another wrestling event after this next one. I'm calling it "One and Done" ... May 3, 2025. I'm not looking to start up the TWA again. I don't intend to do any of that. We're having "RassleCon" from noon to 3:30 in the afternoon and matches at 7:30 that night. Several of my old TWA guys are coming from everywhere. We're doing it at the 2300 Arena.

One of the things we're going to have is a ten-bell salute, which I think is a really big deal, in honor of the 45 wrestlers who worked for me, in some capacity, that have died.

I don't know if you've heard about our banner campaign. Bay Ragni, who was Chubby Dudley in ECW, came up with this idea totally independent of me. It was all his idea. It's unbelievable. They have all these banners at the 2300 Arena. Bay wants to have a banner there with five names on it. He calls it the "Icons of Philadelphia" and the names are D.C. Drake, Larry Winters, Johnny Hotbody, Tony Stetson, and Joel Goodhart. We made a deal with the building management, that if we could get a thousand signatures, we'll have the banner. We sent a link to all the wrestling podcasts that I've appeared on, like the ones I've done with Carmela, Bob Smith. The podcasts are great, but I know I must give them fits because, when I get started, I don't shut up.

I've noticed that.

(laughs) Touché. (laughs) Anyway, we got a thousand signatures just last week [mid-March 2025].

At what point did the idea for doing a final show come to you? What was the genesis of the idea?

It's all Bay Ragni's fault. (laughs) I've known Bay for years. After I did his podcast, he called me up and said, "*By the way, I want a banner at the 2300 Arena,*" and he described what he wanted to do. Now, I had been to the 2300 Arena, but never to watch wrestling. I've been there and I know they had the banners. Tod Gordon's name is there, Rob Van Dam's name is there. Bay said, "*I want the banner for the icons of Philadelphia.*"

I said to him, "*If you're going to do that ...*" — I said it kiddingly — I said, "*You know what? Flair had his last match, Sting had his last match, on a final tour. You know what? I never had the opportunity to announce my last card.*" I said, "*We'll call it 'One and Done'.*" Don't ask me how I came up with the name. It just came off the top of my head. I said, "*Yeah! We're going to do 'One and Done' and we'll do it at the 2300 Arena.*"

Bay says, "*Well, you know the 2300 Arena is going to be expensive.*"

I said, "*I don't care. I do* [music] *shows all the time and I'm spending $30,000 a show. I know guys who try to do shows like this on a shoestring, and that's the problem.*"

I call 2300 Arena and the guy who owns it, or runs it, is a guy named Roger ... nice guy. I called and I said, "*Roger, my name is Joel Goodhart. I don't know if you know who I am.*"

He said, "*Joel Goodhart! I know who you are.*"

We set up an appointment and I laid out my plan. I told him I wanted to do 'One and Done', but if I'm going to do it, I can only do it at the 2300 Arena. The original building that I ran — which was Temple University's McGonagle Hall — has been knocked down. Then we looked at the Civic Center, and that was knocked down. The place where we did our Bar Wars show was gone. None of my original buildings were there for me to use, so I thought, "*2300 Arena is the only major arena where wrestling fans would know where you are and what you are all about.*" He said, "*Fine, what dates do you have?*"

I said, "*Well, I want to do it in the spring because I need a lot of time to put this together.*" So I looked at the dates of May 3 and May 10. Those were the dates he gave me. May 10 was the weekend of Mother's Day, so that was out, so I said May 3. We agreed on a price and we locked in the date. Now, Bay and I — and I'm not kidding you, we had many, many hours of conversation, primarily about what talent to bring in — we're going to have eight matches.

Philadelphia, Pennsylvania: May 3, 2025
2300 Arena, Saturday
- South Philly Street Fight for the TWA Heavyweight Title
  Breaker Morant vs. Chris Wylde
  — This will be the final match of Breaker's career.
- Back to the Future Match, Special Referee Manny Fernandez
  Rock 'n' Roll Express vs. The Backseat Boyz
- TWA Second Generation Match
  Tessa Blanchard vs. Samantha Starr
- TWA Legends Tag Team Match
  "Wildfire" Tommy Rich & Doug Gilbert vs. Shane Douglas & ??
- TWA Alumni Lumberjack Match
  "Hitman" Tony Stetson vs. Michael Tartaglia
  — This will be the final match of Tony's career.
- No Gimmicks Match
  Hannibal the Death Dealer vs. Super Crazy
- Belle 2 Bell Showcase Match, Special Referee Madusa Miceli
  Notorious Mimi vs. Gabby Ortiz
- ECWA Triple Threat Match
  Clutch Rockwell vs. Darius Carter vs. Jay D. Luscious

We're working with three local organizations ... one from Pennsylvania, one from New Jersey, one from Delaware. That's the Tri-State area. The three are going to have their own title matches. They can book it and do whatever they want. And then there's an organization you may have heard of called Belle 2 Bell. It's a ladies wrestling promotion, locally started by Missy Sampson, who came out of Larry Sharpe's Monster Factory. Two of her top girls will be on the card. The last match of the night will be for the TWA heavyweight championship, the last time the belt will be defended ... ever!

On top of all that, we have Madusa Miceli coming in for both the con and the matches. She'll be refereeing the Belle 2 Bell girls' match. Manny Fernandez, one of my favorite people, is coming in. He'll be here for the con, as well. We'll have two local wrestlers, JP and Tommy Grayson — they're known locally as the Backseat Boyz — with their manager Johnny Kashmere, against Rock 'n' Roll. Rock 'n' Roll and Manny are very good friends, so they're looking forward to that match. We'll also have a third-generation match between Tessa Blanchard, Tully Blanchard's daughter, and Baby Doll's daughter, Samantha Starr. They're both phenomenal wrestlers.

Is Tessa with Belle 2 Bell?
No, she's independent. She's Tully Blanchard's daughter and Tully worked for me. Of course, Miranda is Terry Gordy's daughter, who also wrestled for me. So that's the tie-in there.

There's a lot of curiosity about Shane Douglas' mystery partner.
(laughs) Yes! Nobody will expect the guy I'm flying in. It will be a total surprise. We'll also have a match with two guys you may not know because they're local — Chris Wylde against Breaker Morant. I must have said this a hundred times. If I was starting a wrestling organization today, they would be my D.C. Drake and Larry Winters. They are great. They have great chemistry together, and even though 2300 Arena has regulations against fighting into the crowd, they do go outside the ring, but they stay within the fencing. They'll be doing a TWA-style match. So, we're going to have a great card.

At the end of the night, after the show, we'll have a second 10-bell salute, denoting the death of the TWA.

The talent will be at Rasslecon that afternoon, as well. We have quite a few other names coming in for Rasslecon, as well, and some of them might be involved in the matches in some fashion. Almost all my TWA alumni who are still alive will be at Rasslecon. Besides the guys wrestling on the card, we'll have Sandman, Johnny Hotbody, D.C. Drake, Glen Osbourne, Jimmy Jannetty, Michael Bruno, Baby Doll, Don E. Allen. Cujo the Hellhound, who didn't wrestle in the original TWA, but wrestled on the TWA reunion card, will also be at Rasslecon. The guys who refereed for me — Joe Zanolle, Jim Molineaux, Mike Kehner, John Finegan, Rich Ingling — will all be there.

Then there's the ECW talent
Yes. Tod Gordon, the force behind ECW. Bob Artese, the ECW ring announcer will be there, and Joel Gertner. Blue Meanie, Chubby Dudley, Super Crazy, Sabu … I know there must be more.

H.D. Ryder, Ernesto Benefica.
Yes. They're all listed on the website.

That's an amazing lineup of talent and you haven't even mentioned the out-of-town guys who worked for TWA that will be there.
Oh, yes! Tully Blanchard, Ric Flair, Tony Atlas, Bill Apter, Kerry Morton. There are other names that are escaping me right now. I've had calls from a lot of people who want to be on the show. Austin Idol called me because he had been talking to Dr. Tom Prichard and Prichard told him about it. He asked Prichard, *"Why didn't he call me? What's up with that?"*

This was all put together over hundreds of hours of phone calls. So, how did it start, you ask? It was all off the top of my head when Bay Ragni called me about the banners, so it's all his fault. (laughs) I came up with the name in 30 seconds and it just snowballed from there. The one guy I haven't been able to get in touch with is Lawler. He was on several of my shows. I don't know what Lawler's price tag is, but I would have booked him in two seconds.

You lost a lot of money when you promoted the original TWA. What are your goals for this show?

We're charging 20 bucks for Rasslecon 2025, $25 at the door. Our goal is to attract a thousand people, which would be 20 grand. We would also make money on merchandise and vendor table fees. My accountant is going to certify, at the end of the day, whether we made a profit or lost money. If we make money, it will all go to the TWA guys in an equal share. They're all coming in and they're not getting paid. We've all had our health problems. D.C. Drake had a triple bypass. Drake suffered all kinds of injuries and eventually got out of the business. J.T. Smith, who later worked for ECW, wound up with 11 concussions. His doctor told him, *"Don't have a twelfth."* Glenn Osbourne walks with a cane. So, we're not going to get into the ring, but we're going to surround the ring for the Ten-Bell Salute. What I hope to do is, there will be fifteen to 20 guys. If we make a $10,000 profit, we'll each get paid 500 bucks. I hope that's the case because some of the guys need the money. If anyone doesn't need it, or want it, we're contributing the money to the Cauliflower Alley Club.

One of the other things I did was, I had a luncheon here at my house last year on Oct. 28. I had 20 to 25 guys there, all local guys. I didn't bring in guys from out of town. We talked about the "One and Done" show and what we wanted to accomplish. It was phenomenal. I hadn't seen those guys for 32 years. Bay Ragni flew up from Nashville.

The building seats 879, to be exact, and I get unlimited standing-only. That's for all the wrestlers' kids and family, or whoever. We'll give away some tickets, but 879 is the total capacity. What we are doing is, there's 80 seats on the front row that sell for a hundred bucks. The second row 80 seats sell for $75. Then there's 240 general admission seats, those are $25, and the rest of the reserved are $35. So the total gate is about 36,000 if we sell it.

Again, the con is 20 bucks, so if we can get a thousand — and who knows if that's going to happen — but that will be another 20,000. The total gate could be fifty to 60,000. And we'll have merchandise, like our old t-shirts — *"I'm out of the closet, no longer meek, I'm finally admitting I'm a wrestling freak"* — and all that. My goal is, if we get a lot of the old-time smart marks, as I call them, to come, they're going to buy up everything. We're going to have the TWA logo. *"We wrestle, we brawl, we started it all."* Of course, that's a takeoff on my original catchphrase. I'd like that to be the name of the book. We'll have the book signing there. These things will all culminate on May 3rd. It's taken on a life of its own.

That's why I want to get the book done. I wanted to be sure we talk because you're hard to nail down. Scott's in Yellowstone one week, Alaska the next, Pennsylvania Amish country the next. (laughs)

(laughs) Life is short. We're trying to get it all in while our health is still good.

Absolutely! You're enjoying life. You know, I kept seeing pictures on Facebook of the fun you and your wife were having with your grandchildren, and I said to myself, *"I have to have one."* Now I have a ten-month-old grandson who is just adorable.

I'm loving life. I'm 71. I still have my practice. I'm working six days a week. I have a Zoom at 9:30 and one at 11:30, physical therapy at one. Then I go home and I have a Zoom at 3:30, and I do an occasional podcast at seven. And I talk to you from five in the morning until whenever! I have a full day! Staying busy keep you alive. Too many people retire and sit around and their health just goes to pot.

This has been fun, Joel. Your story is fascinating and I've learned a lot.

Thank you for all the time you've put into it. You've taught me a lot, too. You've brought back memories about a lot of things that I had completely forgotten … and some things that I still don't remember.

Joel Goodhart, Tony Stetson, Johnny Hotbody & Bay Ragni
Philadelphia, Pennsylvania | Oct. 28, 2024 | TWA HOMECOMING

Also available from www.crowbarpress.com

This series, created by Scott Teal, features the most detailed books ever published on the history of specific wrestling cities and territories. Each volume contains a definite listing of every wrestling match we could find for each venue, illustrated with hundreds of images of program covers, advertisements, newspaper ads and headlines, and memorabilia. Also included, when available, are gate and attendance figures, match stipulations, and much more. These volumes represent an incredible amount of research that will be referred to over and over by both everyone.

v1 – Wrestling in the Garden, The Battle for New York
by Scott Teal & J Michael Kenyon

v2 – Nashville, Tennessee, volume 1: 1907-1960
by Scott Teal & Don Luce

v3 – Alabama: 1931-1935 by Jason Presley

v4 – Japan: The Rikidozan Years
by Haruo Yamaguchi, with Koji Miyamoto & Scott Teal

v5 – Knoxville, Tennessee, v1: 1905-1960 by Tim Dills & Scott Teal

v6 – Amarillo, Texas, v1: 1911-1960 by Kriss Knights & Scott Teal

v7 – St. Louis: 1873-1927 by Scott Teal

v8 – St. Louis: 1928-1935 by Scott Teal

— Fall Guys: The Barnums of Bounce —
by Marcus Griffin, Annotated by Steve Yohe & Scott Teal

If you're like most people, who think professional wrestling was strictly "kayfabe" in the days before it morphed into "sports entertainment," then think again. In 1937, a book titled Falls Guys: The Barnums of Bounce was published. In the 215 pages written by sportwriter Marcus Griffin, the sport was exposed to the general public and the behind-the-scenes wheeling and dealing by promoters and wrestlers alike were brought to light. It was the first credible book ever published on the subject.

Fall Guys was, and still is, fascinating reading ... with one caveat. A great deal of the book was written by Griffin with an extreme bias for Toots Mondt ... his boss ... and against those whom Toots didn't like. It is filled with inconsistencies, contradiction, and ... yes, downright lies. Nevertheless, the book is the best resource of events that took place during that era, and wrestling scholars have used much of Griffin's writing as a launchpad for their own research.

That being the case, why would anyone want to read this book?

This is the annotated version, in which Yohe & Teal challenge Griffin's statements about events and correct errors that have been repeated through the years in other books and writings. They also add additional detail to the stories and the lives of the book's personalities.

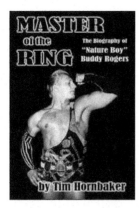

Also available from www.crowbarpress.com
— MASTER OF THE RING —
The Biography of "Nature Boy" Buddy Rogers
by Tim Hornbaker

In 1948, years before the "sports entertainers" like Hulk Hogan, Steve Austin, or "The Rock" were even born, a young man named Buddy Rogers went to the ring in Hollywood Legion Stadium and transformed pro wrestling forever. Billed as the "Nature Boy", Rogers, with his flambouyant personality and underhanded tactics, became an immediate box-office sensation. He was center stage everywhere he appeared, not only in fast-paced matches, but in backstage power plays.

By the late 1950s, he was an unparalleled superstar, but he had one honor yet to achieve ... the National Wrestling Alliance world heavyweight championship. To that point, the contentious environment of wrestling politics stalled his push to the ultimate throne, and only through experience did Rogers overcome the obstacles in his path until, finally, with friends in high places, he was given a title match against champion Pat O'Connor at Chicago's Comiskey Park before a record crowd of 38,000 spectators. By the end of the night, Rogers was the new heavyweight champion of the world! After the match, he strapped on the title belt and stood in the center of the ring, and in his typically arrogant fashion, announced: *"To a nicer guy, it couldn't happen!"*

Backstage assaults, injuries, and other events almost derailed his title reign, and in the midst of his historic run, Rogers suffered serious health problems, which as a cloud over his future on the mat. Since then, wrestling fans have asked countless questions about what really happened on that fabled evening. Author Hornbaker dissects the incident, as well as Buddy's entire life, to answer those questions and clear up some of the misconceptions and lies told about Buddy.

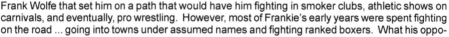

Raising Cain: From Jimmy Ault to Kid McCoy
by Frankie Cain & Scott Teal

Frankie's story isn't only about his life as a wrestler.

Volume 1 takes you on a fascinating journey that began when he was just plain Jimmy Ault, living on Depression-era streets of downtown Columbus, Ohio – learning hustles and cons from Gypsies, sleeping on rooftops, and selling anything he could – all simply to keep from starving. He came into his own and finally began to earn a decent living when prostitutes in Cherry Alley convinced him to work as their protector against the dangers they faced on the streets. Frankie, having fought on the streets almost every day of his young life, was born for the job.

Frankie tells how he discovered pro wrestling and how he helped form the Toehold club, where young boys could mimic and learn the pro style. But it was his introduction to and training by tough shooter Frank Wolfe that set him on a path that would have him fighting in smoker clubs, athletic shows on carnivals, and eventually, pro wrestling. However, most of Frankie's early years were spent fighting on the road ... going into towns under assumed names and fighting ranked boxers. What his opponents didn't realize, though, was that he was there to "put them over," i.e. make them look good and give them a win to enhance their record. While they were trying to knock Frankie out, he was fighting back, but only enough to make it look like a real contest before he did what the promoters brought him there to do.

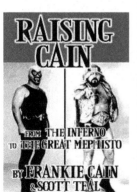

In volume 2, Frankie shares the origins of the masked team known as the Infernos, his transformation into the villain known as the Great Mephisto, being involved in legitimate fights in the dressing rooms with both wrestlers and promoters, fascinating confessions of how life in a business built on greed and power affected him in both body and soul, plus countless road stories and much more.

Frankie's story — presented in his voice just as he shared it with Scott Teal — will transport you back to a time of the true legends of both boxing and wrestling. Brutal, honest, and often hilarious, *Raising Cain* is a look at the life and career of a self-made man who lived his life as none other.

Also available from www.crowbarpress.com

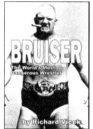    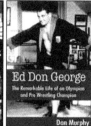

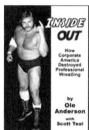 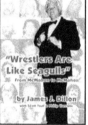  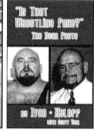 

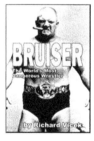    

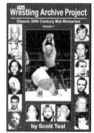 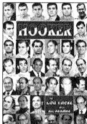   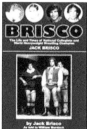